Teacher's Edition

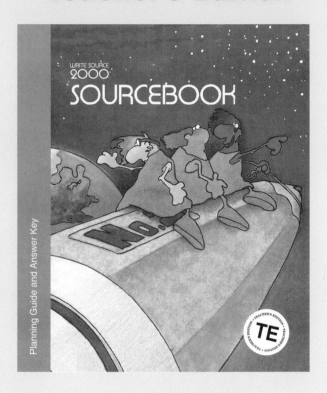

. . . a planning guide for using

SOURCEBOOK 6000

WRITE SOURCE

GREAT SOURCE EDUCATION GROUP

a Houghton Mifflin Company
Wilmington, Massachusetts

About the Teacher's Edition . . .

There are five main sections in the Teacher's Edition. The first section provides teacher's notes for all of the units and activities in the SourceBook. The second section presents all of the writing activities in a framework, or sequence, to help with curriculum planning. The third section provides a suggested timetable of activities for the entire school year. The fourth section offers activities that can be used to reinforce or assess students' mastery of basic skills. And the fifth section contains an answer key for the Student SourceBook. This guide will prove invaluable when planning and scheduling writing and learning activities in your classroom.

Authors: Dave Kemper and Pat Sebranek

Printed in the United States of America

International Standard Book Number: 0-669-43274-1

2 3 4 5 6 7 8 9 10 -RRDW- 02 01 00 99 98 97

TABLE OF CONTENTS

Planning

Teacher's Notes

Teacher's Notes

This section contains notes and objectives for each core writing unit and for each set of writing workshops, language and learning workshops, and writing and learning minilessons in the SourceBook. Teachers will find this information helpful when planning writing and learning activities in their classrooms.

Previewing

TEACHER'S NOTES

PART I
Core Writing Units

CORE WRITING UNITS

OBJECTIVES

Students will . . .

■ *become thoughtfully involved in the process of writing.*

■ *work with the most important types of writing, the innermost core of communication.*

■ *produce at least one significant piece of writing per unit.*

■ *collaborate on their work throughout each unit of study.*

Introduction

The **Core Writing Units** provide students at each grade level with a series of writing assignments addressing many of the basic types of writing covered in the *Write Source 2000* student handbook: paragraphs, essays, autobiographical writing, biographical writing, and creative writing. As students complete their work in these units, they will gain valuable experience with the types of writing tasks they are often asked to carry out in many of their classes. They will also practice the very skills that are at the "core" of the writing process, from selecting subjects to correcting final drafts.

IMPLEMENTATION

All of the Core Writing Units are ready to implement; everything students need to complete their work is included, from step-by-step guidelines to student models. Each page within these units is self-contained, providing students with clearly identifiable starting and stopping points for their work.

The Core Writing Units can serve as the foundation for a middle-school writing program. A yearlong timetable provides a suggested schedule for implementing these units (see pages 36A-39A). However, you may adjust this schedule according to the needs and nature of your students.

GETTING STARTED

A suggested start-up activity is included in the teacher's notes for each core writing unit (see pages 7A-14A). These activities are designed to help students focus their thinking for the work ahead.

CORE WRITING

Writing About Personal Experiences (pages 5-10)

Discussion: This first Core Writing Unit provides students the opportunity to work with autobiographical writing. In the activities, students practice gathering writing ideas as well as developing one subject into a finished personal experience paper. Students will work on evaluating skills as they consider their own and their classmates' writings. Insights gained in sharing these evaluating exercises will be used when writing final drafts.

Objectives:

1. Students will demonstrate the ability to write personal experience stories integrating the details generated in their prewriting activities.

2. Students will do basic evaluation of their initial writing and practice using that feedback in refining and rewriting their first drafts.

RESOURCE: *Write Source 2000* handbook: "Writing About Experiences"

Implementation Guidelines: This unit would work well early in the year since most students are confident enough to write about personal experiences. (In the Yearlong Timetable, this unit is scheduled for Week 3.)

Start-Up Activity: To help students get into a storytelling mood, have them arrange their desks in a circle. Then, using an empty paper towel roll, demonstrate in pantomime one possible object the roll could be. For example, you could use it like a telescope or snorkel. After students identify the general object, share a brief personal story triggered by that image, beginning, "One day . . ." Pass the roll around the class giving each student an opportunity to create a pantomime and share a brief story beginning, "One day . . ."

Suggested Writing Timetable:

DAY ONE Have students participate in the "Start-Up Activity." Introduce "I'm not making this up!" (SourceBook 5). Have students write down their reactions to the questions before discussing the writing with a classmate. Have students do **THE NEXT STEP** with a partner.

DAY TWO Implement "Gathering Ideas for Writing: Sentence Completions" (SB 6). Then have students share their best ideas with each other. Students could also create their own sentence starters, exchange them, and write more completions; or starters could be written on the board, and completions could be volunteered orally.

DAY THREE Implement "Gathering Ideas for Writing: Listing" (SB 7). (If students already have several ideas they want to write about, emphasize listing as a technique for generating details.) **THE NEXT STEP** should help students focus on a writing topic. Assign "Developing One of Your Ideas" (SB 8). Students should begin their first drafts.

DAY FOUR Emphasize the HANDBOOK HELPER (SB 8). Have students continue working with their first drafts. Some students may be ready to begin the evaluation process (SB 8).

DAY FIVE Students should complete the evaluation questions and begin their final drafts. If students complete their final drafts, assign the *extended activity* "Writing About a Pet" (SB 9) or "Writing About a Cooking Experience" (SB 10).

CORE WRITING

Building Paragraphs: Part 1 (pages 11-17)

Discussion: "Building Paragraphs: Part 1" provides students with an opportunity to learn about and practice basic paragraph writing. In the activities, students practice writing topic sentences as well as the narrative paragraph. The skills students develop here will help them with all of their school-related writing.

Objectives:

1. Students will develop a working knowledge of basic paragraph writing.
2. Students will demonstrate the ability to write effective topic sentences and narrative paragraphs.

RESOURCE: *Write Source 2000* handbook: "Building Paragraphs"

Implementation Guidelines: "Paragraph Review and Narrative Writing" is the first of two units devoted exclusively to paragraph writing. It is recommended that this unit be implemented early in the year. Implement the individual activities in a sequence of your own making if this unit seems too writing intensive for your students. (In the Yearlong Timetable, this unit is scheduled for Week 6.)

Start-Up Activity: Write "word" on the board; ask students to identify the next larger unit of meaning in our language (some may say "phrase" or "clause"; most may say "sentence"). Then ask them to continue the sequence: "paragraph," "essay," "report," etc. This activity should help students understand the paragraph's place in our communication system.

Suggested Writing Timetable:

DAY ONE Begin with the "Start-Up Activity." Then have students review the paragraph by completing "The Working Parts" (SourceBook 11-12).

DAY TWO Assign "Understanding Topic Sentences" (SB 13-14). After students complete these two pages, they may do **THE NEXT STEP** (SB 14). Have students develop one of their topic sentences into a paragraph (*Special Challenge*, SB 14). This paragraph should be due the next day.

DAY THREE Implement "Thumbs-Up!" (SB 15) after students review the narrative paragraph in their handbook (078) and read "The Details in a Paragraph" (082-084). Then have students plan and write their own narrative paragraphs (SB 16). Students should prepare first drafts for the next day.

DAY FOUR Ask students to continue working with their narrative stories. They may share their work with a classmate in **THE NEXT STEP** (SB 16). Students should shape their narrative paragraphs into more polished personal stories.

DAY FIVE Have students write another narrative paragraph for "Ten Stories High" (SB 17) following the guidelines for "Writing the Paragraph" (Handbook 081-084). Conclude the work with **THE NEXT STEP** (SB 17).

CORE WRITING

Building Paragraphs: Part 2 (pages 19-24)

Discussion: "Building Paragraphs: Part 2" provides students with an opportunity to learn about basic types of paragraph writing. Students will practice writing both expository and descriptive paragraphs.

Objectives:

1. Students will develop a working knowledge of basic paragraph writing.
2. Students will demonstrate the ability to write both expository and descriptive paragraphs.

RESOURCE: *Write Source 2000* handbook: "Types of Paragraphs"

Implementation Guidelines: "Expository and Descriptive Writing" is the second of two units devoted exclusively to paragraph writing. It is recommended that this unit be used during the quarter following the one in which "Paragraph Review and Narrative Writing" was applied. (In the Yearlong Timetable, this unit is scheduled for Week 12.)

Start-Up Activity: Ask your students to imagine what reading would be like without paragraphs. Share a three- to five-paragraph sample of writing in which paragraphing has been eliminated. Direct students to read the selection and then cut and paste to reestablish paragraphs, or simply indicate where paragraph breaks should occur.

Suggested Writing Timetable:

DAY ONE Have students review "Building Paragraphs" and read about the expository paragraph in the handbook. Ask students to complete the activity on SourceBook 19.

DAY TWO Have students read the model expository paragraph "A 'Tick' in Time" (SB 20). Assign *Now You Try*. Implement **THE NEXT STEP** on the same page.

DAY THREE Have students read about the descriptive paragraph in the handbook and complete "Writing a Descriptive Paragraph" (SB 21). Then they must choose a favorite topic sentence and develop it into a paragraph.

DAY FOUR Students may refer to "Writing About a Place" in the handbook. Next, have them complete "Framing a Picture" (SB 22). Implement **THE NEXT STEP** on the same page.

DAY FIVE Students should review and revise their writing for the week.

Extended Activities: You may encourage motivated students to write a persuasive paragraph. Refer them to the handbook and ask them to try the "Writing Persuasive Paragraphs" *extended activity* (SB 23-24). Some students may want to write letters to the editor.

CORE WRITING

Writing Descriptively About People (pages 25-34)

Discussion: Biographical writing is descriptive writing; it is evaluating, selecting, and connecting details to create a lasting impression of an individual. This unit teaches students how to use details and action verbs in creating a portrait of a particular person.

Objective: Students will learn how to carefully describe people by using concrete details and action verbs.

RESOURCE: *Write Source 2000* handbook: "Writing About a Person" and "The Character Sketch"

Implementation Guidelines: This unit consists of four self-contained but related miniunits:

1. Selecting and collecting details (SourceBook 25-27).

2. Writing a one-paragraph description of a person (SB 28-29).

3. Understanding and using strong verbs (SB 30-31).

4. Writing descriptively about a person in one or more paragraphs (SB 32-34).

(In the Yearlong Timetable, this unit is scheduled for Weeks 15 and 16.)

Start-Up Activity: Gather photographs and posters of people (magazines and old photo albums are good sources). Pass these out to students and ask them to list the characteristics or details that they observe in the pictures. Encourage them to be as thorough as possible in collecting these details.

Suggested Writing Timetable:

WEEK 1

DAY ONE Consider using the "Start-Up Activity" above. Then implement the activities on SB 25 of this unit.

DAY TWO Implement "Selecting and Collecting Ideas for Description" (SB 26). Assign "Arranging Details in a Descriptive Poem" (SB 27) for homework.

DAY THREE Review the poems students developed overnight. Have them read "Reacting to a Short Descriptive Paragraph" (SB 28) and complete *Now You Try*.

DAY FOUR Review and revise first drafts, using the "Revising Checklist" (SB 29). You might want to assign the *Special Challenge* writing activity on this page for homework.

DAY FIVE Hold an in-class revising and editing workshop. Final drafts of the students' one-paragraph descriptions are due on the next school day.

WEEK 2

DAY ONE Implement "Understanding Action Verbs" (SB 30) and "Using Vivid Verbs in Descriptions" (SB 31).

DAY TWO Assign a one- to three-paragraph essay in which students will write descriptively about a person. Begin with "Selecting Another Person to Describe" (SB 32).

DAY THREE Have students read and respond to "Reacting to and Writing a Description" (SB 33). First drafts of description papers are due on the next school day.

DAY FOUR Have students review and revise first drafts. Implement "Revising Your Description" (SB 34), including the *Special Challenge* if you so choose.

DAY FIVE Hold an in-class revising and editing workshop. Have students use the evaluating checklist on SB 34. Final drafts are due on the next school day.

CORE WRITING

Writing Mystery Stories (pages 35-45)

Discussion: Mystery writing serves as an excellent introduction to some of the more complex writing forms. It develops strategies and skills used in cause and effect and problem/solution writing, for instance. In addition, it exercises the students' powers of observation, analysis, assessment, and logic.

Objectives:

1. Students will learn how to observe, collect, and use clues to solve riddles, puzzles, and other kinds of mysteries.

2. Students will gain an understanding of the important role logic plays in writing.

RESOURCE: *Write Source 2000* handbook: "Story Writing"

Implementation Guidelines: The unit consists of four self-contained but related writing miniunits.

1. Creating mood; setting the stage for a mystery (SourceBook 35).

2. Gathering clues (SB 36 37, 43).

3. Planning a mystery story (SB 38-39).

4. Writing a mystery story: a one-paragraph introduction; the rest of the story (SB 40-41).

The *extended activities* are entertaining miniunits providing students with opportunities to practice their evaluating and assessing skills. (In the Yearlong Timetable, this unit is scheduled for Week 22.)

Start-Up Activity: If you do not use "Mysteries on the Move" (SB 45) as a homework assignment, consider using it as a start-up activity. It involves students in creative and imaginative clue-collecting, observation, and mystery-solving exercises.

Suggested Writing Timetable:

DAY ONE Have students read and react to THE FIRST STEP (SB 35). Implement "In the Mood" (SB 35) and "Completing a Mystery Story" (SB 36). Assign "Mysteries on the Move" (*extended activity*, SB 45) for homework.

DAY TWO Review students' work on SB 35-36 and implement "It's a frame-up" (SB 37).

DAY THREE Review "It's a frame-up" and implement "Clues to the Crime" (SB 38) and "Here a Clue, There a Clue" (SB 39).

DAY FOUR Implement "Writing the Introduction for an Original Mystery" (SB 40) and "Writing the Rest of Your Story" (SB 41). Consider using the *extended activity* "The suspense is killing me . . ." (SB 43) or "Where were you the night of . . . ?" (SB 44).

DAY FIVE Have students review and revise first drafts (SB 42). Final mystery stories are due the next school day.

Extended Activity: Here's the real solution to "Where were you the night of . . . ?" (SB 44).

When Mom came home from work, she realized that she was locked out of the house. She went to a friend's house and left messages on the answering machine telling us where she was. When Dad couldn't find us, he called home, but he only got the answering machine. He assumed Mom had come and picked us up for some reason, so he drove home. Forty-five minutes later he arrived home to an empty house. He really panicked when he called Mom; she knew nothing about us. By then it was 2:00 a.m. After listening to *our* phone messages asking where he was, Dad realized he'd left us stranded in a city of a million people. So he headed back to the city. About 4:00 a.m. we were all finally laughing about our nightmare mystery.

CORE WRITING

Comparison and Contrast Essay (pages 47-54)

Discussion: This unit provides students with the opportunity to learn about and practice one type of two-part writing: the comparison and contrast essay. Students will use the Venn diagram to clarify facts and issues and organize their writing ideas. Two-part writing exercises thinking skills and lends itself to many subject areas.

Objectives:

1. Students will develop a clear understanding of the concepts of "compare" and "contrast."

2. Students will gain confidence in using the Venn diagram and will appreciate its usefulness in clarifying facts and issues.

3. Students will demonstrate the ability to write effective three-paragraph comparison and contrast essays.

RESOURCE: *Write Source 2000* handbook: "Developing Essays"

Implementation Guidelines: This unit is designed to be used in the second half of the year since it presents the multiparagraph essay, requiring some previous experience in developing paragraphs. (In the Yearlong Timetable, this unit is scheduled for Week 30.)

Start-Up Activity: Bring in two of the objects from the *Idea 1* and *Idea 2* lists (SourceBook 47). Have students generate as many similarities and differences as they can. They may do this individually and then share the results as a class. Ask how being able to identify such similarities and differences could prove valuable. Have students disuss how they've used a similar process in making their own decisions. Students should realize the benefits of using comparing and contrasting skills in making day-to-day decisions, as well as in completing their class work.

Suggested Writing Timetable:

DAY ONE Begin with the "Start-Up Activity." Implement "Working in Pairs" (SB 47). Introduce "Picturing the Process" and the Venn diagram (SB 48).

DAY TWO Continue with "The Venn Diagram Revisited" (SB 49). Encourage students to take the *Special Challenge* on the same page. Using the Venn diagram will help students develop a comparison and contrast writing idea.

DAY THREE Begin by reading the comparison and contrast essay "Food for Thought" (SB 50). In discussing the essay, have students find the writer's use of personification. Suggest that they experiment with giving their own subjects "personalities." Do REACT (SB 50). Implement "Writing the Comparison and Contrast Essay" (SB 51).

DAY FOUR Students should be working on their essays. Some may be ready to apply the evaluating checklist (SB 52).

DAY FIVE Students should finalize their essays and complete "Reviewing and Revising Your Essay" (SB 52). The *extended activities* "Writing Diamante Poems" (SB 53) and "Writing Contrast Couplets" (SB 54) could be used as all-class breaks from working on individual essays.

CORE WRITING

Writing a Report (pages 55-64)

Discussion: This Core Writing Unit provides students with a complete report-writing experience. Special attention is given to the preliminary steps, especially selecting an interesting subject, locating resources of information, and collecting facts and details. Students will work very closely with "The Classroom Report" chapter in the *Write Source 2000* handbook throughout the unit. The skills and strategies that students learn about and practice here will help them write reports in all of their classes, now and in the future.

Objectives:

1. Students will carry out all of the steps in the report-writing process as described in the handbook.
2. Students will learn about and locate different resources of ideas and information.
3. Students will use note cards to record information.

RESOURCE: *Write Source 2000* handbook: "The Classroom Report," "Personal Research and Writing," "Using the Library," and "Interviewing"

Implementation Guidelines: We suggest that this unit be implemented during the third quarter after students have had some experience with organizing and writing paragraphs. (In the Year-long Timetable, this unit is scheduled for Weeks 25 and 26.)

Start-Up Activity: The first activity in the unit (entitled "Getting Started") asks students to begin their subject search by taking inventory of their special skills, interests, and experiences. (The subjects for the students' reports should come from their own interests and experiences.) Make sure that you have students share their ideas with their classmates.

Suggested Writing Timetable:

WEEK 1

DAY ONE Have students read the introduction to "The Classroom Report" (Handbook 271). If students select the topic of the report, implement "I've always been interested in . . ." (SourceBook 55); if you select the topic of the report, implement "Checking Special Resources for Ideas" (SB 56). (Your students will require references and resources to complete this activity.) Then lead students through **THE NEXT STEP** on the page you assigned.

DAY TWO Begin with "Getting Your First Thoughts on Paper" (SB 57). Conclude with the **REVIEW** on the same page.

DAY THREE Have students read "Collecting: Gathering the Details" (HB 272). Implement "Information Please" (SB 58). *Note: It's a good idea to provide library time for your students at this point. Students may refer to "Using the Library" (HB 290-300) for help in finding information for their reports.*

DAY FOUR Refer students to "Recording Your Information" and "Organizing Your Information" (HB 273-274). Guide students through **THE NEXT STEP** for their planning on day three (SB 58).

DAY FIVE Help your students ask questions about their subjects during "Reading and Taking Notes" (SB 59) or plan the *extended activity* (SB 60) during research time. Conclude the week's activities with "Recording Information" (SB 59).

CORE WRITING *(Continued)*

Writing a Report (pages 55-64)

Suggested Writing Timetable:

WEEK 2

DAY ONE Have students review "Organizing Your Information" (Handbook 274) and then read "Outlining Your Information" (HB 275). Using the note cards developed in Week 1, implement "Preparing to Write" (SourceBook 61). Ask students to develop clear sentence outlines in **THE NEXT STEP** (SB 61).

DAY TWO Read and discuss the "Model Report" (HB 284). Ask students to develop an opening paragraph in "Hooking Your Readers" (SB 62). Read and discuss "Connecting: Writing the First Draft" (HB 276-277). Assign the first draft to be due on the next day (SB 63).

DAY THREE Students may revise their first drafts by reading "Improving the Writing" (HB 278) and reviewing the "Model Report" (HB 284). Encourage students to use the evaluating checklist (SB 64).

DAY FOUR Read "Correcting: A Final Look" (HB 279) for guidelines on writing the final copy. Using the handbook guidelines and model (HB 280-286), implement "Adding a Bibliography, a Title Page, and an Outline" (SB 64) if these are required. Assign the final copy for the next day.

DAY FIVE Students may elect to add charts, graphs, or illustrations to their reports (SB 64). Have students plan a "special information festival" to share their discoveries in **THE NEXT STEP** (SB 64).

TEACHER'S NOTES

PART II
Writing Workshops

PREWRITING STRATEGIES (pages 67-78)

OBJECTIVES

Students will . . .

- *let their thoughts flow freely and rapidly in free writings.*

- *generate clusters of initial thoughts and feelings.*

- *develop spontaneous lists on their own, in pairs, and as a class.*

- *invent spontaneous, unrehearsed conversations.*

- *build a repertoire of prewriting strategies.*

Introduction

The **Prewriting Strategy** units provide students with a comprehensive collection of exploratory writing and thinking activities designed to promote fluency and inventiveness—two critical elements in students' growth as writers. They also introduce students to a number of prewriting techniques (or strategies) that can be used again and again.

Each activity sheet discusses a particular strategy and then has the students work with it in an engaging exercise. The AFTER • WORDS suggest how students might apply what they have learned in their own writing. Students at each level work with many of the same basic strategies but are also introduced to new ones.

IMPLEMENTATION

The Prewriting Strategies can be implemented individually throughout the school year—perhaps biweekly or monthly. They can also be developed into weekly units (see pages 36A-37A) or made available on a "needs be" basis in a writing workshop. The strategies are generally arranged according to level of difficulty. Most of the activities can be completed in 30 minutes.

RESOURCES

The following special points of interest in *Write Source 2000* will help your students complete the prewriting activities:

- "An Invitation to Writing" (topic numbers 004-005)
- "Creating a Writing 'SourceBank' " (033-034)
- "Selecting a Writing Subject" (035-036)
- "Searching and Shaping a Subject" (037-038)

GETTING STARTED

Have students read and react to the introduction in the SourceBook. Also have them review the "User's Checklist" to see if they have used any of the strategies listed.

Special Note: "Prewriting" relates to the selecting and collecting steps in the handbook's discussion of the writing process. (See 012-015.) Share this information with your students.

FORMS OF WRITING (pages 79-94)

OBJECTIVES

Students will . . .

- *become thoughtfully involved in the process of writing.*

- *experiment with personal, subject, creative, and persuasive writing.*

- *work with a number of prewriting strategies.*

- *build an appreciation for the role writing plays in daily life inside and outside of school.*

Introduction

Forms of Writing gives students opportunities to develop a variety of compositions from start to finish. The activities reflect the "catalog" of writing forms in *Write Source 2000*, including personal writing, subject writing, and creative writing.

Every effort has been made to get students actively engaged in writing subjects of their own choosing. In some activities, students are asked to compose in teams or small groups. In others, students are simply given a writing frame to complete. The AFTER • WORDS either ask students to complete the work started in the main activity or challenge students with an enrichment project. For the most part, each Form of Writing will take more than one class period to complete.

IMPLEMENTATION

Forms of Writing can be introduced to your students on a regular basis throughout the school year—perhaps biweekly. They can also be used to enrich an existing writing program. Generally speaking, personal writing and subject writing are stressed more than creative and persuasive writing in the workshops.

RESOURCES

The following sections in the *Write Source 2000* handbook will help your students with the Forms of Writing:

- "Starting Points" (topic numbers 030-041)
- "Writing the Comparison and Contrast Essay" (064-065)
- "Writing About a Person, Place, Object, . . ." (068-074)
- "Personal Writing" (129-149)
- "Subject Writing" (150-219)
- "Creative Writing" (220-263)

GETTING STARTED

Have students read and react to the introduction to Forms of Writing in the SourceBook. A general review of the chapters listed under "Personal Writing," "Subject Writing," and "Creative Writing" in the handbook's table of contents will be helpful as well. Students will be reminded of the variety of writing forms cataloged in their handbooks.

Special Note: Make sure students are aware of the guidelines in the handbook for writing comparison and contrast essays and for writing about people, places, and events.

DRAFTING AND REVISING WORKSHOPS

(pages 95-106)

OBJECTIVES

Students will...

- *become thoughtfully involved in connecting and correcting their ideas in writing.*

- *add "showing" detail to writing.*

- *write figuratively for meaning and effect.*

- *apply reviewing and revising strategies to their writing.*

Introduction

The **Drafting and Revising Workshops** focus on writing as it develops from a rough draft into a revised piece of writing. THE FIRST STEP's give students words of wisdom about the activity that follows or about writing in general. THE NEXT STEP's generally have students apply what they have learned.

These workshops help students write first drafts and review and plan revising strategies. They also ask students to carry out a number of basic writing moves such as adding detail, showing rather than telling, and writing metaphorically. (All of the workshops are cross-referenced with the *Write Source 2000* handbook.)

IMPLEMENTATION

The workshops can effectively be introduced on a "needs be" basis when your students need drafting and revising practice. Or they can be implemented in weekly units (see page 38A).

RESOURCES

The following sections in *Write Source 2000* will help your students complete their work in these workshops:

- "The Writing Process" (topic numbers 023-027)
- "Group Advising" (028-029)
- "Composing Sentences" (090-114)
- "The Art of Writing" (115-123)

GETTING STARTED

Have your students read and react to the introduction to Drafting and Revising Workshops in the SourceBook. Also make sure that you review "The Writing Process" chapter in the handbook with your students. It's important that they have an understanding of the writing process practiced by most experienced writers.

FINAL THOUGHTS

The Drafting and Revising Workshops provide students with a blend of practical advice and firsthand experience, helping them improve their writing ability. The necessary enthusiasm and desire to do so can only come from the students themselves—with your help, of course, and with the help and encouragement of their fellow writers.

SENTENCE-COMBINING WORKSHOPS

(pages 107-122)

OBJECTIVES

Students will . . .

- **build smooth-reading sentences.**

- **become fluent in writing detailed sentences.**

- *improve their overall revising and editing abilities.*

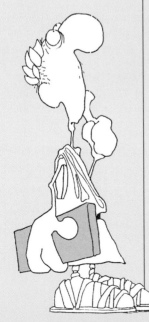

Introduction

The **Sentence-Combining Workshops** will help students develop a sense of sentence style. They are asked to combine sets of basic thoughts using a number of different strategies (combining with ideas, phrases, and clauses). They are also introduced to sentence expanding, a technique that helps students add real meaning to their ideas.

The strategies that your students practice here will help them write with more ease and fluency. They will also begin to appreciate that they do have choices when it comes to expressing their ideas.

IMPLEMENTATION

The individual Sentence-Combining Workshops can be implemented in context when students need stylistic help with their writing. They can also be implemented in weekly units (see page 39A).

RESOURCES

The following sections in *Write Source 2000* will help your students complete their work in these workshops:

- "Composing Sentences" (topic numbers 090-101)
- "Combining Sentences" (102-108)
- "Improving Your Writing" (118-122)
- "The Yellow Pages" (695-718)

GETTING STARTED

Ask students to read and react to the introduction to Sentence-Combining Workshops in the SourceBook. A general review of the chapters related to sentence combining and style in the handbook will be helpful as well. You could also demonstrate (and discuss) a few basic examples of sentence combining on the board.

EDITING WORKSHOPS (pages 123-136)

Introduction

The **Editing Workshops** focus on two important editing concerns—checking for sentence errors and for usage errors. The first set of workshops addresses common sentence errors including sentence fragments, comma splices, run-on sentences, and rambling sentences. The second set of workshops focuses on commonly misused pairs of words *(your, you're)*.

THE FIRST STEP's in each workshop give students words of wisdom about the activity that follows or about editing in general. THE NEXT STEP's generally have students apply what they have learned in a related activity. The skills that students practice in these workshops will help them become better editors of their own writing and better peer editors during writing conferences.

IMPLEMENTATION

These workshops can be implemented in context when students have a need to edit for specific types of errors in their own writing. They can also be implemented in weekly units (see pages 36A and 38A-39A).

RESOURCES

The following sections in the *Write Source 2000* handbook will help your students complete their work in the Editing Workshops:

- "Composing Sentences" (topic numbers 090-101)
- "Understanding Sentences" (695-718)
- "Transition or Linking Words" (089)
- "Using the Right Word" (574-694)

GETTING STARTED

Have students read and react to the introduction to the Editing Workshops in the SourceBook. A general review of the handbook sections related to editing for sentence and usage errors would be helpful as well.

PROOFREADING WORKSHOPS (pages 137-150)

OBJECTIVES

Students will . . .

- *review the rules for capitalization and punctuation.*

- *apply these rules in proofreading exercises.*

- *become familiar with "The Yellow Pages," the proofreader's guide in the handbook.*

- *become thoughtfully involved in the writing process.*

Introduction

In the **Proofreading Workshops,** special emphasis is given to punctuation. Students will, among other things, review or learn about end punctuation, punctuating dialogue, and using commas. In each workshop, THE FIRST STEP's give students words of wisdom about the activity that follows or about proofreading in general. THE NEXT STEP's generally have students apply what they have learned in an extended activity.

As students complete their work, they will come to appreciate "The Yellow Pages" in the *Write Source 2000* handbook as a valuable proofreader's guide. They should always be encouraged (or reminded) to refer to "The Yellow Pages" whenever they have a question about mechanics, grammar, or usage in their own writing.

IMPLEMENTATION

These workshops can be implemented when needed throughout the school year. They can also be implemented in weekly units (see pages 37A-38A).

RESOURCES

The following sections in the *Write Source 2000* handbook will help your students complete their work in these workshops:

- "Proofreading" (topic numbers 026-027)
- "Writing Dialogue" (253-256)
- "The Yellow Pages" (458-795)

GETTING STARTED

Have students read and react to the introduction to the Proofreading Workshops in the SourceBook. A general review of "The Yellow Pages" would be helpful as well. For interesting background information about our system of punctuation, discuss the introduction to "Marking Punctuation" in the handbook (458).

TEACHER'S NOTES

PART III
Language and Learning Workshops

LANGUAGE WORKSHOPS (pages 153-182)

OBJECTIVES

Students will...

- *become thoughtfully involved in the standard use or grammar of the language.*

- *review and work with the eight parts of speech.*

- *address problems with word choice, agreement, and tense.*

- *evaluate their language proficiency.*

Introduction

In every level in the series, at least one **Language Workshop** focuses on each part of speech; special problem areas like subject-verb agreement and pronoun-antecedent agreement are given special attention in separate workshops. THE FIRST STEP's at the beginning of each workshop provide students with important introductory information or interesting food for thought. Many of the workshops continue with a review activity.

Students should be able to complete the main part of each activity in approximately 20 minutes. THE NEXT STEP's provide enrichment activities so students can apply what they have learned in a variety of creative forms and contexts. These activities also provide meaningful work for students who complete the main task before other students. (All of the activities are cross-referenced with *Write Source 2000*.)

IMPLEMENTATION

The Language Workshops can be used on a "needs be" basis throughout the school year. They can also be implemented in weekly units (see pages 37A-39A) or used to enrich an existing language program or as review material.

Workshops for level 6 are introductory in nature; workshops for level 7 take a closer look at the language in action; and workshops for level 8 contain a mixture of new and review material.

RESOURCES

Refer to "What About Grammar?" in the *Write Source 2000 Teacher's Guide* for insights into grammar instruction. (The minilessons in the student SourceBook contain additional language activities.)

The following sections in the *Write Source 2000* handbook will help your students complete these workshops:

- "The Yellow Pages" (topic numbers 458-795)
- "Write 'Agreeable' Sentences" (094-097)
- "Write Clear, Concise Sentences" (098-101)

GETTING STARTED

Have students read and react to the introduction to Language Workshops in the SourceBook. They should be aware that our concern in these workshops is with the standard use of the language—language that an educated and informed public has grown to expect. Each workshop, in essence, looks at the grammar of the standard language, the different roles (parts of speech) words play when they are put to use in semiformal or formal contexts.

READING AND LEARNING STRATEGIES

(pages 183-196)

OBJECTIVES

Students will...

- ■ *become thoughtfully involved in factual reading material.*

- ■ *use charts and categorizing as strategies to help organize reading.*

- ■ *learn how to use the stop 'n' write strategy for difficult reading material.*

Introduction

Each level in the series contains 8-10 **Reading and Learning Strategies** designed to help students with their academic reading. Students will work with all of the tested strategies, including KWL, SQ3R, Question and Answer, Mapping, and so on. Students will also work with memory techniques, maps, graphs, editorial cartoons, the Venn diagram, and locating patterns in reading material.

Most of the important strategies are repeated at each level. However, challenging strategies like SQ3R and locating patterns in material are reserved for level 8.

In most cases, everything students need to carry out their assigned tasks is on the activity sheets themselves or in the handbook. For a few of the activities, they will be asked to read material from other sources (newspapers, textbooks, etc.). The main activities can generally be completed in 30 minutes or less. For the most part, students will work independently. However, they are occasionally asked to work in pairs or small groups. The AFTER • WORDS offer enrichment activities and/or words of encouragement.

IMPLEMENTATION

Consider the needs and nature of your students and implement the Reading and Learning Strategies accordingly. You can implement these strategies in a weekly unit (see page 36A) or individually throughout the school year.

RESOURCES

Refer to "Study-Reading Skills" in *Write Source 2000* for more information and strategies. Also refer to "Writing to Learn" in the *Write Source 2000 Teacher's Guide* for a detailed list of techniques that promote effective study-reading.

GETTING STARTED

Have students read and react to the introduction in the SourceBook. Then have them review the "User's Checklist" to see if they have worked with any of the reading strategies listed. You may also ask students to think and write about their "personal" process of reading assigned material . . . and then share their results.

TALKING AND LISTENING ACTIVITIES

(pages 197-210)

OBJECTIVES

Students will . . .

- *become thoughtfully involved in speaking and listening activities.*

- *prepare and deliver formal and informal speeches.*

- *better understand the dynamics involved in group discussions.*

- *practice listening skills in a variety of contexts.*

Introduction

All three levels of the program contain a series of **Talking and Listening Activities**. The first set of activities focuses on talking or speaking to learn. Students will be asked, among other things, to conduct interviews; to deliver demonstration speeches, campaign speeches, and public service announcements; and to participate in discussions.

The second set of activities asks students to listen for directions, important facts, confusing words, and so on. Simply put, this unit provides students with a wide variety of valuable oral and aural experiences.

IMPLEMENTATION

These activities can be developed into a weekly unit (see page 36A) or implemented individually on a "needs be" basis throughout the school year. We recommend that you encourage students to talk and "actively" listen on a regular basis in your classroom.

Special Note: These activities could enrich existing speech or listening units or perhaps serve as starting points for new units.

RESOURCES

Refer to "Talking to Learn" in the *Write Source 2000 Teacher's Guide* for a variety of talking and listening activities.

Also refer to "Speaking and Listening to Learn" in *Write Source 2000* for more information. Students should refer to this section for all of their talking and listening needs. They should refer to "Group Skills" for insights into the dynamics of group discussions.

GETTING STARTED

Have students read and react to the introduction in the SourceBook. Then have them review the "User's Checklist" to see if they have participated in activities like the ones listed. Follow with a review of the chapters on speaking and listening in their handbooks (389-407).

THINKING WORKSHOPS (pages 211-226)

OBJECTIVES

Students will . . .

- *solve problems, make decisions, form understandings, evaluate information, and build arguments.*

- *utilize all of the language arts to enhance thinking.*

Introduction

Each workshop in this section leads students into a series of basic thinking operations, all part of a higher-level thinking project or "enterprise." The major enterprises are called "Forming Understanding," "Making Decisions," "Solving Problems," "Evaluating Information," and "Building Arguments."

Students can begin most of their work in class. Often, the challenges require that they collaborate in small groups. A few of the workshops may take more than one day to complete. Many of them ask students to develop a form of writing. Others may require interviewing, role playing, and demonstrations. THINKING IT OVER segments ask students to reflect upon their work or to apply what they have learned in an enrichment activity.

Each level contains around 15 **Thinking Workshops**. To make sure that the workshops touch all areas of their lives, students are put into thinking situations that address personal, social, school-related, and global concerns.

IMPLEMENTATION

Introduce the Thinking Workshops on a regular basis (perhaps bi-weekly) or develop weekly thinking units (see pages 37A and 38A). While students will generally be able to work independently, more guidance and collaboration may be required in these activities than in the other parts of the SourceBooks. It's best that students work with this material in sequence since the workshops require progressively more complex levels of thinking.

RESOURCES

Refer to "Teaching Thinking in the '90s" in the *Write Source 2000 Teacher's Guide* for insights into promoting thinking in your classroom. "Thinking to Learn" in *Write Source 2000* (306-359) will help students think their way through the workshops.

GETTING STARTED

Have students read and react to the introduction in the SourceBook. Any of the "Teaching About Thinking" activities listed on pages 116-117 in the *Write Source 2000 Teacher's Guide* will help you produce the right mind-set for the thinking workshops. You might also review the thinking chart in the handbook (330) since it lists the basic thinking skills students will use in the workshops.

VOCABULARY AND WORD PLAY (pages 227-238)

OBJECTIVES

Students will...

- **experience or play with words in a variety of formats.**

- **develop an appreciation for the power of words.**

- **collect interesting words for future use.**

- **become thoughtfully involved in the study of prefixes, suffixes, and roots.**

Introduction

James Moffett states, "Words have sounds, rhythms, spellings, visual shapes—all qualities that can be played with and responded to." And to play with their language is just what students are asked to do in **Vocabulary and Word Play Activities**. They are asked, among other things, to write riddles and slogans and short poems, to explore and appreciate the power of words, and to learn strategies for building vocabularies. All of these activities are designed to help students learn about their language—while having too much fun to realize it.

At each level in the series, there are actually two sets of activities. The first set asks students to experiment and play with the language. The second set focuses on vocabulary building. In these activities students work with prefixes, suffixes, and roots and develop a real "word sense," or understanding of how words are put together.

IMPLEMENTATION

The Vocabulary and Word Play Activities can be implemented individually throughout the school year or in a weekly unit (see page 37A). The vocabulary activities, especially, can enrich an existing unit on vocabulary building or serve as a starting point for a new unit. They ought to be assigned in sequence since they do build on one another.

RESOURCES

Refer to "Building Vocabulary" in the *Write Source 2000 Teacher's Guide* for insights into vocabulary instruction.

The following parts of *Write Source 2000* will help your students build their vocabularies:

- "Use Context Clues" (topic number 370)

- "Improving Vocabulary" (371-384)

GETTING STARTED

Have your students read and react to the introduction to Vocabulary and Word Play Activities in the SourceBook. Also have them list different types of words as part of an introductory discussion. You could ask them to list the longest word they know, the most difficult word, the nicest-sounding word, and so on. Then implement whatever activity seems appropriate for your students.

TEACHER'S NOTES

PART IV

Writing and Learning Minilessons

Covering the important areas

of writing, language, and learning

included in *Write Source 2000*

WRITING AND LEARNING MINILESSONS

(pages 241-260)

OBJECTIVES

Students will ...

- *become thoughtfully involved in all aspects of the writing process.*

- *review or learn about different reading, speaking, thinking, and learning skills.*

- *engage in active and collaborative learning experiences.*

Introduction

The **Writing and Learning Minilessons** can transform any classroom into an active learning environment. (We define a minilesson as a lesson lasting 10-15 minutes and covering a single idea or a basic core of knowledge.) Ideally, each lesson will address a particular need certain students are experiencing. This makes learning much more meaningful and successful.

The first several pages of minilessons focus on "The Yellow Pages" section in the *Write Source 2000* handbook. They address aspects of punctuation, spelling, usage, grammar, and sentence structure. The remaining minilessons address a variety of topics covered in the handbook. (There are over 50 minilessons to choose from.)

IMPLEMENTATION

Minilessons can be delivered from the front of the classroom and include the entire class. However, they work especially well in the writing workshop classroom. Those students who are "stuck" can be pulled together for 10-15 minutes to work on a minilesson related to their problem. Perhaps one group of students needs to know how to punctuate dialogue in stories they are writing. Another group of students may need practice combining sentences, and so on. All this (and more) can be scheduled within one class period. The diverse needs of students can be met by teaching them the skills they need . . . when they need to learn them.

RESOURCES

Students will refer to sections throughout *Write Source 2000* to complete their work in the Writing and Learning Minilessons.

GETTING STARTED

Have students read and react to the introduction in the SourceBook. Then ask students to list parts of the writing process that really cause them problems (selecting an interesting subject, writing dialogue, using commas, and so on). Follow up with a classwide minilesson that addresses one of these problem areas. Mention to students that minilessons will be used throughout the school year to meet their specific *and* immediate learning needs.

Writing Frameworks

Writing Frameworks

This section contains two charts listing the types of writing discussed in the *Write Source 2000* handbook and in the coordinating SourceBooks. The types of writing are listed to indicate a *possible* framework, or sequence, of activities, moving gradually from personal writing to more inventive and reflective writing. Teachers can use these frameworks as a starting point when planning a writing program or when planning individual writing activities.

Selecting

WRITING FRAMEWORK: HANDBOOK

The types of writing covered in the *Write Source 2000* handbook are listed below in a possible sequence or framework of activities, moving from personal writing to writing that becomes more and more public.

	6	7	8
PERSONAL WRITING			
Recording	Writing to Learn (004) Journal Writing (130)	Creating a SourceBank (033) Journal Writing (132)	Learning Logs (409) Journal Writing (132)
Recalling and Remembering	Writing About Experiences (144) Memories of People (149)	Writing About Experiences (144) Memories of Places (149)	Writing Phase Autobiographies (133) Memories of Objects (149)
SUBJECT WRITING			
Introducing	Bio-Poems (158)	The Character Sketch (159)	Writing Phase Biographies (151)
Describing	Descriptive Paragraphs (077) Describing a Person (068)	Descriptive Paragraphs (077) Describing a Place (069)	Describing an Object (070) Describing an Event (072)
Reporting	Writing the Basic News Story (171)	Writing the Feature Story (177)	Writing a News Story (171)
Corresponding	Writing Friendly Letters (196)	Writing Fan Letters (192)	Writing Business Letters (203)
Informing	Narrative Paragraphs (078) Expository Paragraphs (079)	Narrative Paragraphs (078) Expository Paragraphs (079)	Multiparagraph Essays (052) Expository Paragraphs (079)
Searching and Researching	Writing Summaries (184) Library Report (271, 290)	Writing Summaries (184) Report Writing (271)	Writing Summaries (184) Personal Research Paper (265)
CREATIVE WRITING			
Translating	"Invented" Poetry (235)	Free-Verse Poetry (224)	Traditional Poetry (233)
Inventing	Story Writing (237) Writing Mystery Stories (248)	Story Writing (237) Writing Myths (251)	Story Writing (237) Patterned Stories (246)
Scripting	Dialogue Writing (253)	Monologue Writing (253, 245)	Writing Miniplays (257)
REFLECTIVE WRITING			
Analyzing and Classifying	Writing a Comparison and Contrast Essay (064)	Writing About Problems and Solutions (066)	Cause and Effect Writing (066) Writing to Define (071)
Persuading	Persuasive Paragraphs (080)	Writing Pet Peeves (050)	Writing Editorials (178, 074)
Reviewing	One-Paragraph Book Reviews (187)	One-Paragraph Book Reviews (187)	Multiparagraph Book Reviews (187)

WRITING FRAMEWORK: SOURCEBOOKS

This chart lists many of the types of writing found in the *Write Source 2000 SourceBooks*, moving from personal writing to writing that becomes more and more public. The Core Writing Units are in bold type.

	6	7	8
PERSONAL WRITING			
Recording	Collecting Ideas (67-78) Writing for Fluency (85)	Collecting Ideas (69-80) Journal Writing (237)	Collecting Ideas (65-76) Empathizing (213)
Recalling and Remembering	**Writing About Personal Experiences** (5) Writing a Creative Sketch (81) Writing a Monologue (94)	**Writing About Personal Experiences** (5) Observing and Recording (80) The Autobiography (83)	**Writing the Phase Autobiography** (5) Personal Journal Writing (79) Writing Anecdotes (81)
SUBJECT WRITING			
Introducing	**Writing Descriptively About People** (25) Bio-Poems (91)	**Writing a Character Sketch** (27) Writing About People (84)	**Writing the Phase Biography** (23) Character Sketch (87)
Describing	Selecting Details (103) Showing vs. Telling (104)	Describing a Place (85) Describing an Event (92)	Describing an Object (80) Using Sensory Detail (101)
Reporting	Reporting on Events (87)	Finding the Main Idea (183, 184) The Editorial Cartoon (188)	News Stories (82) Objective Writing (223)
Corresponding	Friendly Letters (83) Writing an Invitation (221)	Letter Writing (87) Creative Questions (210)	Letter of Advice (220) Letter to Editor (224)
Informing	**Building Paragraphs 1: Narrative Writing** (11) **Building Paragraphs 2: Expository & Descriptive** (19)	**Building Paragraphs 1: Supporting Details** (13) **Building Paragraphs 2: Planning Strategies** (21)	**Building Paragraphs: Expository Writing** (11) **Building Essays** (17)
Searching and Researching	**Writing a Report** (55) Know-Want-Learn (185) Investigating Local History (219) Summarizing (248A)	**Writing a Report** (55) Know-Want-Learn (182) Summarizing As You Read (186) Personal Research (240)	Oral History (199) Interviewing (200) Paraphrasing (214)
CREATIVE WRITING			
Translating	Phase Poetry (92) Concrete Poetry (229)	A Thinking Poem (205) Analyzing/Translating (220)	Playing with Poetry (232, 233) Bombastic Proverbs (234)
Inventing	**Writing Mystery Stories** (35) Writing Fables (93)	**Writing Myths** (33) Inventing (214)	**Writing a Survival Story** (33) Building a Story (89)
Scripting	Instant Improv (204) TV Skit (220)	Interviewing (195)	Impromptu Miniplay (203) Story of Speculation (212)
REFLECTIVE WRITING			
Analyzing and Classifying	**Writing the Comparison and Contrast Essay** (47) Pro-Con (225) Analyzing a Process (226)	**Writing About Problems and Solutions** (41) Comparison/Contrast (90) Observing/Analyzing (211)	**Cause and Effect Writing** (41) **Writing to Define** (49) Comparing/Contrasting (221)
Persuading	Brainstorming/Persuading (213) Pretending/Persuading (224)	Speaking Persuasively (196)	Arguing/Judging (225) Compromising (227)
Reviewing	Writing Book Reviews (89)	Writing Book Reviews (88)	Writing a Book Review (85) Compiling a Review (86)

Yearlong Timetable

Yearlong Timetable

The lessons in the suggested Yearlong Timetable for level 6 focus on key sets of writing, language, and learning activities in *SourceBook 6000*. Teachers should remember to adjust the timetable to meet the needs of their students and to incorporate other activities and units.

Scheduling

FIRST QUARTER

TIMETABLE 6

RESOURCES:
Write Source 2000 Handbook (HB)
Write Source 2000 Teacher's Guide (TG)
Student SourceBook 6000 (SB)
SourceBook 6000 Teacher's Edition (TE)

WEEK 1
"Getting Started"
HB, "Using the Handbook" page
TG, 9-19 (Teacher's Choice)
SB, 244B

WEEK 2
Writing Workshop: The Writing Process
HB, 011-027, 118-123
TG, 32-33, 62-63
SB, 81-82
TE, 17A

WEEK 3
Core Writing Unit: "Writing About Personal Experiences"
HB, 144-149
TG, 38
SB, 5-10
TE, 7A

WEEK 4
Learning Workshop: Listening Activities
HB, 402-407, 432-449
TG, 51-52, 119
SB, 199-203, 205-209, 249C
TE, 26A

WEEK 5
Writing Workshop: Prewriting (Part 1)
HB, 030-035
TG, 59-79, 144, 151
SB, 69-72
TE, 16A

WEEK 6
Core Writing Unit: "Building Paragraphs: Part 1"
HB, 075-089
TG, 34-35
SB, 11-17
TE, 8A

WEEK 7
Writing Workshop: Editing (Part 1)
HB, 090-093, 477, 484
TG, 35
SB, 126-129, 244A
TE, 20A

WEEK 8
Learning Workshop: Reading and Learning Strategies
HB, 363-370, 811-825
TG, 49-50
SB, 183-186, 190, 193, 260
TE, 25A

WEEK 9
Quarter Wrap-Up

SECOND QUARTER

TIMETABLE 6

RESOURCES:
Write Source 2000 Handbook (HB)
Write Source 2000 Teacher's Guide (TG)
Student SourceBook 6000 (SB)
SourceBook 6000 Teacher's Edition (TE)

WEEK 10

Language Workshop: Nouns and Pronouns
    HB, 118, 719-732, 733-748
    TG, 55, 89-91, 139
    SB, 155-158, 173-174
    TE, 24A

WEEK 11

Writing Workshop: Prewriting (Part 2)
    HB, 035-036
    SB, 73-76
    TE, 16A

WEEK 12

Core Writing Unit: "Building Paragraphs: Part 2"
    HB, 069, 077-089
    TG, 34-35
    SB, 19-24
    TE, 9A

WEEK 13

Writing Workshop: Proofreading (Part 1)
    HB, 253-256, 459-532, 533-546
    TG, 55, 135-139
    SB, 137-143, 247B, 250, 253B
    TE, 21A

WEEK 14

Language Workshop: Vocabulary
    HB, 371-384
    TG, 50, 121-122
    SB, 236-238
    TE, 28A

WEEK 15

Core Writing Unit: "Writing Descriptively About People" (Week 1)
    HB, 068, 159-165
    SB, 25-29
    TE, 10A

WEEK 16

Core Writing Unit: "Writing Descriptively About People" (Week 2)
    HB, 068, 119-120, 159-165
    SB, 30-34
    TE, 10A

WEEK 17

Learning Workshop: Thinking (Part 1)
    HB, 306-310, 330-342
    TG, 47-48, 116-117, 150
    SB, 211-219, 248C
    TE, 27A

WEEK 18

Semester Wrap-Up

THIRD QUARTER

TIMETABLE 6

RESOURCES:
Write Source 2000 Handbook (HB)
Write Source 2000 Teacher's Guide (TG)
Student SourceBook 6000 (SB)
SourceBook 6000 Teacher's Edition (TE)

WEEK 19

Writing Workshop: Revising Writing (Part 1)
HB, 021-027, 128
TG, 34-36, 86-87
SB, 99-103
TE, 18A

WEEK 20

Writing Workshop: Revising Writing (Part 2)
HB, 118-123
TG, 36, 86-87
SB, 104-106
TE, 18A

WEEK 21

Language Workshop: Verbs
HB, 094-096, 749-767
TG, 55, 89-91, 140
SB, 159-166
TE, 24A

WEEK 22

Core Writing Unit: "Writing Mystery Stories"
HB, 237-252
TG, 43
SB, 35-45
TE, 11A

WEEK 23

Writing Workshop: Proofreading (Part 2)
HB, 459-532, 533-546
TG, 55, 135-138
SB, 144-150, 250-254
(teacher's choice)
TE, 21A

WEEK 24

Writing Workshop: Editing (Part 2)
HB, 128, 574-694
TG, 55, 90
SB, 131-136, 256A, 256B
TE, 20A

WEEK 25

Core Writing Unit: "Writing a Report" (Week 1)
HB, 271-274, 290-300, 405-407
TG, 45-46
SB, 55-60
TE, 13A

WEEK 26

Core Writing Unit: "Writing a Report" (Week 2)
IIB, 274-286, 290-300
TG, 45-46
SB, 61-64
TE, 14A

WEEK 27

Quarter Wrap-Up

FOURTH QUARTER

TIMETABLE 6

RESOURCES:
Write Source 2000 Handbook (HB)
Write Source 2000 Teacher's Guide (TG)
Student SourceBook 6000 (SB)
SourceBook 6000 Teacher's Edition (TE)

WEEK 28
Language Workshop: Modifiers
HB, 120-121, 127, 771-787
TG, 55, 89-91
SB, 167-172, 235
TE, 24A

WEEK 29
Language Workshop: Other Parts of Speech
HB, 788-795
TG, 55, 89-91
SB, 175-180
TE, 24A

WEEK 30
Core Writing Unit: "Writing the Comparison and Contrast Essay"
HB, 043-048, 064-065, 089
TG, 34
SB, 47-54
TE, 12A

WEEK 31
Writing Workshop: Sentence Combining (Part 1)
HB, 102-106
TG, 35
SB, 107-114
TE, 19A

WEEK 32
Writing Workshop: Sentence Combining (Part 2)
HB, 107-108, 710, 712, 713
TG, 35, 139
SB, 115-122, 256C
TE, 19A

WEEK 33
Writing Workshop: Editing (Part 3)
HB, 086, 089, 093
TG, 35
SB, 125, 130
TE, 20A

WEEK 34
Learning Workshop: Thinking (Part 2)
HB, 310-330, 343-359
TG, 47-48, 116-117
SB, 220-226, 248B, 249A
TE, 27A

WEEK 35
Forms of Writing: Poetry
HB, 158, 221-236
TG, 42-43, 111
SB, 27, 91, 92, 246A
TE, 17A

WEEK 36
Year-End Wrap-Up

Assessment Activities

Assessment Activities

This section contains six sets of basic skills activities that can be used in a number of different ways. They can be used to strengthen your students' understanding of certain skills or concepts addressed in the writing and language workshops. They can also be used as pretests or posttests to help you assess your students' understanding of these skills or concepts. These activities should not, however, be used to test or measure overall language and writing proficiency. (There are two activities per set.)

Evaluating

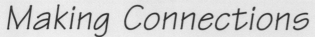

Making Connections

The chart that follows identifies the titles and the subjects of the activities in this section plus the pages of related material in the student SourceBook:

Titles of Assessment Activities	Subjects Covered	Related Pages in *SourceBook 6000*
• Summer Reading • I scream for ice cream!	*Sentence Errors*	125-129
• The Call of the Wild • Let's party!	*Using the Right Word*	131-136
• She's certainly not bashful. • Practice, Practice, Practice	*Capitalization and Punctuation*	139-150
• Fire Drill! • Let's give thanks.	*Parts of Speech*	155-182
• A Capital Offense • Life's Trivial Treasures	*Nouns*	155-158
• The Time of Our Lives • Dealing with Nature	*Verbs*	159-162
• This is highly irregular! • Heads it's WRING; tails it's WRUNG.	*Irregular Verbs*	163-164

SENTENCE ERRORS
Summer Reading

Write *F* in front of each sentence fragment, *CS* in front of each comma splice, *RO* in front of each run-on sentence, and *C* in front of each correct sentence. Also correct each faulty sentence.

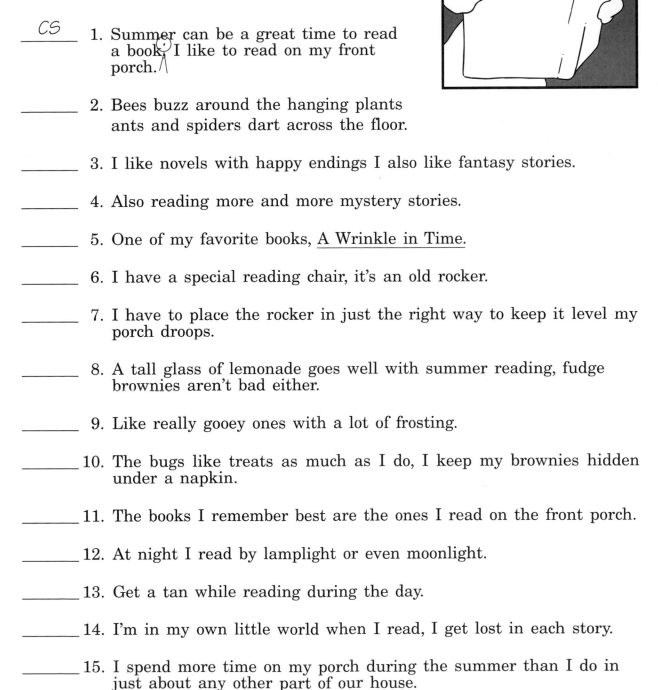

_CS_ 1. Summer can be a great time to read a book I like to read on my front porch.

_____ 2. Bees buzz around the hanging plants ants and spiders dart across the floor.

_____ 3. I like novels with happy endings I also like fantasy stories.

_____ 4. Also reading more and more mystery stories.

_____ 5. One of my favorite books, A Wrinkle in Time.

_____ 6. I have a special reading chair, it's an old rocker.

_____ 7. I have to place the rocker in just the right way to keep it level my porch droops.

_____ 8. A tall glass of lemonade goes well with summer reading, fudge brownies aren't bad either.

_____ 9. Like really gooey ones with a lot of frosting.

_____ 10. The bugs like treats as much as I do, I keep my brownies hidden under a napkin.

_____ 11. The books I remember best are the ones I read on the front porch.

_____ 12. At night I read by lamplight or even moonlight.

_____ 13. Get a tan while reading during the day.

_____ 14. I'm in my own little world when I read, I get lost in each story.

_____ 15. I spend more time on my porch during the summer than I do in just about any other part of our house.

SENTENCE ERRORS

I scream for ice cream!

Write *F* in front of each sentence fragment, *CS* in front of each comma splice, *RO* in front of each run-on sentence, and *C* in front of each correct sentence. Also correct each faulty sentence.

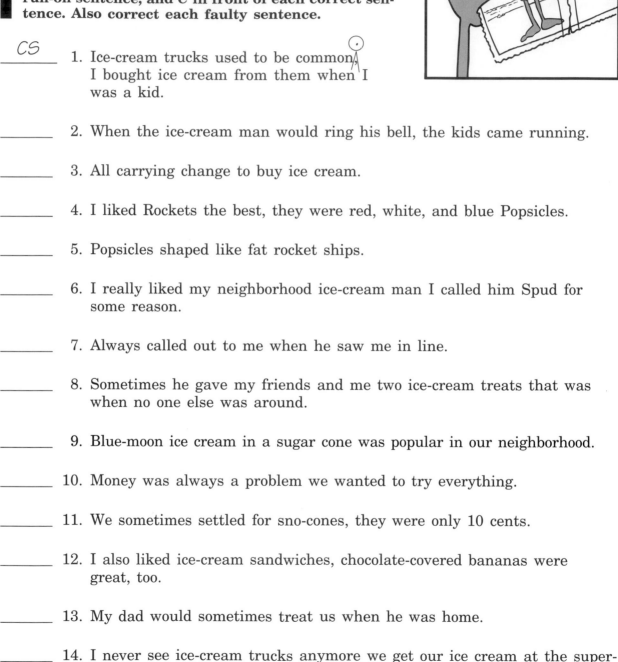

CS   1. Ice-cream trucks used to be common, I bought ice cream from them when I was a kid.

_____ 2. When the ice-cream man would ring his bell, the kids came running.

_____ 3. All carrying change to buy ice cream.

_____ 4. I liked Rockets the best, they were red, white, and blue Popsicles.

_____ 5. Popsicles shaped like fat rocket ships.

_____ 6. I really liked my neighborhood ice-cream man I called him Spud for some reason.

_____ 7. Always called out to me when he saw me in line.

_____ 8. Sometimes he gave my friends and me two ice-cream treats that was when no one else was around.

_____ 9. Blue-moon ice cream in a sugar cone was popular in our neighborhood.

_____ 10. Money was always a problem we wanted to try everything.

_____ 11. We sometimes settled for sno-cones, they were only 10 cents.

_____ 12. I also liked ice-cream sandwiches, chocolate-covered bananas were great, too.

_____ 13. My dad would sometimes treat us when he was home.

_____ 14. I never see ice-cream trucks anymore we get our ice cream at the super-market.

_____ 15. The fun taken out of buying ice cream.

USING THE RIGHT WORD
The Call of the Wild

Draw a line through any underlined word that is incorrectly used and write the correct form above it. Do not change a word that is correct.

Example: Mrs. Isaacson complained that she had

heard
~~herd~~ strange noises coming from under

the hood.

1. The introductory first-aid <u>coarse</u> proved to be very challenging for the young campers. Soda and snacks improved <u>there</u> <u>morale</u>, however.

2. One camper <u>choose</u> jewelry class because she wanted to make a <u>medal</u> bracelet.

3. At night, we were <u>aloud</u> to start enough campfires to light up the <u>hole</u> area.

4. Everyone enjoyed rafting <u>alot</u>, <u>accept</u> for Buford, who got a little "seasick."

5. The nonstop rain ruined <u>quiet</u> a few of our plans and <u>maid</u> a sopping mess inside our leaky tent.

6. I almost died when I stumbled upon <u>an</u> snake slithering <u>among</u> the last two tents.

7. <u>Your</u> not going to believe this, but furry little creatures are not <u>deer</u> to me.

8. We've noticed <u>less</u> deer and no <u>bares</u> on the trails this year.

9. Everyone <u>seamed</u> to enjoy swimming; they liked to tell ghost stories at night, <u>to</u>.

10. Making breakfast over <u>an</u> campfire was a challenge because <u>their</u> was <u>know</u> way to maintain an even, steady flame.

USING THE RIGHT WORD

Let's party!

▌ Draw a line through any underlined word that is
incorrectly used and write the correct form above it.
Do not change a word that is correct.

Example: "~~Your~~ *You're* right, Tasha; a birthday party is
~~to~~ *too* much of a hassle."

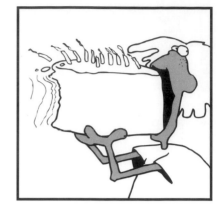

1. At first, I was going to <u>by</u> Tasha a CD player

   for her birthday, but she <u>already</u> has one.

2. A new electronics shop is running a <u>real</u> good sale on CD players starting

   tomorrow <u>mourning</u>.

3. Of <u>coarse</u>, I have no <u>less</u> than <u>too</u> of these devices myself.

4. <u>Their</u> are other things I can do for Tasha's birthday; I'll just have to <u>chose</u>

   from three or four possibilities.

5. I could take her out for an ice-cream sundae, <u>accept</u> <u>deserts</u> are out for

   both of us.

6. <u>It's</u> difficult to diet, but both of us are trying to <u>lose</u> <u>wait</u>.

7. <u>There</u> is always a movie, but I'm not <u>aloud</u> to go to the cinema complex.

8. I could always take her shopping, but we've <u>all ready</u> been to the mall

   <u>quite</u> a few times this summer.

9. Maybe I shouldn't <u>brake</u> tradition; for the <u>passed</u> four years, I've given

   Tasha a book for her birthday.

10. <u>Its</u> an understatement to say she reads <u>alot</u>; I know of no one else <u>whose</u>

    so consumed by books.

CAPITALIZATION AND PUNCTUATION

She's certainly not bashful.

Supply all the capital letters, commas, and end punctuation needed in the following paragraph. Draw a line through any mark of punctuation or capital letter that is used incorrectly.

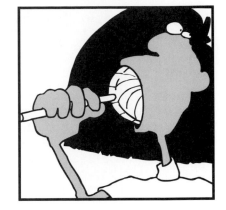

1   ~~w~~e took Amy, my three-year-old baby

2   sister to the disney ice capades last sunday

3   afternoon.   She had never been to a show like that before, Amy

4   went crazy every time she saw new Disney characters and they were

5   all there for her to see people five rows away could hear her yelling,

6   "Mickey," whenever Mickey Mouse was on Center Ice. she squealed

7   with delight when donald duck twirled in midair and came down on

8   one foot Pluto made her break into a peal of giggles when he fell on

9   his behind many of the spectators' around us, when not watching

10 the show, enjoyed watching Amy i can still see her beaming with

11 sticky cotton candy ketchup, and mustard on her face as the show

12 unfolded. after all of the excitement of the Disney production amy

13 quickly became "sleeping beauty" when she hit the backseat of our car

14 what a crazy kid did i enjoy myself that much when i was three.

CAPITALIZATION AND PUNCTUATION

Practice, Practice, Practice

Supply all the capital letters, commas, and end punctuation needed in the following paragraph. Draw a line through any mark of punctuation or capital letter that is used incorrectly.

1   M
    ~~m~~ikala loves playing the violin in her

2   s
    ~~S~~chool Orchestra. She has been playing violin

3   since the sixth grade, but she couldn't play in an orchestra until

4   this year she's a Freshman at cherry valley high school Mikala has

5   orchestra practice right after lunch mrs moseman her orchestra

6   teacher says mikala is very talented Mikala also has private lessons

7   three days a week she wants to play in the boston pops orchestra

8   someday she loves to see professional violinist's whenever she can.

9   Her Mother and Father are very supportive they gave her a quality

10 violin drive her to her private lessons, and encourage her all of the

11 time. Mikala says she is inspired by itzak perlman who had polio

12 when he was four years old, he won the israel talent competition

13 when he was 14 and toured the United States. She dreams of playing

14 just like him one day for now, she's satisfied to be part of the

15 cherry valley high school orchestra.

PARTS OF SPEECH

Fire Drill!

Identify the part of speech for each underlined word. There are three examples for each part of speech, except for the interjection, which has one example. (Two words have been labeled for you.)

1   Our school has a fire *noun* <u>drill</u> about once a

2   month. It seems like *pronoun* <u>it</u> <u>always</u> comes <u>during</u>

3   shop <u>class</u>. I'll be right in the middle of put-

4   ting the <u>final</u> touches on a birdhouse, and then, "BZBZBZBZBZBZBZBZ!"

5   If I'm not in shop class, I'm usually in gym class when the alarm goes

6   off. We all <u>march</u> <u>onto</u> the lawn wearing our "geeky" gym suits. Coach

7   McGirdle <u>runs</u> around blowing his whistle <u>so</u> we remain orderly. "<u>Hey</u>! No

8   chatter <u>in</u> the ranks!" he yells. These fire drills aren't so bad in <u>warm</u>

9   weather, <u>but</u> in winter they are a <u>real</u> bummer. <u>I</u> know they're important,

10 but I can still dislike them. It <u>usually</u> takes the teachers only a few

11 minutes to make sure all the <u>kids</u> are out of the building, <u>yet</u> we seem to

12 stand there <u>forever</u>. On winter days, <u>we</u> almost wish we had a roaring

13 campfire to help us keep warm.

PARTS OF SPEECH
Let's give thanks.

Identify the part of speech for each underlined word. There are three examples for each part of speech, except for the interjection, which has one example. (A few words have been labeled for you.)

adverb
1 I <u>always</u> disliked sitting at the kids' table
   adjective   noun
2 at <u>holiday</u> <u>meals</u>. That meant sitting in a

3 corner <u>of</u> the kitchen at a card table. I disliked

4 it most when <u>I</u> was a teenager. During that time, I always <u>asked</u> my mom

5 if I could sit with the grown-ups, <u>but</u> <u>she</u> always shook her head. Now that

6 I have come of age, so to speak, I get to sit <u>with</u> the adults. However, <u>it's</u>

7 not what I thought it would be. My aunts and uncles usually <u>talk</u> about

8 how much medicine everyone is taking <u>or</u> who has had <u>major</u> surgery

9 recently. <u>Gross!</u> I generally lose my <u>appetite</u> after listening to them for a

10 while. I <u>watch</u> the kids <u>quietly</u> brewing <u>bubbly</u> potions of <u>gravy</u>, olive pits,

11 <u>and</u> soda <u>at</u> their table. Maybe that's where I <u>really</u> belong.

NOUNS

A Capital Offense

▎**Underline the nouns in the following sentences. Write *S* above each singular noun and *P* above each plural noun. (The number of nouns in each sentence is indicated in parentheses.)**

1. On the <u>refrigerator</u> *S* is a <u>list</u> *S* of calorie <u>counts</u> *P*. (3)

2. I left my shoes somewhere in that pile of dirty clothes. (3)

3. Myron has got another one of those nasty summer colds. (2)

4. I bought a six-pack of soda and five bottles of juice for the picnic. (5)

5. We saw a gaggle of geese waddle across the road. (3)

6. Believe it or not, the cows crossed right by the cattle-crossing sign. (2)

7. As you may well know, deer cross roads wherever they want to cross. (2)

▎**Underline the nouns in the following sentences. Write *C* above each common noun and *P* above each proper noun. (The number of nouns in each sentence is indicated in parentheses.)**

1. <u>Mary</u> *P* got a <u>pair</u> *C* of <u>Reebok</u> *P* tennis <u>shoes</u> *C* for her <u>birthday</u> *C*. (5)

2. My parents went to Paris for their wedding anniversary. (3)

3. Todd calls the MTV vote-line every Friday night. (3)

4. I brush my cocker spaniel in the morning. (2)

5. My mom loves that new song by Madonna. (3)

6. I know Dad likes our Siamese cat Mitsi. (3)

7. Mount Rushmore, Washington Monument, and Devils Tower are all national monuments. (4)

8. The White House is the executive residence of the president. (3)

NOUNS
Life's Trivial Treasures

Underline the nouns in the following sentences. Write *S* above each singular noun and *P* above each plural noun. (The number of nouns in each sentence is indicated in parentheses.)

1. My <u>brother</u> [S] always throws his dirty <u>socks</u> [P] on the <u>floor</u> [S]. (3)

2. The chairs look much nicer since they've been reupholstered with such a rich-looking fabric. (2)

3. To exercise my mind, I wrote two entries in my diary. (3)

4. Watermelon is the greatest refreshment ever on hot summer days. (3)

5. Mark told me that there are chicken beaks in some processed meats. (3)

6. Aquarium fish sleep when the light is turned off. (2)

7. Clover is added to grass to make it thicker. (2)

Underline the nouns in the following sentences. Write *C* above each common noun and *P* above each proper noun. (The number of nouns in each sentence is indicated in parentheses.)

1. My <u>dad</u> [C] says I have more <u>shoes</u> [C] than Grant's <u>army</u> [C]. (3)

2. Computers are common sights in American classrooms. (3)

3. Byron actually has five copies of *The Outsiders* in his locker. (4)

4. A volcano erupted in the Philippines yesterday. (2)

5. Yuck, Gino eats cold pizza with anchovies for breakfast. (4)

6. On Friday night, the Hendersons eat fish. (3)

7. A writing handbook is required at Bigfoot Academy. (2)

8. I love large dogs like Great Danes and Saint Bernards. (3)

VERBS

The Time of Our Lives

In the sentences below, underline all the verbs with two lines. Label each action verb with an *A* and each linking verb with an *L*.

1. Doctor Kolar gave͟ (A) my little sister Gracie a shot

   in the arm.

2. The shot, a polio vaccination, was necessary for school.

3. The clinic nurses made the whole experience less frightening.

4. They cracked all kinds of sick jokes.

5. Shots offer protection from harmful illnesses.

6. Shots in the arm are both helpful . . . and painful.

7. Fortunately, the discomfort lasts only a short time.

In each of the following sentences, underline the verbs with two lines. All but three of the sentences contain auxiliary or helping verbs.

1. We had͟ the time of our lives on our first camping trip.

2. Our family had been planning the trip for weeks and weeks.

3. The fish were biting on everything, even balls of bread dough and small

   pieces of liver.

4. We could have eaten fresh fish at every meal.

5. Even our dogs were having a good time, especially on the beach.

6. Our old wooden boat barely stayed afloat.

7. As a result, most of our fishing was done from shore.

8. Except for that, everything about our trip was great.

VERBS
Dealing with Nature

In the sentences below, underline all the verbs with two lines. Label each action verb with an *A* and each linking verb with an *L*.

1. It <u>was</u> another warm July afternoon on a

   Wisconsin dairy farm.

2. The summer sun baked the fields a golden yellow

   color.

3. Holstein cows quietly chewed their cuds.

4. A Labrador retriever found relief from the heat under the back porch.

5. For the fourth week straight, this section of the country went without rain.

6. The dust from the fields irritated everyone's eyes.

7. All of the farms in the area were in need of rain.

In each of the following sentences, underline the verbs with two lines. All but three of the sentences contain auxiliary or helping verbs.

1. Bart <u>was painting</u> their wooden deck along with his mother.

2. Suddenly, Bart heard the screams of his frantic mother.

3. She had stepped on a bees' nest.

4. Bart feverishly slapped at the bees with his paintbrush.

5. His mother jumped up and down at the same time.

6. They must have created quite a scene.

7. For at least 30 seconds, a lot of hollering and hopping was done.

8. Through it all, Bart's mother had suffered no more than two or three stings.

IRREGULAR VERBS
This is highly irregular!

■ **Identify the correct form of the verb in parentheses to complete each sentence. Write your answer on the blank space.**

1. (set) Please _____*set*_____ the piano on that area rug over there.

2. (come) He finally _____ to the end of his lecture.

3. (break) My body feels like it is _____ in five different places.

4. (ring) The telephone _____ many times before Junior answered it.

5. (steal) Someone _____ my bologna sandwich.

6. (go) Have you ever _____ to Great America at night?

7. (bring) No one _____ their favorite music to the party.

8. (fall) Fifty boxes of lightbulbs _____ from the shelf.

9. (ride) I have never _____ on a camel before.

10. (freeze) My older brother and his friend _____ in the tent.

11. (shrink) Since my sweatpants have _____ , I think I'll wear my jeans.

12. (take) The rustler had _____ our favorite llama.

13. (run) The toddler _____ right into the door.

14. (burst) The bubble finally _____ after almost 30 seconds.

15. (begin) Autumn means that the football season has _____ .

16. (become) Mark Twain _____ famous for his understated humor.

17. (drink) Waldo said he had _____ all of his prune juice.

18. (swim) Has Nancy ever _____ in a river?

IRREGULAR VERBS
Heads it's WRING; tails it's WRUNG.

■ **Identify the correct form of the verb in parentheses to complete each sentence. Write your answer on the blank space.**

1. (ride) Only Linda has _____*ridden*_____ on the American Eagle before.

2. (Set) _____ your lunch trays over there next to the soda machine.

3. (drink) I _____ seven glasses of water after mowing the lawn.

4. (drive) Grandma had _____ a car before a driver's license was required.

5. (throw) Has Jan really _____ out our Batman comic books?

6. (run) Our cat _____ away five different times last week.

7. (see) Once my mom _____ my progress report, I knew I was in trouble.

8. (come) Jack never _____ back for his wallet.

9. (shine) Has the sun *ever* _____ in this part of the world?

10. (swim) Yvonne has _____ across the quarry many times before.

11. (ring) The church bells _____ to signal the end of the ceremony.

12. (grow) I've _____ attached to that crazy spider in the corner.

13. (bring) Wally _____ five cupcakes for dessert today.

14. (go) None of us have _____ bowling in years.

15. (shake) Like a fool, Teddie _____ the can of soda before opening it.

16. (burst) Some actors _____ upon the movie scene quite unexpectedly.

17. (break) She's never _____ a promise with her older sister.

18. (ride) Move over! I've _____ shotgun long enough.

Assessment Activities: Answer Key

SENTENCE ERRORS
Summer Reading

Write *F* in front of each sentence fragment, *CS* in front of each comma splice, *RO* in front of each run-on sentence, and *C* in front of each correct sentence. Also correct each faulty sentence.

(Corrections will vary.)

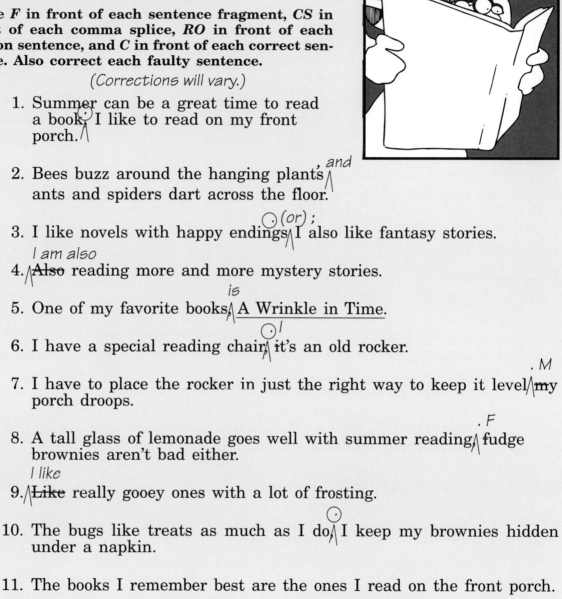

CS 1. Summer can be a great time to read a book ⊙ I like to read on my front porch. ∧

RO 2. Bees buzz around the hanging plants *, and* ∧ ants and spiders dart across the floor.

RO 3. I like novels with happy endings ⊙ *(or)* ; ∧ I also like fantasy stories.

F 4. ∧ *I am also* ~~Also~~ reading more and more mystery stories.

F 5. One of my favorite books ∧ *is* A Wrinkle in Time.

CS 6. I have a special reading chair ∧ ⊙ *I* it's an old rocker.

RO 7. I have to place the rocker in just the right way to keep it level ∧ *. M* my porch droops.

CS 8. A tall glass of lemonade goes well with summer reading ∧ *. F* fudge brownies aren't bad either.

F 9. ∧ *I like* ~~Like~~ really gooey ones with a lot of frosting.

CS 10. The bugs like treats as much as I do ∧ ⊙ I keep my brownies hidden under a napkin.

C 11. The books I remember best are the ones I read on the front porch.

C 12. At night I read by lamplight or even moonlight.

F 13. ∧ *I get* ~~Get~~ a tan while reading during the day.

CS 14. I'm in my own little world when I read ∧ ⊙ I get lost in each story.

C 15. I spend more time on my porch during the summer than I do in just about any other part of our house.

SENTENCE ERRORS

I scream for ice cream!

Write *F* in front of each sentence fragment, *CS* in front of each comma splice, *RO* in front of each run-on sentence, and *C* in front of each correct sentence. Also correct each faulty sentence.

(Corrections will vary.)

CS 1. Ice-cream trucks used to be common⊙ I bought ice cream from them when I was a kid.

C 2. When the ice-cream man would ring his bell, the kids came running.

F 3. *We were all* ~~All~~ carrying change to buy ice cream.

CS 4. I liked Rockets the best⊙*T* they were red, white, and blue Popsicles.

F 5. *They are* Popsicles shaped like fat rocket ships.

RO 6. I really liked my neighborhood ice-cream man⊙ I called him Spud for some reason.

F 7. *He always* ~~Always~~ called out to me when he saw me in line.

RO 8. Sometimes he gave my friends and me two ice-cream treats⊙*T* that was when no one else was around.

C 9. Blue-moon ice cream in a sugar cone was popular in our neighborhood.

RO 10. Money was always a problem⊙*W* we wanted to try everything.

CS 11. We sometimes settled for sno-cones⊙*T* they were only 10 cents.

CS 12. I also liked ice-cream sandwiches⊙*C* chocolate-covered bananas were great, too.

C 13. My dad would sometimes treat us when he was home.

RO 14. I never see ice-cream trucks anymore⊙*W* we get our ice cream at the supermarket.

F 15. The fun *has been* taken out of buying ice cream.

USING THE RIGHT WORD

The Call of the Wild

Draw a line through any underlined word that is incorrectly used and write the correct form above it. Do not change a word that is correct.

Example: Mrs. Isaacson complained that she had

heard
~~herd~~ strange noises coming from under

the hood.

1. The introductory first-aid ~~coarse~~ *course* proved to be very challenging for the young

   campers. Soda and snacks improved ~~there~~ *their* morale, however.

2. One camper ~~choose~~ *chose* jewelry class because she wanted to make a ~~medal~~ *metal*

   bracelet.

3. At night, we were ~~aloud~~ *allowed* to start enough campfires to light up the ~~hole~~ *whole* area.

4. Everyone enjoyed rafting ~~alot~~ *a lot*, ~~accept~~ *except* for Buford, who got a little "seasick."

5. The nonstop rain ruined ~~quiet~~ *quite* a few of our plans and ~~maid~~ *made* a sopping

   mess inside our leaky tent.

6. I almost died when I stumbled upon ~~an~~ *a* snake slithering ~~among~~ *between* the last

   two tents.

7. ~~Your~~ *You're* not going to believe this, but furry little creatures are not ~~deer~~ *dear* to me.

8. We've noticed ~~less~~ *fewer* deer and no ~~bares~~ *bears* on the trails this year.

9. Everyone ~~seamed~~ *seemed* to enjoy swimming; they liked to tell ghost stories at

   night, ~~to~~ *too*.

10. Making breakfast over ~~an~~ *a* campfire was a challenge because ~~their~~ *there* was

    ~~know~~ *no* way to maintain an even, steady flame.

USING THE RIGHT WORD

Let's party!

▌ Draw a line through any underlined word that is
incorrectly used and write the correct form above it.
Do not change a word that is correct.

Example: "~~Your~~ *You're* right, Tasha; a birthday party is

~~to~~ *too* much of a hassle."

1. At first, I was going to ~~by~~ *buy* Tasha a CD player

   for her birthday, but she <u>already</u> has one.

2. A new electronics shop is running a ~~real~~ *really* good sale on CD players starting

   tomorrow ~~mourning~~ *morning*.

3. Of ~~coarse~~ *course*, I have no ~~less~~ *fewer* than ~~too~~ *two* of these devices myself.

4. ~~Their~~ *There* are other things I can do for Tasha's birthday; I'll just have to ~~chose~~ *choose*

   from three or four possibilities.

5. I could take her out for an ice-cream sundae, ~~accept~~ *except* ~~deserts~~ *desserts* are out for

   both of us.

6. <u>It's</u> difficult to diet, but both of us are trying to <u>lose</u> ~~wait~~ *weight*.

7. <u>There</u> is always a movie, but I'm not ~~aloud~~ *allowed* to go to the cinema complex.

8. I could always take her shopping, but we've ~~all ready~~ *already* been to the mall

   <u>quite</u> a few times this summer.

9. Maybe I shouldn't ~~brake~~ *break* tradition; for the ~~passed~~ *past* four years, I've given

   Tasha a book for her birthday.

10. ~~Its~~ *It's* an understatement to say she reads ~~alot~~ *a lot*; I know of no one else ~~whose~~ *who's*

    so consumed by books.

CAPITALIZATION AND PUNCTUATION

She's certainly not bashful.

Supply all the capital letters, commas, and end punctuation needed in the following paragraph. Draw a line through any mark of punctuation or capital letter that is used incorrectly.

1   *W* ~we~ took Amy, my three-year-old baby

2 sister, to the ~d~*D*isney ~i~*I*ce ~c~*C*apades last ~s~*S*unday

3 afternoon. She had never been to a show like that before. Amy

4 went crazy every time she saw new Disney characters, and they were

5 all there for her to see. *P*people five rows away could hear her yelling,

6 "Mickey," whenever Mickey Mouse was on ~C~*c*enter ~I~*i*ce. ~s~*S*he squealed

7 with delight when ~d~*D*onald ~d~*D*uck twirled in midair and came down on

8 one foot. Pluto made her break into a peal of giggles when he fell on

9 his behind. *M*many of the spectators, around us, when not watching

10 the show, enjoyed watching Amy. *I*i can still see her beaming with

11 sticky cotton candy, ketchup, and mustard on her face as the show

12 unfolded. *A*after all of the excitement of the Disney production, *A*amy

13 quickly became "*S*sleeping *B*beauty" when she hit the backseat of our car.

14 *W*~w~hat a crazy kid! *D*did *I*i enjoy myself that much when *I*i was three?

CAPITALIZATION AND PUNCTUATION
Practice, Practice, Practice

Supply all the capital letters, commas, and end punctuation needed in the following paragraph. Draw a line through any mark of punctuation or capital letter that is used incorrectly.

1   M
     ~~m~~ikala loves playing the violin in her

2   S   O
   ~~S~~chool ~~O~~rchestra. She has been playing violin

3   since the sixth grade, but she couldn't play in an orchestra until

4   S   f   C   V   H   S   .
   this year⌄she's a ~~F~~reshman at ~~c~~herry ~~v~~alley ~~h~~igh ~~s~~chool⌄Mikala has

5   Mrs. M   ,
   orchestra practice right after lunch⌄~~mrs~~ ~~m~~oseman⌄her orchestra

6   ,   M   .
   teacher⌄says ~~m~~ikala is very talented⌄Mikala also has private lessons

7   S   B   P   O
   three days a week⌄she wants to play in the ~~b~~oston ~~p~~ops ~~o~~rchestra

8   S
   someday⌄she loves to see professional violinist~~'~~s whenever she can.

9   m   f   T
   Her ~~M~~other and ~~F~~ather are very supportive⌄they gave her a quality

10   ,
   violin⌄drive her to her private lessons, and encourage her all of the

11   I   P   ,
   time. Mikala says she is inspired by ~~i~~tzak ~~p~~erlman⌄who had polio

12   H   I   T   C
   when he was four years old⌄~~h~~e won the ~~i~~srael ~~t~~alent ~~c~~ompetition

13   when he was 14 and toured the United States. She dreams of playing

14   F
   just like him one day⌄for now, she's satisfied to be part of the

15 C   V   H   S   O
   ~~c~~herry ~~v~~alley ~~h~~igh ~~s~~chool ~~o~~rchestra.

PARTS OF SPEECH
Fire Drill!

Identify the part of speech for each underlined word. There are three examples for each part of speech, except for the interjection, which has one example. (Two words have been labeled for you.)

1 Our school has a fire <u>drill</u> *(noun)* about once a

2 month. It seems like <u>it</u> *(pronoun)* <u>always</u> *(adverb)* comes <u>during</u> *(preposition)*

3 shop <u>class</u> *(noun)*. I'll be right in the middle of put-

4 ting the <u>final</u> *(adjective)* touches on a birdhouse, and then, "BZBZBZBZBZBZBZ!"

5 If I'm not in shop class, I'm usually in gym class when the alarm goes

6 off. We all <u>march</u> *(verb)* <u>onto</u> *(preposition)* the lawn wearing our "geeky" gym suits. Coach

7 McGirdle <u>runs</u> *(verb)* around blowing his whistle <u>so</u> *(conjunction)* we remain orderly. "<u>Hey!</u> *(interjection)* No

8 chatter <u>in</u> *(preposition)* the ranks!" he yells. These fire drills aren't so bad in <u>warm</u> *(adjective)*

9 weather, <u>but</u> *(conjunction)* in winter they <u>are</u> *(verb)* a <u>real</u> *(adjective)* bummer. <u>I</u> *(pronoun)* know they're important,

10 but I can still dislike them. It <u>usually</u> *(adverb)* takes the teachers only a few

11 minutes to make sure all the <u>kids</u> *(noun)* are out of the building, <u>yet</u> *(conjunction)* we seem to

12 stand there <u>forever</u> *(adverb)*. On winter days, <u>we</u> *(pronoun)* almost wish we had a roaring

13 campfire to help us keep warm.

PARTS OF SPEECH

Let's give thanks.

Identify the part of speech for each underlined word. There are three examples for each part of speech, except for the interjection, which has one example. (A few words have been labeled for you.)

adverb
1 I <u>always</u> disliked sitting at the kids' table

adjective *noun*
2 at <u>holiday</u> <u>meals</u>. That meant sitting in a

preposition
3 corner <u>of</u> the kitchen at a card table. I disliked

pronoun   *verb*
4 it most when <u>I</u> was a teenager. During that time, I always <u>asked</u> my mom

conjunction *pronoun*
5 if I could sit with the grown-ups, <u>but</u> <u>she</u> always shook her head. Now that

preposition   *pronoun*
6 I have come of age, so to speak, I get to sit <u>with</u> the adults. However, <u>it's</u>

verb
7 not what I thought it would be. My aunts and uncles usually <u>talk</u> about

conjunction   *adjective*
8 how much medicine everyone is taking <u>or</u> who has had <u>major</u> surgery

interjection   *noun*
9 recently. <u>Gross!</u> I generally lose my <u>appetite</u> after listening to them for a

verb   *adverb*   *adjective*   *noun*
10 while. I <u>watch</u> the kids <u>quietly</u> brewing <u>bubbly</u> potions of <u>gravy</u>, olive pits,

conjunction *preposition*   *adverb*
11 <u>and</u> soda <u>at</u> their table. Maybe that's where I <u>really</u> belong.

NOUNS

A Capital Offense

Underline the nouns in the following sentences. Write *S* above each singular noun and *P* above each plural noun. (The number of nouns in each sentence is indicated in parentheses.)

1. On the <u>refrigerator</u> [S] is a <u>list</u> [S] of calorie <u>counts</u> [P]. (3)

2. I left my <u>shoes</u> [P] somewhere in that <u>pile</u> [S] of dirty <u>clothes</u> [P]. (3)

3. <u>Myron</u> [S] has got another one of those nasty summer <u>colds</u> [P]. (2)

4. I bought a <u>six-pack</u> [S] of <u>soda</u> [S] and five <u>bottles</u> [P] of <u>juice</u> [S] for the <u>picnic</u> [S]. (5)

5. We saw a <u>gaggle</u> [S] of <u>geese</u> [P] waddle across the <u>road</u> [S]. (3)

6. Believe it or not, the <u>cows</u> [P] crossed right by the cattle-crossing <u>sign</u> [S]. (2)

7. As you may well know, <u>deer</u> [P] cross <u>roads</u> [P] wherever they want to cross. (2)

Underline the nouns in the following sentences. Write *C* above each common noun and *P* above each proper noun. (The number of nouns in each sentence is indicated in parentheses.)

1. <u>Mary</u> [P] got a <u>pair</u> [C] of <u>Reebok</u> [P] tennis <u>shoes</u> [C] for her <u>birthday</u> [C]. (5)

2. My <u>parents</u> [C] went to <u>Paris</u> [P] for their wedding <u>anniversary</u> [C]. (3)

3. <u>Todd</u> [P] calls the MTV <u>vote-line</u> [C] every Friday <u>night</u> [C]. (3)

4. I brush my <u>cocker spaniel</u> [C] in the <u>morning</u> [C]. (2)

5. My <u>mom</u> [C] loves that new <u>song</u> [C] by <u>Madonna</u> [P]. (3)

6. I know <u>Dad</u> [P] likes our Siamese <u>cat</u> [C] <u>Mitsi</u> [P]. (3)

7. <u>Mount Rushmore</u> [P], <u>Washington Monument</u> [P], and <u>Devils Tower</u> [P] are all national <u>monuments</u> [C]. (4)

8. The <u>White House</u> [P] is the executive <u>residence</u> [C] of the <u>president</u> [C]. (3)

NOUNS

Life's Trivial Treasures

▎Underline the nouns in the following sentences. Write *S* above each singular noun and *P* above each plural noun. (The number of nouns in each sentence is indicated in parentheses.)

1. My <u>brother</u> [S] always throws his dirty <u>socks</u> [P] on the <u>floor</u> [S]. (3)

2. The <u>chairs</u> [P] look much nicer since they've been reupholstered with such a rich-looking <u>fabric</u> [S]. (2)

3. To exercise my <u>mind</u> [S], I wrote two <u>entries</u> [P] in my <u>diary</u> [S]. (3)

4. <u>Watermelon</u> [S] is the greatest <u>refreshment</u> [S] ever on hot summer <u>days</u> [P]. (3)

5. <u>Mark</u> [S] told me that there are chicken <u>beaks</u> [P] in some processed <u>meats</u> [P]. (3)

6. Aquarium <u>fish</u> [P] sleep when the <u>light</u> [S] is turned off. (2)

7. <u>Clover</u> [S] is added to <u>grass</u> [S] to make it thicker. (2)

▎Underline the nouns in the following sentences. Write *C* above each common noun and *P* above each proper noun. (The number of nouns in each sentence is indicated in parentheses.)

1. My <u>dad</u> [C] says I have more <u>shoes</u> [C] than Grant's <u>army</u> [C]. (3)

2. <u>Computers</u> [C] are common <u>sights</u> [C] in American <u>classrooms</u> [C]. (3)

3. <u>Byron</u> [P] actually has five <u>copies</u> [C] of *The Outsiders* [P] in his <u>locker</u> [C]. (4)

4. A <u>volcano</u> [C] erupted in the <u>Philippines</u> [P] yesterday. (2)

5. Yuck, <u>Gino</u> [P] eats cold <u>pizza</u> [C] with <u>anchovies</u> [C] for <u>breakfast</u> [C]. (4)

6. On Friday <u>night</u> [C], the <u>Hendersons</u> [P] eat <u>fish</u> [C]. (3)

7. A writing <u>handbook</u> [C] is required at <u>Bigfoot Academy</u> [P]. (2)

8. I love large <u>dogs</u> [C] like <u>Great Danes</u> [P] and <u>Saint Bernards</u> [P]. (3)

VERBS
The Time of Our Lives

▌In the sentences below, underline all the verbs with two lines. Label each action verb with an *A* and each linking verb with an *L*.

1. Doctor Kolar $\overset{A}{\underline{\underline{gave}}}$ my little sister Gracie a shot

   in the arm.

2. The shot, a polio vaccination, $\overset{L}{\underline{\underline{was}}}$ necessary for school.

3. The clinic nurses $\overset{A}{\underline{\underline{made}}}$ the whole experience less frightening.

4. They $\overset{A}{\underline{\underline{cracked}}}$ all kinds of sick jokes.

5. Shots $\overset{A}{\underline{\underline{offer}}}$ protection from harmful illnesses.

6. Shots in the arm $\overset{L}{\underline{\underline{are}}}$ both helpful . . . and painful.

7. Fortunately, the discomfort $\overset{A}{\underline{\underline{lasts}}}$ only a short time.

▌In each of the following sentences, underline the verbs with two lines. All but three of the sentences contain auxiliary or helping verbs.

1. We <u><u>had</u></u> the time of our lives on our first camping trip.

2. Our family <u><u>had been planning</u></u> the trip for weeks and weeks.

3. The fish <u><u>were biting</u></u> on everything, even balls of bread dough and small

   pieces of liver.

4. We <u><u>could have eaten</u></u> fresh fish at every meal.

5. Even our dogs <u><u>were having</u></u> a good time, especially on the beach.

6. Our old wooden boat barely <u><u>stayed</u></u> afloat.

7. As a result, most of our fishing <u><u>was done</u></u> from shore.

8. Except for that, everything about our trip <u><u>was</u></u> great.

VERBS
Dealing with Nature

▌ In the sentences below, underline all the verbs with two lines. Label each action verb with an *A* and each linking verb with an *L*.

1. It was another warm July afternoon on a
   Wisconsin dairy farm.
   (L over "was")

2. The summer sun baked the fields a golden yellow
   color.
   (A over "baked")

3. Holstein cows quietly chewed their cuds.
   (A over "chewed")

4. A Labrador retriever found relief from the heat under the back porch.
   (A over "found")

5. For the fourth week straight, this section of the country went without rain.
   (A over "went")

6. The dust from the fields irritated everyone's eyes.
   (A over "irritated")

7. All of the farms in the area were in need of rain.
   (L over "were")

▌ In each of the following sentences, underline the verbs with two lines. All but three of the sentences contain auxiliary or helping verbs.

1. Bart was painting their wooden deck along with his mother.

2. Suddenly, Bart heard the screams of his frantic mother.

3. She had stepped on a bees' nest.

4. Bart feverishly slapped at the bees with his paintbrush.

5. His mother jumped up and down at the same time.

6. They must have created quite a scene.

7. For at least 30 seconds, a lot of hollering and hopping was done.

8. Through it all, Bart's mother had suffered no more than two or three stings.

IRREGULAR VERBS
This is highly irregular!

Identify the correct form of the verb in parentheses to complete each sentence. Write your answer on the blank space.

1. (set) Please ____*set*____ the piano on that area rug over there.

2. (come) He finally ____*came*____ to the end of his lecture.

3. (break) My body feels like it is ____*broken*____ in five different places.

4. (ring) The telephone ____*rang*____ many times before Junior answered it.

5. (steal) Someone ____*stole*____ my bologna sandwich.

6. (go) Have you ever ____*gone*____ to Great America at night?

7. (bring) No one ____*brought*____ their favorite music to the party.

8. (fall) Fifty boxes of lightbulbs ____*fell*____ from the shelf.

9. (ride) I have never ____*ridden*____ on a camel before.

10. (freeze) My older brother and his friend ____*froze*____ in the tent.

11. (shrink) Since my sweatpants have ____*shrunk*____ , I think I'll wear my jeans.

12. (take) The rustler had ____*taken*____ our favorite llama.

13. (run) The toddler ____*ran*____ right into the door.

14. (burst) The bubble finally ____*burst*____ after almost 30 seconds.

15. (begin) Autumn means that the football season has ____*begun*____ .

16. (become) Mark Twain ____*became*____ famous for his understated humor.

17. (drink) Waldo said he had ____*drunk*____ all of his prune juice.

18. (swim) Has Nancy ever ____*swum*____ in a river?

IRREGULAR VERBS
Heads it's WRING; tails it's WRUNG.

■ **Identify the correct form of the verb in parentheses to complete each sentence. Write your answer on the blank space.**

1. (ride) Only Linda has _____*ridden*_____ on the American Eagle before.

2. (Set) _____*Set*_____ your lunch trays over there next to the soda machine.

3. (drink) I _____*drank*_____ seven glasses of water after mowing the lawn.

4. (drive) Grandma had _____*driven*_____ a car before a driver's license was required.

5. (throw) Has Jan really _____*thrown*_____ out our Batman comic books?

6. (run) Our cat _____*ran*_____ away five different times last week.

7. (see) Once my mom _____*saw*_____ my progress report, I knew I was in trouble.

8. (come) Jack never _____*came*_____ back for his wallet.

9. (shine) Has the sun *ever* _____*shone*_____ in this part of the world?

10. (swim) Yvonne has _____*swum*_____ across the quarry many times before.

11. (ring) The church bells _____*rang*_____ to signal the end of the ceremony.

12. (grow) I've _____*grown*_____ attached to that crazy spider in the corner.

13. (bring) Wally _____*brought*_____ five cupcakes for dessert today.

14. (go) None of us have _____*gone*_____ bowling in years.

15. (shake) Like a fool, Teddie _____*shook*_____ the can of soda before opening it.

16. (burst) Some actors _____*burst*_____ upon the movie scene quite unexpectedly.

17. (break) She's never _____*broken*_____ a promise with her older sister.

18. (ride) Move over! I've _____*ridden*_____ shotgun long enough.

SourceBook Answer Key

SourceBook Answer Key

SourceBook Answer Key

This section contains answers to appropriate units, workshops, and minilessons in *SourceBook 6000*. (Answers are not given for activities if students' responses will vary.)

Monitoring

... a resource of student workshops, activities, and strategies to accompany

WRITE SOURCE
2000

WRITE SOURCE

GREAT SOURCE EDUCATION GROUP

a Houghton Mifflin Company

Wilmington, Massachusetts

A FEW WORDS ABOUT SOURCEBOOK 6000

WRITE SOURCE 2000

A Guide to
Writing, Thinking,
& Learning

■ **Below are some of the people who developed your SourceBook.**

Authors: Pat Sebranek
Dave Kemper
Randall VanderMey

Contributing Teachers:
Pat Andrews
Laura Bachman
Gina Camodeca
Carol Elsholz
Candice Fortmann
Tom Gilding
Mary Gregory
Janis Hartley
Phyllis Jaeger
Bev Jessen
Bonnie Knoblauch
Dale Ann Morgan
Peg Rifken
Kelly Saaf
tilli
ock

e
Gordon
is Krenzke

Before you begin . . .

it is important for you to know that your *SourceBook 6000* must be used with the *Write Source 2000* handbook. The handbook provides guidelines, examples, and models; the SourceBook provides many opportunities to put that information into practice. It's also important for you to know how all of the activities in the SourceBook are organized.

Part I contains seven core writing units that address many of the important forms of writing covered in the handbook, including auto-biographical and biographical writing, paragraphs, essays, and stories.

Part II contains many different workshop activities that will help you at all stages of the writing process, from prewriting to proofreading.

Part III contains language workshops that will help you better understand how words work, and learning workshops that will help you become a better thinker, study-reader, speaker, and listener.

Part IV, way in the back of the book, features a series of minilessons that relate to all of the different areas of writing, language, and learning covered in your handbook.

What makes "shopping" in your SourceBook so worthwhile is that the activities come in so many different shapes and sizes; there is something to please everybody. All you and your teacher have to do is decide what units and workshops best meet your needs. We're sure that all of your shopping experiences in this SourceBook will help you improve as a writer and as a learner.

TABLE OF CONTENTS

Part I: Core Writing Units

Part II: Writing Workshops

Part III: Language and Learning Workshops

Part IV: Writing and Learning Minilessons

PART I
Core Writing Units

CORE WRITING

Writing from Start to Finish

The **Core Writing Units** provide you with a series of seven extended writing activities addressing many of the basic types of writing covered in the *Write Source 2000* student handbook: autobiographical writing, paragraphs, essays, and stories. As you complete your work in these units, you will be gaining valuable experience with the types of writing tasks you are often asked to carry out in your classes, as well as in most writing assessment tests. You will also be practicing the very skills that are at the "core" of the writing process, from selecting subjects to correcting final drafts.

It's important to know that everything you need to complete your work is included, from step-by-step guidelines to student models. In addition, each page within these units is self-contained, providing you with clearly identifiable starting and stopping points for your work. This will make it easy for you to stay on task from one day to the next. Upon completion of each unit, you will have produced at least one important piece of writing.

Getting Started

User's Checklist

Check your progress as you work on these **Core Writing Units.**

☐ **Writing About Personal Experiences**
I'm not making this up!

☐ **Building Paragraphs: Part 1**
Paragraph Review and Narrative Writing

☐ **Building Paragraphs: Part 2**
Expository and Descriptive Writing

☐ **Writing Descriptively About People**
de•scribe: to represent or depict something in words

☐ **Writing Mystery Stories**
Whodunit?

☐ **Writing the Comparison and Contrast Essay**
Working in Pairs

☐ **Writing a Report**
I've always been interested in . . .

**AFTER •
WORDS** | Does your teacher expect you to turn in a writing portfolio at the end of the grading period? If so, reserve some space in it for the writing you complete in these units.

WRITING ABOUT PERSONAL EXPERIENCES

I'm not making this up!

THE FIRST STEP • No one can write about experiences in your own life better than you. You are the expert! In this unit you will put this expertise to good use since you will be asked to think and write about memorable experiences from your past. In the process, we expect that you will learn something about using good details in writing, speaking in your natural writing voice, and sharing writing ideas with your classmates. (We also expect that you will have some fun along the way.)

READ: As you read the following model by Mike Ekelman, try to picture the experience as it develops.

> *One day last summer, my mom was downstairs washing clothes, and my cat Muter jumped into the dryer without my mom knowing it. My mom put a pile of wet clothes on top of my cat, closed the door, set the timer, and turned on the dryer. All of a sudden she heard a helpless meowing. My mom called me down to find the source of the noise. As I walked down the stairs, I could hear it, too. The meowing grew louder and louder and more frightened sounding. I opened the dryer and there was Muter. Her black hair was standing on end. She looked like one of those pictures of a person who had put her finger in an electric outlet. She fled upstairs. From then on, we've never let Muter downstairs.*

REACT: Use the following set of questions to help you react to this model experience. (Share your responses with a classmate.)

● What do you like best about this writing?

● Does the writing contain enough detail? That is, can you picture the experience as it unfolds?

● Could the writer have started his writing in a different way? How so?

   ● What would be a good title for this personal story?

      ● Does this model remind you of any experiences from your past?

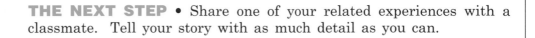

THE NEXT STEP • Share one of your related experiences with a classmate. Tell your story with as much detail as you can.

■ Gathering Ideas for Writing: Sentence Completions

COMPLETE: To help you think about some of your own memorable experiences, complete as many of the following open-ended sentences as you can.

1. I was so scared the first time I _____

_____

_____ .

2. My favorite vacation or trip was _____

_____

_____ .

3. I'll never forget when _____

_____ .

4. I was so embarrassed when _____

_____ .

5. I got so mad when _____

_____ .

6. The most difficult thing I ever did was _____

_____ .

7. The worst thing I ever did was _____

_____ .

8. One time, while eating at a restaurant, I _____

_____ .

THE NEXT STEP • Share your sentence completions with a classmate (or your entire class). Listening to someone else's experiences may help you remember even more of your own memorable experiences.

■ Gathering Ideas for Writing: Listing

THE FIRST STEP • Freely **listing** ideas as they come to mind (personal brainstorming) is another effective way to gather ideas for writing. If you really let yourself go as you list, you will be amazed at the number of ideas you will uncover.

LIST: Pick a specific time in your life—living in an old neighborhood, a series of visits to the doctor's office, adjusting to a new member in the family, and so on. Then list below any experiences that come to mind when you think of that time. Work freely and rapidly. (If a totally unrelated experience comes to mind, that's fine. List it.)

Special Note: You might want to make a contest out of this activity by seeing if you can fill in this entire space within, say, 5 minutes.

THE NEXT STEP • Underline any ideas in your list that surprise you. Put a star next to any ideas that would make good subjects for experience papers. Share your results with your classmates. (See who was able to create the longest list.)

■ Developing One of Your Ideas

SELECTING: You now have two sets of ideas to choose from for a personal experience paper. (You've completed a series of open-ended sentences and created a list of related experiences.) Spend a few minutes reviewing each set of ideas, and then select one of these experiences as the subject for your writing.

Identify Your Subject Here:

_____

WRITING THE FIRST DRAFT: On your own paper, write a first draft of your work by recording the important details related to the experience as they come to mind, one right after another. (Keep writing until you have said all that needs to be said. Your work might be one paragraph in length or longer.)

Special Note: Most of the important details should already be clear in your mind. But don't be surprised if you uncover some hidden details as you write. Make sure that you include all of the important sights, sounds, smells, and feelings related to this experience.

HANDBOOK HELPER	Refer to "Writing, About experiences" in the index if you need more help with your writing. (Read the student model in that section.)

EVALUATE: The following checklist will help you review and revise your first draft. (Use this same checklist to evaluate your classmates' work.)

____ **Organization:** Are all of the details arranged in a clear and logical order, as things happened during the experience?

____ **Detail:** Are enough details included in the writing to help readers get a clear picture of the experience?

____ **Mechanics:** Has proper attention been given to neatness and accuracy? (Consider readability, sentences, spelling, punctuation, and so on.)

____ **Style:** Does the paper read smoothly and clearly from start to finish? What has the writer done to make her or his work enjoyable to read?

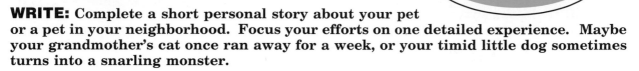

■ Writing About a Pet

extended **ACTIVITY**

Pet Lore

WRITE: Complete a short personal story about your pet or a pet in your neighborhood. Focus your efforts on one detailed experience. Maybe your grandmother's cat once ran away for a week, or your timid little dog sometimes turns into a snarling monster.

Note: If you can't think of a pet story, write about some other animal-related experience. (Use the space below for your first draft. Write your final copy on your own paper.)

THE NEXT STEP • Put your desks or chairs in a circle and, one by one, share your work with your classmates. Everyone likes to hear a good animal story.

■ Writing About a Cooking Experience

What's Cooking?

extended
ACTIVITY

COLLECT: In the space provided below, list at least four of your most memorable kitchen creations—entire meals, desserts, main dishes, sandwiches, etc. (Even if you're not a gourmet chef, you have at least put together a few interesting sandwiches in your time. You should have no trouble thinking of ideas for your list.)

A Recipe for Remembering

WRITE: On your own paper, write freely for 5 minutes about one of the creations from your list. Make sure to write nonstop. Include a lot of sights, sounds, smells, and tastes in your writing.

Food for Thought

Write a title for your free writing—a title that effectively summarizes your kitchen experience.

THE NEXT STEP • Share your work with a classmate. Then continue working with your writing until you shape it into a more polished personal story.

BUILDING PARAGRAPHS: PART 1
Paragraph Review and Narrative Writing

THE FIRST STEP • Raise your hands if you've never been asked to write a paragraph.... Aha, just as I thought. There are no hands in the air. Writing paragraphs in school is a sure bet—as sure as paying taxes will be when you become an adult. You've probably described different rooms, explained how to make things work, and retold important personal stories. These are all common paragraph-writing assignments.

   The activities in this section are designed to help you with this building block of writing. In some cases (as in this activity), you will review basic paragraph writing. In other cases, you will work with paragraphs in completely new ways.

The Working Parts

COMPLETE: **Complete the following statements by referring to the opening two pages in "Building Paragraphs" in your handbook.**

1. The three basic parts of a paragraph are the _____ topic sentence _____

   _____ at the beginning, the _____ body _____ or middle of

   the paragraph, and the _____ closing _____ or _____ clincher _____ sentence at

   the end.

2. A paragraph focuses on one specific _____ topic _____, which can be developed

   in the form of a story, a description, an explanation, or an _____ opinion _____ .

3. Here is a simple formula for writing effective topic sentences:

   A specific _____ subject _____ **+ a specific** _____ feeling _____ **or**

   _____ attitude _____ **= a good topic sentence**.

4. The _____ body _____ is the main part of the paragraph. This is where

   you tell the reader about your topic by including _____ specific _____

   _____ details _____ .

5. The _____ closing (clincher) _____ sentence reminds the reader what the topic of the

   paragraph is really all about.

■ Reviewing Paragraphs *(continued)*

READ: Carefully read the sample paragraph below. Note that the three basic parts of this paragraph are labeled.

A Very Dangerous Business

Topic Sentence

This might come as a surprise to you, but doing homework can be a very dangerous business. Just last night as I began to work on a math worksheet, three dangerous felons grabbed me from behind and stuffed me into the trunk of a rusty, old car. After driving for quite a while, the car came to a sudden stop, and my kidnappers left the car. I knew I had to do something quick, or it would be too late. I didn't want to yell and alert the

Body

kidnappers, so I wrote a note on the back of my worksheet and stuck it through one of the rust holes in the car. Fortunately, a passerby saw the note and notified the police. Soon after, the police came and captured the kidnappers. Since the police kept my worksheet as evidence, I couldn't complete my homework.

Closing Sentence

Tonight I'm going to make sure all of the doors and windows are locked before I start working.

You won't believe what happened to me!

Special Challenge: Take a normal, everyday experience like doing homework, walking to school, taking a test, or playing a game, and turn it into a "tall" tale like the model paragraph. Label the three basic parts in your finished paragraph.

■ Understanding Topic Sentences

Controlling Your Writing from the Start

THE FIRST STEP • If you allowed things to get totally out of control, you might

- finish off three bags of Oreo cookies,
- wear your polka-dotted pajamas to school,
- or call in a search party to help you find your bed under the mess in your room.

None of these things have ever happened to you, I'm sure. (If you did wear your pajamas to school, I don't want to know about it.) So let's move on to something much more practical.

Have you ever written something in which the ideas seemed to go all over the place like a glass of spilled milk? I'll bet you have. From time to time, all writers produce pieces that lack focus, that seem to be a bit out of control. This can be a serious problem, especially when you are asked to write a very controlled piece of writing like a **paragraph**.

The best way to keep a paragraph under wraps is to start with a focused topic sentence. A good topic sentence focuses on a specific subject and clearly states your feelings or attitude about that subject.

CHECK: Which of the following two ideas would make a good topic sentence?

> *Sir Arthur is a gerbil.*
> *Sir Arthur is my "baddest" pet gerbil.*

Discussion: Obviously, the second idea would work best. It contains a specific subject (Sir Arthur) plus a specific attitude (is my "baddest" pet gerbil). The first idea simply states a flat, uninteresting fact.

CHECK: Put a ✔ next to any of the following ideas that would make good topic sentences. (Share your results.)

1. ✔ Mr. Smith always has mischief in his eyes.

2. ____ Robert makes blueberry pancakes.

3. ____ Ms. Pitts grows apricots.

4. ✔ Spiral notebooks can be hazardous to your health.

5. ✔ Our student council has worked miracles this year.

6. ____ Our toaster is broken.

■ Understanding Topic Sentences *(continued)*

CREATE: Write focused topic sentences for the following general subjects:

HANDBOOK HELPER	Refer to "Paragraph, Basic parts" in the handbook index for a formula for writing your examples.

(A friend) _____

_____

_____

_____

(A machine) _____

_____

_____

_____

(A piece of clothing) _____

_____

_____

_____

(A subject of your own choosing) _____

_____

_____

_____

THE NEXT STEP • Exchange papers with a classmate. Make note of at least one topic sentence in each other's work that would make a good starting point for a paragraph. Afterward, share effective topic sentences with other members of the class. (Write them on the board for all to see.)

Special Challenge: Develop one of your topic sentences into a paragraph complete with effective supporting details. (Again, refer to the handbook if you need help with your paragraph writing.)

■ Model Narrative Paragraph

Thumbs-Up!

THE FIRST STEP • Reading, writing, speaking, and listening all lead to learning, right? These are the *language arts* you practice daily in school. You also practice another method of learning both inside and outside of school—learning through firsthand experience. This method may be the most important one of all.

READ: **The following model describes an unusual lesson the writer learned through a firsthand experience. Read and enjoy.**

Learning the Hard Way

I learned to treat my spiral notebooks with a great deal of respect one day in eighth grade. During fifth-hour science class, one end of the wire holding my notebook together managed to corkscrew its way into my thumb. (Don't ask me how.) After I couldn't get it out, I showed Mr. Gibson, my teacher, what had happened. He clipped the wire from the notebook and tried unsuccessfully to pull the other part out of my thumb. He then sent me to the gym so Mr. Zold could have a go at it. After he failed, I went to the office. It was decided there that I should go to the hospital, so my mother was notified. Surprisingly, I didn't have much pain through all of this, but I sure felt foolish sitting around with a wire sticking out of my thumb. Once my mother picked me up, she had me in the emergency room at St. Luke's Hospital in no time at all. After examining my injury, the doctor froze my thumb and twisted the wire out with some kind of medical pliers. Yuck! From that day on, I always covered the spiral part of my notebooks with tape.

How about you? What have you learned through experience? Let's find out on the next page.

■ Planning and Writing Narrative Paragraphs

Calling All Learning Experiences!

SHARE: Share some learning experiences (including unusual ones) with a classmate. Then each of you select one experience to write about in a narrative paragraph. In your writing, make sure to identify what you learned. (Use the space below for planning your paragraph and writing your first draft.)

Special Note: Refer to the model on the previous page to help you with your writing. Also refer to "Narrative paragraph" in the handbook index for another model.

Paragraph Work Space

_____

_____

_____

_____

_____

_____

_____

_____

_____

_____

_____

_____

THE NEXT STEP • Share your work with a classmate. Then continue developing your writing until you shape it into a more polished personal story. (Write your finished product on your own paper.)

■ **Planning and Writing a Narrative Paragraph**

Ten Stories High

THE FIRST STEP • Let's say you had a blast visiting your Aunt Matilda in her high-rise apartment. What's one of the first things you would want to do afterward? You'd want to tell someone about the experience. Everyone likes to share personal stories. It's part of human nature.

When you re-create one of these stories on paper, you are writing a **personal narrative**. Read the narrative paragraph in the handbook for a model of this type of writing. (Refer to "Narrative paragraph" in the index.)

A High-Flying Adventure

PLAN & WRITE: Write a narrative paragraph about a memorable experience that took place somewhere well above ground level. You might have traveled by plane, ridden a double Ferris wheel, visited a tall building, crossed a bridge, jumped from a tree, etc. You get the picture, right?

Note: Make sure that your paragraph begins with a good topic sentence and ends with an effective closing thought. Also make sure you have included plenty of detail in the body of your writing. (Use the space below to plan your paragraph; do your actual writing on your own paper.)

Topic Sentence: _____

_____

Detail: _____

Detail: _____

Detail: _____

Detail: _____

THE NEXT STEP • Share the results of your high-flying adventure with a classmate. Make note of at least one thing you liked in each other's work. Then, if you feel especially brave, share your writing with the entire class.

BUILDING PARAGRAPHS: PART 2
Expository and Descriptive Writing

THE FIRST STEP • Are people on a negative kick lately or what? All I hear are complaints and criticisms. The weather is either too hot or too cold. Everything costs too much money. The streets aren't safe anymore. Well, I've had it up to here with this kind of talk. (That's my complaint.) I want to hear some good news for a change.

WRITE: **In a paragraph, write about a class that you really like, a thoughtful or helpful person that you know, a place in your city that you really appreciate, a worthwhile group or organization you're associated with, or any other related subject. (Use the space below to plan your paragraph; do your actual writing on your own paper.)**

Note: Make sure that your paragraph begins with a good topic sentence and ends with an effective closing thought. Also make sure you have included plenty of supporting details in the body of your writing.

Topic Sentence: _____

_____

Detail: _____

Detail: _____

Detail: _____

Detail: *(Optional)* _____

Closing Sentence: _____

_____

THE NEXT STEP • Share your work with a classmate. Paragraphs that are particularly upbeat should be shared with the entire class.

■ Writing a How-To Paragraph

It's only natural.

THE FIRST STEP • In an **expository paragraph**, you share your knowledge about something. You *present* facts or directions, *explain* ideas, or *define* terms. By their very nature, expository paragraphs are instructive. They often tell readers what to do first, second, third, and so on.

READ: **What follows is an expository paragraph explaining how to remove a common tick from your skin. (Now, don't laugh! Ticks can transmit diseases that are harmful to humans. Ever hear of Lyme disease?) As you read this model, note how the information is tightly organized (*first of all, instead, then, finally*).**

A "Tick" in Time

It takes time and patience to remove a tick once it has attached itself to your skin. First of all, do not try to pull it off with force. A portion of its head will break off and remain inside the flesh. This can eventually cause an irritating sore. Instead, cover the animal (ticks are animals, not insects) with rubbing alcohol, heavy salad oil, or petroleum jelly, and wait until it relaxes its grip. Then carefully remove the tick with a tweezers. Finally, wash the affected area thoroughly with soap and water. Follow these same steps whenever you see a tick on your skin.

➤ *Now You Try*

WRITE: **In a paragraph, explain how to do something related to the outdoors. For example, you might know (or want to learn) how to treat poison ivy, build a campfire, trail ride on a mountain bike, plant a tree, or . . . the sky's the limit! (Use your own paper for your work.)**

Special Note: If you're really not into the great outdoors, write about another subject. You might even refer to your handbook for ideas; it's full of how-to information.

THE NEXT STEP • In a writing group or as a class, share paragraphs and see who has written the most detailed, amusing, or helpful explanations.

■ **Writing a Descriptive Paragraph**

In the Middle of the Action

THE FIRST STEP • In descriptive writing, you share your sensory impressions of a person, a place, a thing, or an idea with your readers. (*Sensory* simply means "dealing with your senses.") If your description is clear, your readers should be able to see what you see, hear what you hear, and feel what you feel.

CREATE: Write a topic sentence for each of the general subjects listed below. Each one is a potential subject for a descriptive paragraph. (Use the following example as a guide for your work.)

Example: *My sister's car is a real junkyard dog.*

(A specific subject [My sister's car] + a specific feeling or attitude about it [is a real junkyard dog] = a good topic sentence.)

(A person you respect or admire) _____

_____

(A specific part of the day) _____

_____

(A familiar piece of furniture) __ _____

_____

(A particular pastime) _____

_____

(A topic of your own choosing) _____

_____

WRITE: Put a check next to one sentence that you especially like. Share your work with a classmate and see if he or she agrees with your choice. Then write a descriptive paragraph for this topic sentence. (Refer to "Descriptive paragraph" in the handbook index for a model.)

Remember: In descriptive writing, a reader should see what you see, hear what you hear, and feel what you feel.

■ **Completing a Descriptive Writing Frame**

Framing a Picture

WRITE: Complete the following paragraph frame with descriptive words and phrases. The specific subject of your writing can be a favorite room, a secret meeting place, a vacation spot, or so on. (Make minor changes in the frame if needed.)

My Special Place

Whenever I am feeling _____ or _____ ,

I go to _____ .

It's a _____

place for (to) _____ .

When I'm there, I always look for (or see) _____

_____ .

It usually makes me feel _____

and _____ .

At times, I hear _____ or _____

_____ in this special place.

If I take a deep breath, I sometimes smell _____

_____ .

I know of no other place like _____ .

THE NEXT STEP • Review your writing after you complete the frame. Make note of any parts that could be improved if more details were added or other changes were made. Also have a classmate read and react to your work.

Special Challenge: Rework your writing until it more effectively describes your special place. (Use your own paper.)

■ **Writing Persuasive Paragraphs**

extended
ACTIVITY

Sound Off!

THE FIRST STEP • When you write a story, you are, among other things, trying to convince your readers that you have a good tale to tell. When you share information in expository writing, one of your goals is to get your readers to accept your facts or explanations.

When you write persuasively, your one and only purpose is to present a convincing argument. A persuasive piece might tell a good story, it might be colorful and informative, but it must always be convincing.

Where's the beef?

COLLECT: List potential subjects for a persuasive paragraph. Basically you're look-ing for things that you have strong feelings about. Think of school-related subjects like the canceling of the late bus for after-school activities. Also consider important community-related issues like new park regulations. And don't overlook popular leisure-time topics like skateboarding, shopping for clothes, etc.

Focusing Your Efforts

FOCUS: Select a subject from your list and shape it into a topic sentence for a persuasive paragraph. *Remember:* A topic sentence should identify your subject and state an attitude or a feeling about it. (Use the space provided below.)

Helpful Hint: If at all possible, state your topic sentence in positive rather than negative terms. Instead of *Noon hours stink at Goode Middle School,* try *Goode Middle School needs a more organized noon hour.* You'll find it much easier to develop an effective paragraph with a positive topic sentence.

Your Topic Sentence: _____

_____

_____

_____

■ **Writing Persuasive Paragraphs** *(continued)*

extended
ACTIVITY

COLLECT: List below some important facts and
details that support your topic sentence.

_____

_____

_____

_____

_____

_____

Note: Ask your classmates to review your planning. They might suggest a way to strengthen
your topic sentence, or they might supply you with additional supporting details.

Get it in writing.

**WRITE: On your own paper, develop your subject into a persuasive paragraph. See
your handbook for a model persuasive paragraph. (Refer to "Persuasive paragraph"
in the index.)**

Special Note: Organize your details in the most convincing order. (It's generally a good idea
to save your best point for last.)

THE NEXT STEP • Exchange your work with a classmate. Decide
if your partner has presented a convincing argument. Make note of
points you feel are especially strong . . . or not so strong.

Special Challenge: Revise your paragraph if, in fact, you feel your argument could be
stronger.

WRITING DESCRIPTIVELY ABOUT PEOPLE

de•scribe: *to represent or depict something in words*

THE FIRST STEP • The first activity in this unit is a test. But don't worry; it's not a typical test looking for right and wrong answers. This one is designed to evaluate your descriptive abilities. (And it may be one of the most enjoyable "tests" you will ever take.)

CREATE: **Draw a crazy-looking creature, someone or something that comes completely from your own imagination. (You can, of course, base your work on what you know about creatures and animals.) Or you can use magazine clippings to create your creature. You could, for example, combine the head of a monkey with the body of an ostrich, and so on. (Use the space provided below or your own paper for your work.)**

Special Note: Do not let anyone see your drawing just yet! This is very important.

WRITE: **On a separate sheet of paper, describe the appearance of your creature in writing. Base your description on the following points:**

- Give your readers the big picture first. That is, let them know how big or small, long or tall, the creature is.

- Describe its specific features in an orderly way. Start at the top of its head (if it has one) and work your way down to its feet (if it has any).

- Highlight some of its normal as well as its abnormal features.

THE NEXT STEP • Exchange written descriptions (not the drawings) with a classmate. Then try to draw a picture of each other's creatures, following the details provided in the writing. Compare the new drawings with the original ones to evaluate or test each other's descriptive abilities.

■ **Selecting and Collecting Ideas for Description**

Giving a Facial

THE FIRST STEP • Now that you have your descriptive juices flowing, let's move on to a more realistic activity. Picture the many faces of the people you know. Is there one face that stands out in your mind, one that you would really like to describe? Consider the faces of baby brothers or sisters, parents, friends, neighbors, celebrities, and so on.

SELECT & COLLECT: Choose one special face to think and write about descriptively. Then, in the space provided below, collect as many details as possible about your subject's face. Include every feature you can think of, from hairstyle to chin line.

THE NEXT STEP • Carefully review your list to make sure you haven't missed any details. Also make sure that you've captured all of your subject's features as accurately as possible. (Take a second or third look at your subject—either in person or in a photograph—to make sure that your details are accurate.)

■ Arranging Details in a Descriptive Poem

WRITE: Use all of the details you collected in the last activity as the starting point for a descriptive poem about your subject. (Refer to the model and the writing frame below to guide you in your work.)

> *Aunt Adeline*
> *Neat, chestnut bun*
> *Pulls against smooth forehead.*
> *Inquiring eyebrows overhang*
> *Blue pools, wide and deep,*
> *That float on high cheekbones,*
> *Separated by a long, straight nose.*
> *Pinkish lips form "O" in surprise,*
> *Above a no-nonsense chin.*

Discussion: Notice how carefully the subject is described in this model. The descriptions in your poem should be selected and written with the same amount of care.

WRITING FRAME

Use this frame as a general guide for your work. You don't have to describe all of the features listed here. (Use the blank spaces below for the first draft of your poem.)

_____ (first name/nickname)

_____ (hair)

_____ (forehead)

_____ (eyebrows)

_____ (eyes)

_____ (cheekbones)

_____ (ears)

_____ (nose)

_____ (mouth)

_____ (chin)

_____ (last name)

■ Reacting to a Short Descriptive Paragraph

READ: The paragraph below was developed from the model poem in the last activity. As you read, notice how the details are logically arranged.

> Aunt Adeline's <u>dark</u>, chestnut-colored <u>hair is always combed straight back and tied into</u> a neat bun <u>at the back of her head</u>. Her smooth forehead <u>wrinkles when she is puzzled about something</u>. Her eyebrows shoot up in a question mark, and her eyes turn deep blue. Her long, straight nose <u>forms an exclamation mark</u>, and her round, pink lips <u>make the point</u>. Aunt Adeline always wears a red silk scarf tied in a knot at her Adam's apple, and it shakes whenever she is surprised. <u>By the look of things, I'm not sure Aunt Adeline is the type of person who likes surprises.</u>

Discussion: The topic sentence comes at the end of this paragraph in the form of a summary statement. Also note that all of the details focus on Aunt Adeline's features when she is surprised.

REACT: Use the following checklist to help you react to this paragraph. (Share your responses.)

1. Put a ✔ next to the descriptive sentences you like the best. Put an ✘ next to the ones you like second best.

2. Underline any details in this paragraph that are not found in the descriptive poem. Why do you suppose the writer added these details?

   (Answers will vary.) To make her writing flow smoothly

3. What would be a good title for this model?

   (Answers will vary.) Serious Aunt Adeline
   My No-Surprises Aunt

➤ *Now You Try*

WRITE: Write a one-paragraph description of your subject's face, using the details in your descriptive poem as a starting point for your work.

Special Note: Try to focus your description around a certain look—maybe a look of surprise, anger, happiness, etc. Also remember to include a topic sentence in your paragraph. (Do all of your work on your own paper.)

■ Revising Checklist

REVISE: Use this checklist to help you improve your first draft. (Use the same checklist to evaluate your classmates' work.)

_____ **Organization:** Is the paragraph organized around a topic sentence?

_____ **Detail:** Does the description seem to focus on a certain look? Do the details effectively capture this look?

_____ **Style:** Do the sentences flow smoothly and read clearly?

_____ **Mechanics:** Has the proper attention been paid to neatness and accuracy?

HANDBOOK HELPER	Improve your first draft by using stronger, more colorful words. See "Writing, Improving" in the index for ideas.

Special Challenge: What's the best way to put the finishing touch on a piece of writing? By thinking of a good title for it. At the end of "The Writing Process" chapter, the handbook tells you to think of a title as fish bait: _"It should look juicy, it should dance slightly, and it should have a hook in it."_ In other words, a title should attract the readers' attention and lead them right into your writing.

COMPLETE: For practice, write titles for the following "works of art." (Share your results.)

1. Suppose someone has just written a song about you. What would be a good one-word title for this song?

   Title: _____

2. Suppose someone has written your biography. What would be a title for this book?

   Title: _____

3. Now suppose you have just written a newspaper article about life in your school. What would be the title of this article?

   Title: _____

THE NEXT STEP • Now go back to your descriptive paragraph and write an effective title for it. (If it already has a title, make sure that it hooks your readers' attention.)

■ Understanding Action Verbs

Something in the way she moves . . .

THE FIRST STEP • Capturing a person on paper can be more than just a physical description. You can also capture a person in action. Thus, it's a good idea to sharpen your ability to use words that *describe* motion: **ACTION VERBS**.

The more exact and vivid the verbs are in your writing, the easier it is for your readers to see what your subject is doing. Which sentence creates the clearer picture in your mind?

> *Toni walked to the front of the room.*
>
> *Toni bounced to the front of the room.*

Hopefully you picked the second one. *Bounced* creates a clearer picture. The stronger verb *bounced* suggests that Toni is eager to move—maybe she is about to receive some very good news.

➤ *Now You Try*

LIST: Provide more action-packed examples of the verbs listed in the first column. (The first one has been done to get you started.)

threw:	hurled	tossed	lobbed
said:			
sat:			
ran:			
looked:			
ate:			

THE NEXT STEP • Try not to prop up your verbs with modifiers. If you use strong, clear action verbs, you don't need them. Here's an example:

> **"Get off my seat," Susan *said angrily*.**
> **"Get off my seat," Susan *snapped*.**

See? The vivid verb *snapped* does the job of two words (*said angrily*).

■ Using Vivid Verbs in Descriptions

Put some "muscle" in your writing.

READ & REACT: Review the following descriptive paragraph, noting all of the words that are underlined. These are the verbs. (In one case a verb and modifier are underlined.) Cross these words out and replace them with strong, active, *muscle-bound* verbs . . . the kind of verbs with lifetime memberships at a fitness center.

(Answers will vary.)

The Shaq ~~plays~~ [*attacks*] the game of basketball. When he ~~runs~~ [*charges*] down the court, the fans ~~cheer loudly~~ [*explode*]. And when he ~~puts~~ [*stuffs*] the ball through the net, the whole gym ~~reacts~~ [*erupts*]. No basketball player in the game ~~interests~~ [*mesmerizes*] people so much.

Now read through the paragraph again with the new verbs. See what a difference that makes?

| **HANDBOOK HELPER** | Refer to "Verb, Vivid" in the index for more information. Pay special attention to the "Helpful Hint" about using and misusing "to be" verbs like *is, are,* and *was*. |

REVIEW: Now take another look at the descriptive paragraphs you wrote earlier (or another piece of writing). Circle all of your action verbs. (Ask a classmate to help you if you're not sure of all of your verbs.) Replace some of these verbs with more muscle-bound examples, and see what an improvement these changes make in your writing. (Share your results.)

Special Challenge: Look for a sports column in your local newspaper or an article in *Sports Illustrated* that contains a lot of **vivid verbs**. (Sportswriters know how to describe action.) Share this writing with your classmates.

■ Selecting Another Person to Describe

THE FIRST STEP • So far in this unit, you've discovered some ways to describe people by using specific details and strong action verbs. (You've also learned about writing effective titles.) Now it's time to put all these skills to work in another description.

SELECT: Choose another person, someone who has made a difference in your life, to describe in one or more paragraphs.

COLLECT: Once you have a subject in mind, write freely about this person in the space provided below. Write honestly and openly, recording ideas as they come to mind. (Think of the different things this person has done, your relationship with this person, and so on.)

_____

_____

_____

_____

_____

_____

_____

_____

_____

_____

_____

_____

_____

_____

THE NEXT STEP • Review your free writing, underlining ideas (and actions) that you might like to use in your description. (Share your results.)

■ Reacting to and Writing a Description

READ: The following description focuses on the subject's actions rather than on how this person looks. As you read, note how these actions really describe the person on the inside. (Also make sure to read the side comments for this model.)

Grandma King

Notice the clear topic sentence.

If I could, I would give everyone a grandma like Grandma King. Grandma King was the kind of grandma who always had fresh-baked sugar cookies in a jar on her kitchen counter or an extra stick of Wrigley's spearmint in her purse just when I needed it most. When I was sick, Grandma would bed me down on her

Specific details and verbs bring this subject to life.

green sofa and just about spoon-feed me tea or Campbell's chicken noodle soup. If I was feeling up to it, she'd whip up a grilled cheese sandwich and a chocolate shake. Sometimes the food smelled a little like the Vicks VapoRub she'd put on my throat, but I never minded. Grandma King always let me watch soap operas at her house (and didn't squeal to Mom), always said I had

The closing sentence echoes the topic sentence.

the best voice in the choir, and always kept my secrets. Is it any wonder I wish everyone had a Grandma King?

HANDBOOK HELPER

Refer to "Descriptive paragraph" in the index for another model. Notice how this description also focuses on the actions of the subject.

WRITE: Complete the first draft of your description on your own paper. In your writing, focus on an important action or actions that really describe your subject on the inside. The topic sentence for your paragraph should effectively introduce your subject because of his or her actions. The supporting sentences should contain specific details and action-packed verbs.

Helpful Hint: Let the following statement be your writing guide: A descriptive paragraph should give a single, clear picture of a subject.

■ Revising Your Description

EVALUATE: The following checklist will help you review and revise your work. (Use this same checklist to evaluate your classmates' work.)

Organization: Does the paragraph begin with a clearly stated topic sentence? Do the supporting sentences focus on one or more of the subject's actions?

Detail: Are these actions effectively described? Does the writing contain vivid verbs?

Style: Does the writing "speak" with honest feelings? Does the title add to the overall effect of the writing?

Mechanics: Has proper attention been given to neatness and accuracy? (Consider readability, sentences, spelling, punctuation, and grammar.)

Special Challenge: The descriptive paragraph in the handbook includes an illustration of the subject, Mr. Brown. (Seeing Mr. Brown certainly adds something to this writing.)

Think of the best way to illustrate the subject of your own action-based description. You might want to show this person involved in a specific action or "paint" a different type of picture (a snapshot, a portrait, a graphic design, etc.). Work on this illustration on your own paper. Upon completion, combine the two—your paragraph and illustration—into an effective composition. (Again, refer to the paragraph and illustration in the handbook for ideas.)

Special Note: If you like how your finished product turns out, present it as a gift to the subject of your writing. (That is, of course, if you have described your subject in positive terms.)

WRITING MYSTERY STORIES
Whodunit?

THE FIRST STEP • Have you ever solved a mystery? You're not sure? Well, I bet you have. What about the time you lost your notebook—and found it after retracing your steps around your home? Or what about the time your mother couldn't find her car keys—and you discovered them inside a grocery bag after asking her some questions? Each of us solves little mysteries every day. We look at different situations, collect clues, study our information, and come up with possible answers or solutions.

In this unit, you will be given many opportunities to plan and solve different types of mysteries. As you complete your work, you will practice and polish your skills of observation, description, analysis, and creativity. Your work in this unit will help you with your writing in all of your classes, especially when you are asked to explore problems and solutions or causes and effects. Mystery writing is really a combination of creative and analytical writing.

In the Mood

READ: **To get into the mystery-writing mood, freely list ideas related to each word below. These are words often associated with mystery writing. (Work on this activity with a classmate if your teacher allows it.)**

Example: **gloomy**   *dark, ugly, scary, spiderwebs, spooky, rainy*

crimes _____

clues _____

suspects _____

detectives _____

haunted mansions _____

_____ **?** _____

_____ **?** _____

THE NEXT STEP • Share lists with your classmates. Think of mysteries you have read about, seen, or experienced that involve some of these ideas.

■ Completing a Mystery Story

READ & WRITE: After reading the following starter, study the picture below for clues that would help you solve the mystery. Then write the second half of the story on your own paper. The name of your detective and how he or she solves the crime is up to you.

The telephone on my desk rang loudly. It was old Mrs. McFuddle complaining that a thief had broken into her house.

"Where were you when it happened?" I asked.

"Where was I? Why I was at home, of course!"

"Did you hear anything?"

"What's that?" she yelled.

"Hear! Did you hear anything?"

"If I'd heard anything, I wouldn't be calling you now. I would've called you then, you fool!"

"Okay. Well, did the thief take anything?"

"Did he fake something? How should I know—I was sleeping."

I decided to try another tactic.

"Is anything missing, Mrs. McFuddle?"

"Certainly something is missing. My new leather shoe. That stinking thief took one of my new leather shoes."

"Anything else?"

"No . . . yes! That no-good rat stole the pie I baked for the church social. It was cooling on the living-room windowsill."

"Let me see if I've got this right, ma'am. A thief came into your house while you were sleeping and stole one leather shoe and a pie. Is that about it?"

"Well . . . no, . . . there is more." (YOU FINISH THE STORY)

THE NEXT STEP • Share stories with your classmates. Pay special attention to the way each writer has built her or his story (working in suspects and clues, building suspense, and solving the mystery).

■ **Completing a Mystery Writing**

It's a frame-up.

READ: After reading the following story starter, continue the story by filling in the blank spaces with characters and clues listed at the bottom of the page. Then, on your own paper, keep the story going by working in a reason for the crime, possible suspects, clues, and a solution. (Share your work with your classmates.)

It was a cold and wet night. The wind whipped through the trees, bending and shaking the long branches. Inside my grandmother's house the lights flickered and dimmed. My sister and I huddled under the thick blankets clutching Grandma's photo album. "Keep this safe," she had said before she left. Suddenly, there was a loud *CRASH!* The lights flickered one last time, and then we were in darkness. From the hall, came the heavy sound of running feet.

The door opened slowly. There stood _____ .

My sister _____ and I _____ ,

burying the album deep within the blankets.

"Give me the album," _____ whispered and

grabbed it from beneath the bedding.

Opening to the first page, _____ took

_____ from behind (his, her, its) back and

_____ . Slowly, _____ pulled

_____ from _____ . Then . . .

grandmother	fainted	a lottery ticket	my father
screamed	a diamond	the stranger	choked
a computer disk	my mother	giggled	a small key
laughed crazily	cut	a deposit box key	he
slit	the binding	she	tore
cover	the shadow	a gun	front page
the voice	a knife	a letter opener	an ice pick
a pair of scissors	the man	a screwdriver	the album

■ **Reviewing a Mystery-Story Plan**

Clues to the Crime

THE FIRST STEP • Mystery stories are built around a problem or crime that has to be solved. Once a writer identifies a problem to solve, he or she can start planning the other parts of the story.

READ: Carefully read the following plan for a children's mystery called *Danger in Tibet* by Robert Quackenbush (Pippin Press, 1989).

MYSTERY PLANNING GUIDE

Problem/Crime A character named Willard is missing after climbing Mt. Everest, and his room at the inn at the foot of the mountain has been ransacked.

Possible Suspects
Nevel Tree Duck (owner of the inn)
Trempe (a housekeeper)
Salum (Willard's climbing guide)

Motive (possible reason for the crime)
* The owner of the inn, the housekeeper, or both might want something belonging to Willard.

Detective/Crime Solver Inspector Miss Mallard is Willard's aunt.

Important Clues
* Muddy footprints *below* but not *in* Willard's room
* A map to a special city and an empty police report folder in Willard's room
* Trempe's hot temper

Solution to the Crime
Using the map, Miss Mallard finds Willard in the special city, which he is trying to protect from a criminal. Miss Mallard returns to the inn and arrests Trempe who, she decides, has faked the footprints below Willard's room.

The Key Clue: Trempe became extremely upset when Salum attempted to enter the inn with muddy feet. Thus, Miss Mallard believes that as he tried to set up the crime, Trempe couldn't bring himself to fake muddy footprints *in* Willard's room.

Special Note: This is a basic outline of the characters and plot. The actual story was developed in much more detail with dialogue, descriptions, and other actions.

■ **Planning a Mystery Story from Scratch**

Here a Clue, There a Clue

COLLECTING: Begin planning an original mystery story by filling in the following mystery planning guide. (Refer to the previous page to see how one writer planned his story.)

Special Note: You don't have to fill in all of the categories before you start your writing. Some things can't be figured out until the actual writing takes place. Also expect to make changes in this guide as your story develops.

MYSTERY PLANNING GUIDE

Problem/Crime *(This can be something as minor as a missing baseball glove, or as serious as a missing person. Include the name of the victim in your explanation.)*

Possible Suspects *(List at least two characters—people, animals, or creatures—as possible suspects in your mystery.)*

Motive *(Identify reasons why the suspects might have caused the problem or committed the crime.)*

Detective *(Identify the chief investigator. It could be yourself or someone you make up.)*

Important Clues *(List any objects, ideas, remarks, or observations that might lead to a solution to the crime.)*

Solution to the Crime *(Decide how the detective will solve the crime.)*

THE NEXT STEP • Share your plan with a classmate. Ask your partner for help if you are having trouble figuring out some of the basic parts of your story.

■ Writing the Introduction for an Original Mystery

WRITE: After filling in the chart on the previous page, use the space provided below to work on the introductory paragraph (or the first part) of your mystery. (Refer to the opening paragraph of the mystery on page 37 for a model.)

Special Note: The introduction should identify, describe, or actually play out the problem that must be solved in the story. Also, a feeling of suspense or puzzlement should be created. In effect, the opening of a mystery should hook the readers so they will want to read on to see "whodunit." (Mysteries are usually told from the point of view of the detective.)

Writing Work Space

_____

_____

_____

_____

_____

_____

_____

_____

_____

_____

_____

_____

_____

_____

THINKING IT OVER • For some writers, the introduction of a story is the real key. Once they feel comfortable with the first scene or two, the rest of the story seems to fall into place. For others, the introduction will not become important until the rest of the story is worked out. Keep these points in mind as you work on the first part of your story.

■ Writing the Rest of Your Story

COLLECTING: Work space is provided here for you to continue your story. Keep the following points in mind as you develop your mystery.

● Try to have at least two possible suspects in your mystery.

● Include believable clues to the problem or crime.

● Don't let things happen too quickly. Have your detective talk to different people, think things out, describe different things, and perhaps face a dead end or two during the story.

● And most importantly, don't become frustrated if your story doesn't work out perfectly. Just do the best that you can do.

HANDBOOK HELPER   Refer to "Story writing" in the index for additional help with your writing.

Additional Writing Work Space

■ Reviewing and Revising Your Writing

EVALUATE: Use the checklist below to review and revise your writing. (Use this same checklist to help you evaluate your classmates' stories.)

Special Note: If your original mystery doesn't seem to be working out, consider reviewing and revising one of the other mysteries you have started in this unit. (However, make sure you get your teacher's approval beforehand.)

_____ **Organization:** Does the opening of the story effectively introduce a problem or crime? Does the main part of the story work itself out (not too quickly) in an organized way?

_____ **Detail:** Have people, places, clues, and actions been developed in enough detail?

_____ **Style:** Does the story read like a mystery (including the thoughts of the main character, a feeling of suspense, and so on)?

_____ **Mechanics:** Has proper attention been given to neatness and accuracy? (Consider readability, sentences, spelling, usage, and grammar.)

Additional Comments: (when reviewing a classmate's work)

_____ Identify one or more things that you really like about this mystery.

_____ Identify one or two changes that you would recommend in this story.

THE NEXT STEP • Share your final story with your classmates. (Maybe your teacher will make multiple copies of some of these stories.)

■ Possible Starting Points for Mystery Stories

extended **ACTIVITY**

The suspense is killing me . . .

THE FIRST STEP • Use one of the following story ideas as the starting point for a real-life mystery story. Work on this story with a classmate if your teacher allows it. (Do your work on your own paper.)

You're pacing in the school parking lot. It's been at least an hour since your mother was supposed to pick you up after school. Practice ended right on time, and all the other kids have already left. In the growing darkness of a late winter afternoon, you're beginning to wonder what has happened.

One sweltering day at the water park two of your friends shout to you, "Hey, we're going to get something to drink." You think nothing of it as you watch them disappear into the sea of swimmers. However, an hour later, when they still haven't returned, you begin to wonder what has happened.

When you do a final count, your collection of _____ comes up one short. You turn the house upside down looking for the missing item. You had all of them this morning, but now one is missing. You begin to wonder what has happened.

(Your own idea?) _____

_____

_____

_____

_____

■ **Mystery Writing**

Where were you the night of . . . ?

READ: Obviously not all mysteries are full of brilliant detectives like Sherlock Holmes. Many mysteries involve real people just like you. Here's a true mystery:

> One night Dad dropped off my sister and me at the huge auditorium for a concert. Mom was working late at the office. Because of concert delays, the main group didn't get on stage until after 10:30. We told Dad the concert would be over by 11:00, and lots of people did leave about midnight; however, we stayed until the very end. When we went outside, there was no Dad in the parking lot. When we called home—at 1:00 a.m.—we only got the answering machine. What could have happened?

REACT: Write your version of what could have happened to Dad and how this mystery finally was solved. (Use the space below for your planning and first draft. Write the final version of your explanation on your own paper.)

> When Mom came home from work, she realized that she was locked out of the house. She went to a friend's house and left messages on the answering machine telling us where she was. When Dad couldn't find us, he called home, but he only got the answering machine. He assumed Mom had come and picked us up for some reason, so he drove home. Forty-five minutes later he arrived home to an empty house. He really panicked when he called Mom; she knew nothing about us. By then it was 2:00 a.m. After listening to our phone messages asking where he was, Dad realized he'd left us stranded in a city of a million people. So he headed back to the city. About 4:00 a.m. we were all finally laughing about our nightmare mystery.

THE NEXT STEP • After sharing your explanations, ask your teacher to read to you the real solution to this problem.

Special Challenge: Write the start of one of your own real-life mysteries to exchange with a classmate. Then write an explanation for each other's mystery. (Discuss your results.)

■ **Mystery Writing**

Mysteries on the Move

extended **ACTIVITY**

THE FIRST STEP • Flying down the freeway, or just bumping down a city street, you have encountered mysterious messages on personal license plates. While you may not be quick enough to unravel these mysteries as they speed by at 65 miles per hour, here's a chance to practice your detective skills at a slower speed.

WRITE: In the following activity, you must decipher the messages on the license plates. (The first one is done for you.) *Hint:* Try sounding out letters, numbers, and words. Clues are often hidden in sounds.

Occupations:	*Science:**	*Sayings:*
2 T H B I Z	P B F T	10 S H U N
dentist	*lead foot*	*tension/attention*
T C H E R	G O 4 A U	W H O D N T
teacher	*go for gold*	*whodunit*
P R Y V T I	F E M A N	R U 4 M E
private eye	*iron man*	*Are you for me?*

*(Refer to the "Periodic Table of the Elements" in your handbook index for help.)

WRITE: Now create your own license plate mini-mysteries. Exchange them with classmates to see if they can decipher your clues.

WRITING THE COMPARISON AND CONTRAST ESSAY
Working in Pairs

THE FIRST STEP • How many things have you already compared today? You may have compared two different types of cereal—perhaps Cheerios and Froot Loops—to decide what to eat for breakfast. Or you may have compared your orange button-down shirt and your favorite green T-shirt to decide what to wear. Each time you make a decision about what you eat, what you wear, what you watch, what you say, and what you believe, you are comparing and contrasting things. In this unit, you will compare and contrast at least three pairs of related items using a graphic organizer called a Venn diagram. Later, you will write about one of these pairs of items in a comparison and contrast essay.

SELECTING: Look at the items in the list below. Notice how they are alike and how they are different. Now add at least three more related items in the spaces provided.

Idea 1	Idea 2
Granny Smith apple	Red Delicious apple
jean jacket	winter jacket
mountain bike	racing bike
soccer ball	football
Saturday	Sunday

_____   _____

_____   _____

_____   _____

_____   _____

THE NEXT STEP • Share your list with a classmate. Did each of you add *related* items to the list? Which items do you like best in each other's list?

■ **Using the Venn Diagram**

Picturing the Process

THE FIRST STEP • One of the most effective ways to explore the similarities and differences between two related items or ideas is to use a Venn diagram. As you can see in the example below, a Venn diagram consists of two interlocking circles. In the area marked **1,** you list words and phrases that relate only to one of the items. In the area marked **2,** you list words and ideas that relate only to the other item. In the area marked **3,** you list words and ideas that relate to both items.

Special Note: The ideas in areas **1** and **2** name ways that the items differ, or *contrast*. The ideas in area **3** name ways they are alike, or *compare*.

CANNED FRUIT
- processed
- soft
- sometimes syrupy
- tastes like the can

1

- sweet
- good snack
- source of vitamin C

3

FRESH FRUIT
- in natural state
- crisp texture
- clean taste
- nothing added

2

SELECT & COLLECT: Choose one pair of items or ideas from the previous page to compare and contrast using the Venn diagram below. (If you find one pair of words difficult to diagram, try another pair.)

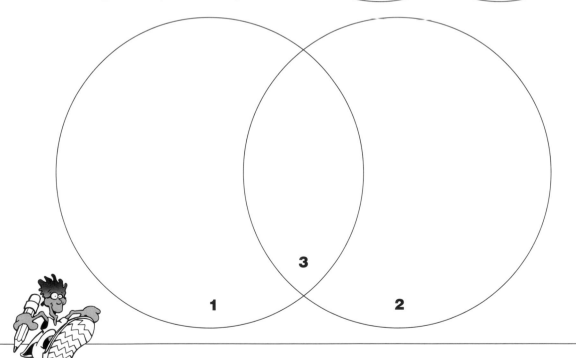

1

3

2

THE NEXT STEP • Share your work with a classmate. Ask your partner if she or he can think of any additional ways to compare and contrast your subjects.

■ The Venn Diagram Revisited

REVIEW: Carefully review the following list, putting a check next to two or three of these statements that would be interesting to compare and contrast. Discuss your choices with a classmate. (Consider the reasons for your choices in your discussion.)

List of Comparison and Contrast Ideas

People/Animal Category

Charles Barkley is different from Michael Jordan.

Janet Jackson is different from Paula Abdul.

A regular friend is different from a "best" friend.

A club is different from a gang.

In baseball, a thrower is different from a pitcher.

Object Category

A rug is different from a carpet.

McDonald's food is different from Hardee's food.

Microwave ovens are different from conventional ovens.

Idea Category

Listening is different from hearing.

Studying is different from learning.

Fear is different from terror.

Confidence is different from conceit.

Special Challenge: Use the spaces below if you would like to make up "comparison statements" of your own.

_____

_____

_____

SELECT & COLLECT: Select one of your choices from above to explore in another Venn diagram. (Use your own paper for your work.)

THE NEXT STEP • Share the results of your second diagram. Then apply the Venn diagram to still another pair of related words (perhaps another one of your choices from above). *Remember:* Practice makes perfect.

■ Reading and Reacting to a Comparison and Contrast Essay

READ: As you read this comparison and contrast essay, notice how each paragraph deals with the subject (two types of apples) in a special way. Also pay careful attention to the side notes. (The writer used a Venn diagram to plan this essay.)

Food for Thought

The opening sentences introduce the subject. The special qualities of one item are discussed in the rest of this paragraph.

No bag lunch is complete unless it contains a juicy apple. Two of the most popular apples rolling out of today's lunch bags are Granny Smith and Red Delicious. The words *Granny Smith* call to mind warm kitchens and sugar cookies. How odd that it is the name for such a big, robust apple. As with most green apples, a Granny Smith is on the tart side. The first time you bite into one, its tartness can catch you by surprise. But after that, each new bite is a refreshing treat. One of the real strengths of this apple is its staying power. Seldom will you find a Granny Smith softened or bruised.

The special qualities of the other item are discussed in paragraph two.

The Red Delicious is a thing of beauty, a classic apple with few peers. It is a tall apple, starting out broad shouldered, then gradually and gracefully tapering to a narrow base. If the Red Delicious were an athlete, it would be a basketball player, probably a scoring forward. The Red Delicious almost always lives up to its name when you bite into one, because it delivers a delicious, sweet taste. If this apple has a flaw, it is in its texture, which can occasionally be soft and mealy.

The two items are compared in the final paragraph.

Both the Granny Smith and Red Delicious are healthy and satisfying treats, whether they are part of lunch or a between-meals snack. Both apples are, in fact, large enough to be meals unto themselves. This makes them popular with adults as well as children. It also helps that they are almost always available in stores from one season to the next. That they are always boldly displayed in grocery produce sections also attests to their popularity. It would be safe to say that for many people, these two apples have become as American as apple pie itself.

REACT: Draw a Venn diagram on your own paper, listing at least two or three comparisons and contrasts made about the two subjects in this essay. (Share your responses.)

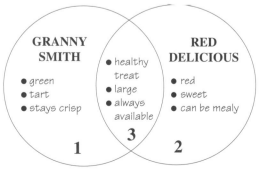

■ Writing the Comparison and Contrast Essay

SELECTING & CONNECTING: Choose one pair of ideas that you have worked with in a Venn diagram to write about in a comparison and contrast essay. Your essay should consist of three paragraphs following the guidelines listed below. (Also refer to the model on the previous page for ideas.)

WRITING GUIDELINES

Paragraph One: The first paragraph should include information listed in area 1 in the Venn diagram. (This is information that relates only to one of the items.)

Special Note: The first paragraph should also include an opening sentence or two to introduce the subject of your essay.

Paragraph Two: The second paragraph should include information listed in area 2 in the Venn diagram. (This is information that relates only to the other item.)

Paragraph Three: The final paragraph should include information listed in area 3. (This is information that shows how the two items are alike, or *compare*.)

Special Note: The final idea in this paragraph should bring the essay to an effective conclusion.

WORK SPACE

(Use this space to begin the planning and writing of your essay. Do the rest of your work on your own paper.)

_____

_____

_____

_____

_____

_____

_____

_____

■ Reviewing and Revising Your Essay

EVALUATE: The following checklist will help you review and revise your writing. (Use this same checklist to evaluate your classmates' work.)

____ **Organization:** Is the writing organized into three clear paragraphs, contrasting and then comparing the two related items? Is the information in each paragraph organized and easy to follow?

____ **Detail:** Are all of the important points supported with specific details? Are there enough important similarities and differences included in the writing?

____ **Style:** Does the essay include effective opening and closing thoughts? Does the essay read smoothly and easily?

____ **Mechanics:** Has proper attention been given to neatness and accuracy? (Consider readability, sentences, spelling, usage, and grammar.)

Additional Comments: (*when reviewing a classmate's work*)

____ What do you like best about this comparison and contrast essay? (List two things.)

____ Do you have any suggestions for improvements? (List any of these ideas.)

Special Challenge: In a paragraph, explain *how* and *why* the Venn diagram works (or doesn't work) so well as a prewriting strategy. Also consider how it can be used in all of your classes and in areas other than writing (reading, studying, etc.). Do your writing on your own paper.

■ Writing Diamante Poems

extended
ACTIVITY

THE FIRST STEP • A *diamante poem* begins with one subject at the top of its diamond shape and ends with an opposite subject at the bottom. It has seven lines and does not rhyme.

READ: Carefully read the examples below to see how the diamante poem develops from one line to the next.

Cat

cuddly, furry

purring, sleeping, eating

hunter, feline, canine, friend

barking, playing, chasing

friendly, loyal

Dog

Summer

warm, nice

swimming, biking, playing

friends, parks, ball, snow fight

sledding, skating, skiing

white, fluffy

Winter

City

noisy, busy

growing, crowding, moving

building, streets, trees, barn

charming, mellowing, relaxing

slow, peaceful

Country

Discussion: Notice that lines two and six describe the opposite subjects. Lines three and five list action words (*-ing* words) about each opposite. The first half of line four lists nouns related to the first subject; the second half lists nouns related to the second subject.

WRITE: Now write your own diamante poem using the examples above as your guide. (Do your writing on your own paper.)

■ Writing Contrast Couplets

➤ *Now You Try*

WRITE: Write at least two contrast couplets. (A couplet is two rhyming lines, each containing the same number of syllables.) The first line in a contrast couplet includes two words that are opposites. The second line makes a comment about the first. (Space is provided below to plan and write the first drafts of your couplets. Use your own paper for your final drafts.)

Examples:

It really doesn't matter if you're young or old.
There's always someone to say: "Do as you're told."

If they are short, or tall, or somewhere in between,
Kin of every shape and size—all are really keen.

THE NEXT STEP • Share your couplet with a classmate. Then create one or two additional contrast couplets as a team.

WRITING A REPORT
I've always been interested in . . .

THE FIRST STEP • Writing a report is as easy as . . . following the basic guidelines in the handbook. And that is just what you will do in this unit. You will select a specific subject to investigate, collect facts and details from different resources, and connect all of your ideas in writing. (You can find these guidelines by referring to "Report, The Classroom" in the index.) The skills that you practice here will help you write reports in all of your classes.

Getting Started

If you have a strong personal feeling about your subject, it becomes much easier to write an effective report—one that you can feel proud to share. So it is important that the subject for your report comes from your own experiences or interests. The activities on the next two pages will help you select a subject with personal appeal.

COMPLETE: Fill in this chart by taking inventory of your special skills, interests, and experiences. (List as many ideas as you can.)

Things I like to do: *(skateboard? sing?)* _____

_____

Things I'm good at: *(math? drawing?)* _____

_____

Things I like to read about: *(different countries? sports figures?)* _____

_____

Places I've visited: *(theme parks? different cities?)* _____

_____

People, places, and events I'd like to know more about: _____

_____

THE NEXT STEP • Underline two or three ideas in your list that you may want to explore and write about in a report. Share these ideas with your classmates.

■ Selecting a Subject

Checking Special Resources for Ideas

THE FIRST STEP • To help you think of even more ideas for your report, refer to one of the following resources: an encyclopedia index, a current edition of the *Readers' Guide to Periodical Literature*, or a resource recommended by your teacher.

Special Note: An encyclopedia index lists every subject covered in a complete set of encyclopedias. The *Readers' Guide* lists every subject covered in major magazines for a given period of time. (Refer to "Readers' Guide" in the handbook index for more information.)

LIST: **Use one of the resources just described (or a recommended resource) to find possible subjects for your report. List at least two interesting ideas for each category.**

People: _____

_____

Places: _____

_____

Objects: _____

_____

Events: _____

_____

Ideas: _____

_____

IDENTIFY: **Put a check next to the two ideas in this chart that interest you the most as report subjects. (Share your work with a classmate.)**

THE NEXT STEP • Now review all of the ideas you have listed in the opening exercises. Select one of these ideas to be the subject of your report. Write your choice on this line: _____

■ **Starting the Searching Process**

Getting Your First Thoughts on Paper

RECORD: Use the space provided below (or your own paper) to record your first thoughts about your subject. Here are some ways to start: Explain why this subject interests you, explore what you already know about it, identify what else you would like to know, and so on. (Write freely and rapidly, recording ideas as they come to mind.)

_____

_____

_____

_____

_____

_____

_____

_____

_____

_____

_____

_____

_____

_____

REVIEW: As you review your first thoughts, you will begin to see how much you know about your subject, and how much you need to find out. Underline any specific ideas that you may want to use or refer to later on. For example, any questions you asked about your subject may help you plan your reading and note taking.

■ Locating Resources

Information Please

THE FIRST STEP • If your subject is fairly new (like rollerblading), you may find most of your information in magazine articles, pamphlets, and interviews. If your subject is more "established" (like stunt flying), you may have more luck with reference books and other nonfiction books. Try to collect facts from at least two or three different sources of information for your report. (Your teacher may set guidelines for the number of resources you must use.)

LOCATE: To get the collecting process started, identify different resources that would help you learn about your subject. Try to list specific titles, names, or places for at least three of the categories listed below.

Special Note: You will have to use the card catalog, the *Readers' Guide to Periodical Literature*, and the vertical file in your library to complete this activity.

Resources Planning Sheet

People to interview:

Reference books:

Other nonfiction books:

Magazines:

Pamphlets and booklets:

Other (videos, places to visit, etc.):

THE NEXT STEP • Decide which resource you will use first to learn about your subject. Then get ready to conduct your research, using the information in the next activity as your guide.

■ **Collecting Information**

Reading and Taking Notes

ASK QUESTIONS: To help you organize your fact finding, write a number of important questions (at least four or five) about your subject that you would like to answer in your report. List each of these questions on separate note cards or half sheets of paper. Then, anytime you find a fact that helps answer one of your questions, record this information on the right note card.

Remember: These questions should focus on different parts of the subject you would like to know more about. Check your "first thoughts" writing on page 57 in this unit for ideas.

Examples:

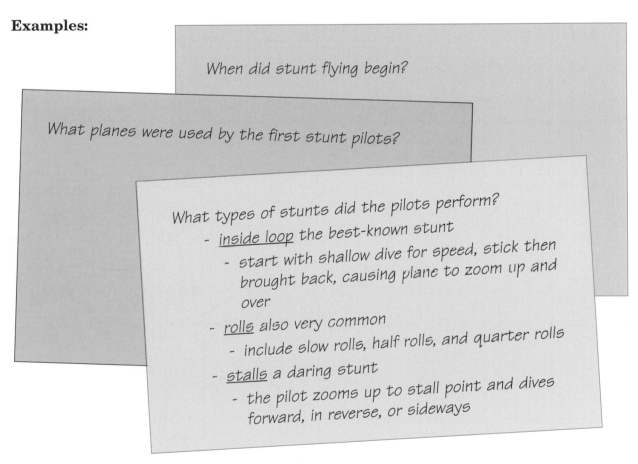

When did stunt flying begin?

What planes were used by the first stunt pilots?

What types of stunts did the pilots perform?
- <u>inside loop</u> the best-known stunt
  - start with shallow dive for speed, stick then brought back, causing plane to zoom up and over
- <u>rolls</u> also very common
  - include slow rolls, half rolls, and quarter rolls
- <u>stalls</u> a daring stunt
  - the pilot zooms up to stall point and dives forward, in reverse, or sideways

(Refer to "Report, Sample note cards" in the handbook index for more examples.)

RECORDING INFORMATION · List information on the note cards clearly and neatly, using phrases instead of complete sentences. Use your own words as much as possible. If you want to quote someone, make sure to record the person's words just as you found (or heard) them. Also make sure to record the person's name.

■ **Conducting an Interview**

Learning from an Expert

THE FIRST STEP • Interviewing someone who knows a
lot about your subject is one of the most valuable and enjoyable ways to collect new
information. You can learn all about the interviewing process in the handbook. (Refer to
"Interviewing" in the index.) To plan for your interview, fill out a worksheet like the one below.

Interview Planning Worksheet

Person's name: _____

Phone number: _____

Date, time, and location of interview: _____

Brief description of this person's job or interest in your subject: _____

_____

List questions that you would like to ask. (Your questions
should require more than a yes or no answer.)

1.

2.

3.

4.

5.

6.

7.

THE NEXT STEP • Before you conduct an official interview for your report, interview a classmate or friend about his or her favorite pastime.

■ **Organizing Your Information**

Preparing to Write

THE FIRST STEP • Once you have collected all of your information, the next step is to organize your ideas for writing. Here's a simple plan that will help you do this.

SELECT: Choose the information on one note card to be the main idea in your report. Be sure to focus on an important part of your subject, as does this main idea in a report on stunt flying: "Early stunt flying was exciting for spectators, but very dangerous for the pilots." (In the space below, write the main idea of your report.)

Main Idea: _____

_____

ARRANGE: Organize your other note cards in the best possible order. Keep the main idea of your report in mind as you order the cards. (If the information on one of the note cards doesn't seem to fit, leave it out.)

OUTLINE: Next, on your own paper, organize your notes into a rough outline. Begin by listing the questions on your note cards in the order that you have just arranged them. Leave enough space after each question to list important facts and details from each note card. Follow this form:

Subject: _____

Question: _____
       – (important facts and details)
       –
       –
       –

Question: _____
       –
       –
       –
       –

THE NEXT STEP • If you need to write a formal outline, rewrite your first version into a clear *sentence outline.* For example, turn a question like "What types of stunts did the pilots perform?" into a statement like "Stunt pilots performed three basic types of stunts." (Refer to "Report, Sample outline" in the index for specific guidelines for using Roman numerals—I., II., III., etc.—and capital letters.)

■ Connecting: Writing the Opening Paragraph

Hooking Your Readers

THE FIRST STEP • To write the first draft of your report, follow the basic information as you have outlined it—plus add an opening and a closing paragraph. It is that simple.

The Opening Paragraph

The first paragraph should say something interesting or surprising about your subject so readers will want to read your report. (See *"Ways to Begin . . ."* below.) The introduction should also introduce the main idea of your report. You may then explain or develop this main idea in more detail in the body of your report.

Ways to Begin a Report . . .

- **Share** a personal experience related to your subject.
- **Open** with an important quote from a book or an interview.
- **Begin** with a surprising fact or detail.
- **Tell** a brief story about your subject.
- **Describe** your subject to help readers see it in living color.

WRITE: Use the space provided here (or your own paper) to plan and write your opening paragraph. (Share your opening paragraph with at least one of your class-mates to see if it provides an effective hook.)

■ **Connecting: Completing the First Draft**

Sharing Your Ideas . . . On Paper!

CONTINUE: Write the main part of your report using your outline as a guide. Each important point (or question) in your outline becomes a topic sentence for a paragraph in your report. The details under each important point become supporting sentences. (Use the space below to get started on this part of your report.)

Special Note: Don't be afraid to add new ideas (not included in your outline) as you write. Some of your best thinking about your subject may occur during the writing process.

_____

_____

_____

_____

_____

_____

_____

_____

_____

_____

_____

_____

(Refer to "Report, Model report" in the handbook index if you need help with your writing.)

COMPLETE: Add a closing paragraph to your report, if needed. This paragraph should summarize the main points in your report and leave readers with a strong final statement about your subject.

■ Reviewing and Revising Your Writing

EVALUATE: Use the checklist below to review and revise your writing. (Use this same checklist to help you evaluate your classmates' reports.)

____ **Organization:** Are all of the paragraphs organized in an effective way? Is the main point of each paragraph clear? Are all of the supporting details organized in the best order?

____ **Detail:** Are there enough details to give readers a clear understanding of the subject?

____ **Style:** Is there a main idea about the subject emphasized? Does the report contain effective opening and closing paragraphs?

____ **Mechanics:** Is the writing neat and accurate? (Check for complete sentences, spelling, punctuation, and grammar.)

Adding a Bibliography, a Title Page, and an Outline

If you are required to include a bibliography (works cited page), a title page, and an outline with your report, see your handbook for guidelines. (Refer to "Report, Bibliography" in the index for this information.)

Adding Other Elements

You might want to add charts, graphs, photographs, or illustrations to your report. If that is the case, make sure that you present this information as clearly, neatly, and accurately as you can.

Do I need to add more details?

THE NEXT STEP • Share your finished report, perhaps as part of a special information festival in which you and your classmates share interests and new discoveries.

PART II
Writing Workshops

PREWRITING STRATEGIES

Getting Started

Picking Berries

For many young writers, getting started is the most difficult part of writing. The blank page—all clean, white, and scary—can stop young writers in their tracks. This is often true because young writers don't realize that writing is SUPPOSED to be a messy, trial-and-error process. You, as a young writer, are not supposed to do all the writing in your head and then put perfect prose on perfect paper.

When you begin a writing project, you should think of the blank page as a practice field where you can let your ideas go without having to worry about how they look, sound, or hang together. This stage of writing is like picking berries. You go into the tangled briar patch that is your mind, pick some thoughts and ideas, and drop them into the basket (the paper). Then, when you're finished doing that, you sift through the ideas, looking for the "keepers."

The activities in this section will introduce you to some tried-and-true **Prewriting Strategies**, such as free writing, listing, and clustering. These methods of idea gathering are used by professional writers all the time. Once you get the hang of these strategies, you'll be able to put them to good use throughout the rest of your school days and beyond.

User's Checklist

Check your progress as you work on these **Prewriting Strategies.**

☐ **Free Writing** • *"I'll admit it. I . . ."*

☐ **Free Writing** • *"I can't believe I did that!"*

☐ **Clustering** • *"That's all, folks!"*

☐ **Clustering** • *A Blustery Cluster*

☐ **Listing** • *"If I were a parent . . ."*

☐ **Listing** • *Cockroach for a Day*

☐ **Brainstorming** • *Environmentally Friendly*

☐ **Observing, Recording** • *From Head to Toe*

☐ **Story Frames** • *"Honest, Officer, I was framed . . ."*

☐ **Story Starters** • *"Now you keep it going."*

FREE WRITING

"I'll admit it. I . . ."

Everyone responds differently to the first day of school. Some kids think it's no big deal, some would do anything to get out of it, some are thrilled, some are nervous . . . How did you feel on the first day of school this year? What did you do? What did you wear? Tell us about it—in a free-flowing way—with as much detail as you can remember.

PREWRITING STRATEGY

Free writing *is the simplest form of prewriting. You just put your pen or pencil to the paper and keep it there. The key to this prewriting strategy is to let your ideas flow. Keep on writing (try not to even pause) until all the thoughts you have on the subject have flowed onto the page.*

AFTER • WORDS

Unless it is very personal, exchange your writing with a classmate. Notice in your own work and in your classmate's where the writing seems dry or unnatural. Until you get the hang of *free writing*, you will probably not be able to stop yourself from pausing and hesitating. Keep working at it!

PREWRITING STRATEGY

Free writing *is one of the best forms of prewriting, especially for personal writing topics. When you free-write, you simply open up your mind and let the thoughts pour out—freely. Once you start, you should keep writing until all your thoughts on the topic are down on paper.*

FREE WRITING
"I can't believe I did that!"

We've all done things that we later wish we hadn't. Have you ever done or said something so embarrassing that you can barely stand to think about it? Something that still gives you that butterflies-in-your-stomach, warm-faced feeling every time you do think of it? Tell us about it. Write quickly and without hesitation.

AFTER • WORDS

Use free writing the next time you need to "test" yourself in one of your other subjects. Free writing (also called *stop 'n' write*) is an excellent way to see just how much you really know about a topic.

PREWRITING STRATEGY

Clustering *is a prewriting strategy that serves many purposes. It is a good strategy for gathering information on a writing topic. Clustering is also great for coming up with a narrowed-down or specific writing topic. Either way, clustering helps you "see" your thoughts and how they are related to one another.*

CLUSTERING

"That's all, folks!"

Do a cluster on the topic of cartoons. You can include your favorite cartoons from when you were little, the ones you still like, or your favorite Disney films. As with any cluster, let your pen connect one thought to another to another to ... Use your own paper if you run out of room.

TIP Refer to the "Clustering" section of your handbook for more information and a model. You'll notice in that model that the ideas flow from "running" all the way to "Plastic Earlobe." Take that cue and, in your cluster, let your ideas run their course—don't limit them.

cartoons

AFTER • WORDS
Now go back to the cluster and pick out the details that would work well in a paragraph or short essay about cartoons.

Remember: You can re-cluster (pick a new "nucleus word" from one of the details) if you feel your first cluster isn't working well.

PREWRITING STRATEGY

You may already use **clustering** *as a prewriting strategy. If not, anyone who has can tell you what a great way it is to gather your thoughts about a writing topic. Clustering allows you to write down everything you know about a topic, look it over, and then organize those details quickly and simply.*

CLUSTERING
A Blustery Cluster

Clustering, like free writing, is such a useful prewriting strategy that it's worth a second (and third and fourth and . . .) run-through. In the space below, do a cluster about storms. Remember to include as many details and related bits of information as you can. Let your mind (and cluster) take you in a variety of directions.

AFTER • WORDS
Go back and look at the general type of details you wrote down in your cluster. Would these details work best in

■ a story about a stormy night that gave you the willies,

■ a poem about "stormy feelings," or

■ a science paper about weather?

Decide what sort of writing you'd like to do with the details in your cluster.

storms

LISTING

"If I were a parent . . ."

When parents make kids do things that seem un-reasonable, most kids say to themselves, "When I become a parent, I won't make **MY KIDS** do that." You will probably change your mind, however, when you DO become a parent. In fact, if you could be the mom or dad right now, and your parents were the kids, you'd probably make them do a lot of the same things you are not thrilled about.

Make a list of chores and rules you would im-pose on your parents if you could. (Hey! Have fun with the list, but use good taste and common sense, too.)

PREWRITING STRATEGY

Listing *is one of the most popular prewriting strategies because it is so direct and simple. It works especially well when you have plenty of ideas but need to see them down on paper before you begin writing.*

AFTER • WORDS
Now write a paragraph, poem, or short story about what you think it would be like to be a parent. Include some ideas about why you think your parents impose the rules they do. Be as creative as you can and try to re-create the thoughts (and words) of your parents.

1._____

_____

2._____

_____

3._____

_____

4._____

_____

5._____

_____

6._____

_____

7._____

_____

PREWRITING STRATEGY

Listing *is a quick and simple way to get your ideas down before beginning to write. Listing works well for creative writing topics or topics in history, science, etc.*

LISTING
Cockroach for a Day

A famous writer named Franz Kafka wrote a story called *The Metamorphosis* about a man who wakes up to find that he's turned into a bug. If you could spend a day as something other than a human being, what would you like to be?

Make a list of the possibilities. You can include animals, vegetables, insects, etc.

1. _____

2. _____

3. _____

4. _____

5. _____

6. _____

Now go back and pick one of the things on your list. Make a new list of the characteristics and habits of the thing you picked. For instance, if you picked a panther, you could include facts like these: runs fast, eats raw gazelle, sleeps in trees, etc.

My day as a _____

1. _____

2. _____

3. _____

4. _____

5. _____

6. _____

AFTER • WORDS

Poof! You're a . . . whatever. Write a poem or short story about a day as whatever you picked to be. Include as much detail from your second list as you can.

PREWRITING STRATEGY

Brainstorming *is a prewriting strategy much like listing, except that brainstorming is a way of collecting ideas from a group of people. Like pitching pennies into a wishing well, everyone throws in their ideas freely and, almost like magic, you have a well full of ideas from which to draw.*

BRAINSTORMING
Environmentally Friendly

Everybody is talking about the environment these days. From McDonald's Happy Meals to Downy fabric softener, the things we buy seem to show that many people are trying to produce and use more environmentally friendly products. Together with your class or writing group, brainstorm for a list of all the things you commonly throw away, either individually or as a group.

Throw away:

Now choose a few of the things on your list, and make a new list of ways in which you could use these things, instead of throwing them away. Make sure the suggestions on this list are specific—items you could make from "garbage," for instance.

New uses:

AFTER • WORDS
Brainstorm for ways you could share your ideas with the rest of your school. Perhaps your brainstorming will actually result in a number of new recycling projects for you and your fellow students.

OBSERVING, RECORDING
From Head to Toe

Many young writers have trouble filling their writing with enough details, not because they don't know what details are, but because they don't seem to notice the details all around them. To improve your sight, you should simply practice noticing details and recording them with precision.

For instance, look down at your feet. Starting with the tips of your shoes, write down what you are wearing. Record every small detail. Don't write down "sneakers." Instead, write down "white Nike high-tops with black and white laces, a hole over my right big toe, four scuff marks, and the left tongue tucked crookedly. . . ." Just keep those details coming. And remember, we're talking from head to toe . . . or is that toe to head?

AFTER • WORDS

Exchange your recorded observation with a classmate. Take a good look at each other; then look at what your partner wrote down. Is there anything missing? Help each other complete the observations to the point where a fashion artist could draw your outfit down to the last detail.

PREWRITING STRATEGY

Sometimes your teacher or a classmate will prepare an open-ended story or "story frame" for you to complete. This can be an excellent way to start a short story, a play, or an adventure story.

STORY FRAMES
"Honest, Officer, I was framed . . ."

A story frame is an open-ended, fill-in-the-blank story. A story frame can be a great way to get started writing a short story. By the time you finish filling in the blanks, you are off and running with the plot of an exciting story.

Put yourself in the middle of the following short story. Because the story depends totally on the way in which you fill in the blanks, we can't even tell you what kind of story it is. I guess you COULD say it's a mystery story—at least it is to us.

The Pit, the Pendulum, and the ___Pit Bull___ *(noun)*

___Gina___ *(your name)* woke sometime after midnight to ___eerie___ *(adjective)* silence. S/he listened, sure s/he had heard ___dog-snoring___ *(noun)* just a moment before. Getting out of bed, s/he walked ___gingerly___ *(adverb)* out of the bedroom and down the stairs toward the ___kitchen___ *(noun)*. ___Gina___ *(your name)* spotted a ___fuzzy mound___ *(noun)* in the corner. Moving ___blithely___ *(adverb)*, s/he grabbed the ___cast-iron___ *(adjective)* ___frying pan___ *(noun)* and headed toward the ___corner___ *(noun)*. Just then ___Gina___ *(your name)* heard a ___sleepy___ *(adjective)* ___whimpering___ *(noun)* and quickly turned around to find a ___puppy___ *(noun)* staring at her/him. S/he felt pretty ___amazed___ *(adjective)* at that point and decided to . . .

AFTER • WORDS

On your own paper, finish the story. Work with a classmate or writing group if your teacher allows it.

Special Challenge:

Create a story frame of your own and exchange it with a classmate.

PREWRITING STRATEGY

For as long as storytelling has been around, the technique of "beginning in the middle of things" has also been around. Beginning at a spot in the story where a character is facing a challenge is a great way for a storyteller to reach out and capture a reader or listener.

STORY STARTERS

"Now you keep it going."

Caught up in his own thoughts of what had happened that day, David fidgeted with the button on his cuff, not paying much attention to the party. The memory of Georgianne's angry words kept his stomach churning the appetizers he had just eaten. He looked up to find Georgianne staring at him while Mrs. Frumply complimented her on the dress she was wearing. Just as he was about to escape from the room to avoid talking to her, she . . .

As readers, we are drawn into the action of this passage because it is "action in progress," and because we don't have all the information we need to make sense of it. We don't know what happened between David and Georgianne, just as we are uncertain as to what will happen next. The suspense captures both the storyteller and the reader.

Hook 'em good!

Write a story starter of your own. Try to write it in the style you like to read, whether that's a mystery, a romance, or a good old-fashioned ghost story.

AFTER • WORDS
Exchange story starters with a classmate. Finish the story and give it back (or read it) to your classmate.

Special Challenge:
As a special challenge, finish the above starter with the help of your classmate (or perhaps a writing group). You may find that group input can make storytelling a snap.

FORMS OF WRITING

A Writing Variety Pack

We know as well as you do that variety *does* add spice to life. That's why we included such a wide array of activities in the **Forms of Writing** section. Among other things, you'll be asked to introduce yourself in a creative character sketch and "immortalize" a family member or friend on a historical marker. You'll also be asked to write a poem about an athletic event as well as create a fable modeled after one of Aesop's famous works. Taken as a whole, there is a lot here for you to enjoy.

These special activities engage you in personal, subject, and creative writing—the three major categories of writing covered in the handbook. They are designed to expand your writing knowledge and challenge your creative ability.

Special Note: Your handbook contains guidelines and models for a variety of writing forms, including many of those addressed in this section. Review the table of contents or page through the writing sections and see for yourself.

Getting Started

User's Checklist

Check your progress as you work on these **Forms of Writing.**

☐ **Writing a Creative Sketch** • *May I introduce myself?*

☐ **Writing Friendly Letters** • *A Day in the Life of Today's Students*

☐ **Writing for Fluency** • *Hey! Motormouth!*

☐ **Creating a Historical Marker** • *. . . and on this very spot!*

☐ **Writing a Book Review** • *Writing About Reading*

☐ **Writing a Bio-Poem** • *Introducing . . . !*

☐ **Writing Phrase Poetry** • *Phrases . . . Nothing More than Phrases . . .*

☐ **Are You Fable Able?** • *Working with Aesop*

☐ **Writing a Monologue** • *But what were you thinking?*

AFTER • WORDS We encourage you to experiment with many different forms of writing both inside and outside of school. *Remember:* Variety is the spice of life.

WRITING A CREATIVE SKETCH
May I introduce myself?

Congratulations. You've just been named one of this country's outstanding creative thinkers. A leading national magazine wants to run a story about you and the other individuals who have received this honor. In preparation for the story, one of the magazine's editors has asked you to submit a brief personal sketch (a paragraph about yourself).

Naturally, you want to make your sketch a creative one, but you're not quite sure what to say. The following activity is just what you need to get your creative juices flowing. Read on and see what we mean.

Answer the following questions to the best of your creative ability. Then ask yourself one or two additional questions. (Use the lines provided in this activity for a neat final copy of your answers.)

1. What will your address be sometime in the distant future? (Maybe you'll be living in another dimension in some faraway solar system.)

   _____

   _____

   _____

2. What are three things you can do as well as anybody else? (Maybe you're very skilled at crossing *t*'s.)

   _____

   _____

   _____

   _____

3. What two things have never happened to you? (Maybe you've never been hit by a falling piano.)

   _____

   _____

   _____

   _____

4. What doesn't your best friend know about you? (Maybe you've never revealed one of your secret passions: pineapple on pizza.)

_____

_____

_____

5. What five people don't you personally know? (Maybe you've never met Princess Di or Dick Tracy.)

_____

_____

_____

_____

_____

6. What other questions "need" to be asked and answered about you? (Think of at least one question and answer it.)

_____

_____

_____

Right-Brain Writing

Use the information that you've collected to help you write your personal sketch. (Use your own paper.)

Special Note: Don't begin your writing in an ordinary way. That is, don't say something like _My name is Ozzie Sanchez, and I'm a student at McKinley Middle School._ You're a creative kid, remember? Instead, try something like the following:

> _Call me Three Z. Several months ago, I decided that the three z's in my name, Ozzie Sanchez, say a lot about me. I'm zany, zippy, and . . ._

AFTER • WORDS	Share your answers to the questions and your sketch with a classmate. Make note of the "zany" and "zippy" ideas you like in each other's work.

WRITING FRIENDLY LETTERS

A Day in the Life of Today's Students

Let's suppose you were selected to participate in a special exchange called "A Day in the Life of Today's Students." Each student involved in this program is required to share his or her normal experiences for one school day with a student in another part of the country.

Logging Your Way

To make this job easier for you, we have designed the following log for you to complete. You simply select a day to "log." (Make sure you carefully review the log before you use it.)

Date:

Name:

Grade:

Name and Address of Your School:

Describe what you are wearing today.

Note: Complete the next four parts at the specified times.

It's 8:30 a.m. Identify where you are and describe how you feel.

It's 10:30. Identify where you are and what you see.

It's lunchtime. Describe what you're eating.

It's 1:30. Identify where you are and where you'd rather be.

Identify your best or worst class for the day. Explain your answer.

Describe a challenging or unusual assignment you are working on in one of your classes.

Describe something funny, interesting, or frustrating that happened this day.

Let me introduce myself.

In a letter addressed "Dear Student," describe a day in your life as a student. Include as much information from your log as you can, so someone reading your letter could learn a lot about you, the student. (Feel free to include additional information as well.) Make sure to follow the guidelines for writing friendly letters described in your handbook. (Refer to "Letters, Friendly letters" in the index.)

AFTER • WORDS Share logs and letters with your classmates. Note if any of your classmates have feelings about school that are similar to your own.

WRITING FOR FLUENCY

Hey! Motormouth!

Here's a chance to prove or improve your long-windedness. (Long-windedness is the ability to write or speak forever on a certain topic.)

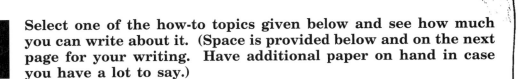

Select one of the how-to topics given below and see how much you can write about it. (Space is provided below and on the next page for your writing. Have additional paper on hand in case you have a lot to say.)

EXPLAIN HOW TO . . .

- draw a straight line
- pour a glass of milk
- eat a bowl of cereal
- sit in a chair
- look in a mirror
- (a topic of your own choice)

GUIDELINES

1. You must write on only one of the suggested topics.
2. You must do your writing in one sitting of 15 minutes.
3. What you write must make sense and in some way discuss *how to do* your selected topic.

TIP Don't think too much about your topic—just write freely and rapidly. New ideas will pop into your mind as you go along.

**AFTER •
WORDS**
Exchange your writing with a classmate. Count the number of words your partner has written. Then find the real motormouth in your classroom by comparing word counts with all of your classmates.

Special Challenge: Consider this writing a first draft; develop it into a finished how-to paper.

CREATING A HISTORICAL MARKER

. . . and on this very spot!

You've just been chosen to keep a record of important events experienced by family members and close friends. Start by listing at least four names in the space provided below. (These should be people you either see every day or can contact by local phone—parents, brothers and sisters, aunts and uncles, cousins, or neighborhood friends.)

Special Challenge: Include the name of one ancestor in your list. (An ancestor is a relative from long ago that a parent or grandparent has told you about.)

1.

2.

3.

4.

5.

6.

Recording Information

Record at least one memorable experience or event for four of the people you've listed. How will you get this information? Talk to each of the people. Get them to tell you about a "time they'll never forget." Consider the 5W's (*who, what, when, where,* and *why*) when recording facts and details about the experience. (Begin your recording in the space below. Use your own paper for the remainder of your work.)

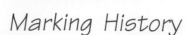

Marking History

Select one individual's experience to memorialize on a historical road marker. (Historical markers are placed at the location of important events.) Include enough facts and details to ensure that passersby will fully appreciate the experience. (Remember the 5W's.)

Special Note: The design and wording of your historical marker is up to you. (Plan your markers on your own paper; use the space provided here for your finished product.)

AFTER • WORDS	Create a historical marker featuring a memorable experience from your own past.

WRITING A BOOK REVIEW

Writing About Reading

Teachers want to know what understandings you have formed while reading a book. That is why they have you write book reviews (reports). A **book review** is a special type of persuasive writing in which you state an opinion about a certain feature(s) in a book, and then support this statement with specific facts and details from the reading. The subject for a book review usually comes from one or more of the four main parts of a book—the *plot*, the *characters*, the *setting*, or the *theme*.

Meaningfully Engaged

In the space provided below, list two or three possible subjects for a review of a book you've read recently.

Special Note: **Your handbook lists many ideas to help you think of subjects. These ideas are arranged according to the four main parts of a book mentioned above. (Refer to "Book review (report)" in the handbook index. Once you turn to this section, you'll find the list under "Finding an Idea for Your Review.")**

What's the big idea?

Select one of the subjects from above to be the focus of a paragraph-length book review. Then, in the space provided below, write your topic sentence. On the next page, list facts and details from the book that support the subject of your writing.

Note: **Refer to the model plan in "The Book Review" section of the handbook for help. (It appears under the heading "Model Book Review.")**

Plan

Topic Sentence: _____

_____

_____

Supporting Facts and Details: _____

_____

_____

_____

_____

_____

_____

Write your review on your own paper. Make sure that everything you say in your paragraph supports your topic sentence. (Use the model one-paragraph book review in the handbook as your guide.)

AFTER • WORDS

Share your finished product with a classmate. Make sure your partner's review focuses on a specific subject related to his or her book. Also make sure that the subject of the review is effectively supported with facts and details.

WRITING A BIO-POEM
Introducing . . . !

In a bio-poem, introduce a close friend, a family member, a famous individual, or perhaps a character from a book. Just make sure you select someone you know very well. (Refer to "Bio-Poem" in the handbook index for writing guidelines. Also refer to the model bio-poem below.)

Special Note: Make minor changes in the writing guidelines to meet your personal needs. For example, your bio-poem doesn't have to be exactly 11 lines long, and it doesn't have to include the exact number of ideas called for in certain lines. (Use your own paper for your work.)

Becca

Becca
Energetic
Sister of Maggie and John
Lover of gymnastics, tuna sandwiches, and
   saxophones
Who feels good when working out,
   watching movies, and having parties
Who needs lunch money, hair spray,
   and her pink marker
Who gives her friends pencils and her
   teachers frustration
Who fears she forgot something, she'll
   get bit by a little monster, or that
   the world will come to an end
Who would like to see Robyn get a pencil
   case, Janae return her pink
   marker, and the country of Guatemala
Resident of Burlington
Dalrymple

AFTER • WORDS	Share your poem with at least one of your classmates. If at all possible, display the finished products so everyone can read them. Write additional bio-poems if you enjoyed this activity. For special occasions, they make good gifts.

WRITING PHRASE POETRY
Phrases . . . Nothing More than Phrases . . .

First, a question. Do you know a prepositional phrase when you see one? If your answer is "yes," you're ready for work. So hold your nose, close your eyes, and plunge into the directions. If your answer is "no," read the rest of this introduction before you take the plunge.

A **prepositional phrase** is a neat little package of words that begins with a preposition (no surprise there!) and ends with the nearest noun or pronoun. *At my wit's end* and *with my spacey lab partner* are prepositional phrases. Now on to the directions.

Write a poem about an athletic event of some type. Think of "sporty" things you do on your own, with a group of friends, in gym class, or as part of an organized team. Consider anything from a bike ride to a pickup basketball game, from a swim meet to a soccer match. Here comes the hard part: Express your ideas in only one way—in prepositional phrases. (Use the space below for the final version of your poem.)

Special Note: Refer to "Phrase poetry" in the handbook index for a model. This phrase poem tells a simple story about a cross-country run.

AFTER • WORDS Share your poem with at least one classmate. Then, if possible, display all of the poems on a bulletin board for everyone to enjoy.

ARE YOU FABLE ABLE?
Working with Aesop

Select two characters from the following list that would best fit the fable below.
Afterward, circle the lesson at the bottom of the page that is best taught by this fable.
(Share your results.)

mouse	peacock	fox	slave	rabbit (hare)
grasshopper	ant	woodsman	stork	donkey
ox	mother	frog	wolf	dog
young boy	father	sheep	a plant	young girl

Title: The _____ and the _____

A young _____ hopped into his home, eager to talk to his father.

"Father!" he exclaimed. "I have just seen the biggest and strongest animal. He is

as wide as a big oak tree and strong enough to move huge rocks."

The father _____ said, "Oh, you must have seen Farmer

Brown's _____, who works his fields. Don't be too impressed with

that animal. I can puff myself up to that size whenever I want."

"Please let me see you do it," begged the young _____ .

The father huffed and puffed until he eventually burst into

tiny pieces.

Fable Lessons
- Do not trust flatterers.
- Little friends may prove to be great friends.
- Do not count your chickens before they are hatched.
- Self-pride may lead to self-destruction.
- It is easy to be brave at a safe distance.
- One cannot be first in everything.

AFTER • WORDS	Write your own fable. If you wish, select characters and a lesson to be taught from the lists on this page.

WRITING A MONOLOGUE

But what were you thinking?

Select a recent time—sitting in a dentist's chair while your mouth turned numb, daydreaming during social studies class, etc.—and re-create your thoughts and feelings at that time by writing a MONOLOGUE. A monologue is a special type of conversation an individual has with him- or herself.

Example: The thoughts (in italics) that follow re-create a very tense time for a boy during the first week of the basketball season. (This is part of a student monologue.)

Boy, it was a lot easier last year. I thought for sure I'd made the A team. This year it's so much harder. I wonder what's so different? The guys are almost all the same, and I've been practicing. Today I'm not doing that badly. Hopefully, I'll make it this year.

"Come on, Briggs, let's play tight defense!" barked Coach Anderson.

I wonder if Coach is yelling at me or trying to help me out. I wonder what I'll do if I don't make it. I better not think that way. There are guys worse than me out here.

Some Thoughts on Thinking

Say enough in your monologue so a reader can share in your thoughts and feelings. In a sense, your monologue should be a brief story with a beginning, a middle, and an end. (Use your own paper for your work.)

AFTER • WORDS Exchange monologues with a classmate and enjoy each other's one-way conversation. Then read the award-winning model short story in your handbook. (Refer to "Story writing, Model story" in the index.) The entire action in this story is played out in the mind of the main character, which makes it a short story in monologue form.

Special Challenge: Write your own fictional story in monologue form.

DRAFTING AND REVISING WORKSHOPS

Hard-Hitting Writing

Learning to write well is a little bit like learning how to hit a baseball or softball. Some people can hit the ball well without any help, while others need a little coaching. In the same way, some people have no trouble putting their thoughts on paper, while others need the guidance of their teachers and classmates.

The **Drafting and Revising Workshops** that follow will help you practice many of the skills that lead to "hard-hitting writing."

You'll practice writing and reviewing first drafts, learn about improving paragraphs, and come to understand what it means to show rather than tell in writing. Before you know it, you'll be hitting line drives time after time in your paragraphs, reports, and stories.

Special Note: See the revising section in the first full chapter in your handbook for a detailed description of the revising process from first step to last.

User's Checklist

Check your progress as you work on these **Drafting and Revising Workshops.**

☐ **Writing a First Draft** • *An Outpouring of Words*

☐ **Reviewing First Drafts** • *And the winner is . . .*

☐ **Reviewing a Paragraph** • *King Corn*

☐ **Reviewing & Revising Paragraphs** • *Scout's Honor*

☐ **Selecting and Using Details** • *The Bear Facts*

☐ **Showing Versus Telling** • *"Touchy, Feely" Writing*

☐ **Using Figurative Language** • *Deflating and Inflating*

AFTER • WORDS

If you ever expect to make it in the major leagues as a writer, here's what you must do: practice writing regularly, read a lot, and approach "coaching" activities like these with a serious attitude.

WRITING A FIRST DRAFT
An Outpouring of Words

THE FIRST STEP • Write your first drafts as freely as possible. Work in many of the facts and details you have collected about your writing subject, but also be open to interesting thoughts and feelings that happen to enter your mind as you write. Your first draft should be the source of some unexpected discoveries.

Read the following portions of two first drafts. As you read, decide which one seems more freely written.

❑ My spring break was enjoyable. I did a lot of fun things with my friends. I also saw most of my relatives. We had them over for a meal on Sunday. After dinner, we watched some home videos . . .

❑ Spring break was awesome this year because we went to my grandma's house in Georgia and I got to hang around with all of my cousins. Jake's my oldest cousin, and he took me for a ride on his Harley Sportster. You can ride motorcycles in March in Georgia 'cause it's warm. One night after a great meal, we watched a basketball game. The Bulls, my favorite team, won. Jake bet me a dollar they'd lose, so I even had some money in my pocket. I put the dollar in my Harley-for-my-16th-birthday fund . . .

Discussion: The first example is accurately written, but also very dull. It appears to have been written in a very careful and cautious way. The second example represents a more free-flowing first draft. It certainly needs some work, but it also shows a lot of personality and promise—just what you're looking for in a first draft.

Free and Easy

■ **Read what your handbook has to say about writing first drafts and then complete the sentences that follow. (Refer to "Writing process, First draft" in the index.)**

Let your _____ pen _____ or _____ pencil _____ do the

talking and connecting. Don't hesitate. Just write.

If you have trouble staying with your writing, _____ time _____ yourself.

Write in short, spontaneous bursts of _____ 3 _____ to

_____ 5 _____ minutes and see what you can discover.

Write as much of your first draft as possible in your first

_____ sitting _____ while all of your collecting is fresh in your mind.

➤ *Now You Try*

■ **Write a free-flowing first draft about a fun-related topic. If you've worked on the two previous workshops, you should have a topic in mind. You should also have collected some related thoughts and feelings to use in your writing. (Do your work on your own paper.)**

Helpful Hint: Follow the advice the handbook gives for writing first drafts. (See the first part of this workshop.) And remember that a first draft does not have to be perfect.

TIP If you don't have a specific topic to write about, use one of the following sentence starters to get you going:

To me, fun means . . .

I know I'm having fun when . . .

Here's what I know about fun . . .

THE NEXT STEP • Review your first draft and mark any parts that you really like. Have a classmate review your writing as well. Then, if you feel good about your progress, continue working with your writing until you shape it into a finished product. (Refer to "Revising" in the index for help.)

REVIEWING FIRST DRAFTS

And the winner is . . .

THE FIRST STEP • What do readers enjoy in a piece of writing? That depends. Some readers may like writing that is clear, crisp, and to the point. Other readers may like writing that is more indirect, that makes them figure some things out for themselves. And still others may like writing that "sings" with beautiful, well-chosen words. (Of course, most readers like a combination of things.) What do you enjoy in a piece of writing? Let's find out.

Carefully read the paragraphs that follow. (All three are sections of student writing.) Then rank the paragraphs, putting a "1" next to the paragraph you think is best and so on.

3 When I was about four years old, I was alone in our family room. For some reason, I was looking underneath the couch, and I spotted a strange object. I grabbed it, only to discover too late that it was a large fishing hook. I screamed for my mom as the hook bit into my thumb. She tried to pull it out but only succeeded in pushing it in a little farther. Our neighbor took me to the doctor, and the doctor had to cut it out. When I got home, my brother was mad because I let the doctor throw the hook away.

2 James could see himself now, roughly swinging his ten-speed around. He was mad and neither knew nor cared where he went. He simply got on his bike and took off. If he had been thinking more clearly, he would have turned to see the old Chevy swerving from one side of the road to the other. It wasn't until the car was almost upon him that he turned. A frightened face stared at him from behind the windshield. He smelled burning rubber before the squeal of brakes blocked out everything else. When the car hit the bike, James was tossed into space. He remembered the pale, full moon before he crashed to the ground. Then everything went dark.

1   On Thursday, the 9th of October, our language arts class went on a hike. We walked along the golf course until we came to a cement bridge over a stream. We sat by the fast, raging water. When I really concentrated, it felt like I was flowing with it. There were big, colorful rocks watching me watch them. When I looked the other way, I could see golfers struggling to win. Upstream there was water falling to where it thought it should be. At the edge of the woods, sticky burrs waited for us to come so they could hitch a ride. Then there was the bridge daring us to write on it. I could see most people took the dare. And when I looked up, I could tell the sky was thinking about rain. We walked through a tunnel of trees back to school.

THE NEXT STEP • Underline words, phrases, and ideas that you really liked in the paragraph you ranked as the best piece of writing. Then share the results of your ranking and underlining with a class-mate. Afterward, share your findings with the entire class.

REVIEWING A PARAGRAPH

King Corn

Read the model paragraph that follows. Then, in pairs, small groups, or as a class, *discuss* the paragraph's strengths and weaknesses. Use the questions that follow the model to help you conduct your discussion.

    Mr. King was my seventh-grade teacher. One time he told us one of his corny jokes, and the whole class started throwing spitballs at him. It took us 10 minutes to clean up the mess. Another one of his favorite tricks was to pick a "volunteer" for a quick trivia contest. When we studied gender, he was unbelievable. For example, he would lower his voice and talk like a real rough guy when we covered masculine gender. Whenever he got sick of "playing school," we'd have one of his famous drills. He'd have us stand at attention, march outside, and talk and relax for 15 minutes. Mr. King was a great teacher.

Points to Consider

- ❑ Does the paragraph begin with a strong and clear topic sentence?
- ❑ Does the paragraph contain enough detail? Are there places where more detail is needed?
- ❑ Are there any ideas or details that don't really belong in this paragraph?
- ❑ Do you like the way this paragraph is written? Does it hold your interest?
- ❑ Does the paragraph end with an effective closing sentence?

THE NEXT STEP • After your discussion, rate the paragraph by circling one of the numbers that follow. (Number 5 represents the highest rating; number 1 represents the lowest rating.)

5   4   3   2   1

Then on your own paper, explain your answer. In your explanation, refer to some of the points that were raised in your discussion. (Share your results.)

REVIEWING & REVISING PARAGRAPHS
Scout's Honor

THE FIRST STEP • In the process of planning and writing a paragraph (essay, story, etc.), a writer makes a promise to write about a particular topic of interest and to support that topic with details arranged in an orderly manner. If the finished product is appealing and clear to his or her readers, a writer's promise has been kept. On the other hand, if a writer produces a less than effective paragraph, readers will feel let down.

Read the following paragraph carefully. The topic sentence is starred. Put a ✔ next to the four ideas that support the topic sentence, and put an ✘ next to the two that don't belong in the paragraph at all.

★Sojourner Truth was a slave, a preacher, and a great spirit. ✔ She criticized the practice of slavery and the lack of opportunities for women. ✘ The Thirteenth Amendment to the Constitution ended slavery in 1865. ✔ She was born into slavery in 1797 and didn't gain her freedom until 1827. ✘ By 1723, blacks made up 15 percent of New York's population. ✔ Her influence on people's thinking became nationwide when she published the story of her life in 1850. ✔ Once this brave woman gained her freedom, she felt it her duty to share her concerns about oppressed people.

THE NEXT STEP • Rewrite this paragraph on your own paper, making any necessary changes so it reads smoothly and logically. Include only the starred and checked ideas in your rewrite. Make sure to arrange the sentences in the best possible order. (Share your finished product with a classmate.)

SELECTING AND USING DETAILS
The Bear Facts

THE FIRST STEP • There is a lot of "talk" in language arts classes about the importance of details in writing. Your teachers tell you again and again to include lots of details in your stories and paragraphs. But just adding details isn't enough. You have to add *related* details that *support* the subjects of your paragraphs and stories.

Read the topic sentence written below. Then carefully read through the list of details that follows. Put a check next to the four details that best support the topic sentence.

Topic Sentence: *Bears are generally thought of as meat-eating animals, but they really eat a wide variety of foods.*

✔ ____ hunt mice, ground squirrels, and other small animals

✔ ____ catch fish with their strong claws in shallow streams

____ try to avoid fights and run from danger

____ can live for 30 years

✔ ____ enjoy feeding on ants, birds' eggs, and grubs

____ weigh one-half to one pound when born

✔ ____ are fond of honey and will rip apart beehives to get at it

____ spend much of the winter sleeping

____ give birth to cubs during the mother's winter sleep

THE NEXT STEP • On your own paper, write a paragraph using the details you have chosen to support the topic sentence. (Make sure to arrange the details in the best possible order.) Add connecting words (*however, although, in addition,* etc.) where needed. (Refer to "Transitions" in the handbook index for a complete list of these words.) Also add a closing sentence.

SHOWING VERSUS TELLING

"Touchy, Feely" Writing

THE FIRST STEP • When you're talking to a friend, you use your hands, facial expressions, and tone of voice to bring life to your ideas. You can bring life to your writing by including strong, active words that show rather than tell your readers certain things.

Well-known author Sterling North wrote in a lively, "showing" style. In his book *Rascal*, for example, North doesn't just tell us that he found a litter of baby raccoons; he shows the babies to us:

Telling Sentence: *We found four baby raccoons.*

Showing Writing: *In plain sight, within the den, we found four baby raccoons, a month old perhaps. The entire litter of kits might easily have fitted within my cap. Each tail had five black rings. Each small face had a sharp black mask. Eight bright eyes peered up at us, filled with wonder and worry. And four inquiring little mouths whimpered questions.*

█ Now it's your turn. Pick one of the telling sentences that follow and expand it into a showing paragraph. (Use the model above to help you with your writing.)

The dog is one of a kind.   The _____ was a disaster.

_____ class was a riot.   The last movie I saw was great (horrible).

My brother (sister) drives me crazy.   A topic of your own choosing

Helpful Hint: Your goal is to help your readers see your writing subject in living color. You won't be able to do this by rushing through one draft. Showing writing takes time and effort.

Answers will vary.

THE NEXT STEP • Put your writing on display so all of your classmates can see it and appreciate it.

USING FIGURATIVE LANGUAGE
Deflating and Inflating

THE FIRST STEP • We pepper our language with figures of speech: *Mr. Smith blew his top. She's got a screw loose. What am I, chopped liver?* Figures of speech such as these are fun and effective ways to use the language. You will work with two specific figures of speech in this activity—*understatement* and *hyperbole.* Be prepared for some creative amusement.

Examples:

> *Father lost all of the spring in his step when he saw the mature spider move across the ceiling.*

The sentence shown here is so "straight-faced" or serious that it calls attention to itself. This is an example of **understatement**, an intended attempt to downplay an idea.

> *Father had a coronary when he saw the big-as-a-Buick bug booking across the ceiling.*

The second sentence is an example of **hyperbole**, an intended overexaggeration for effect. Obviously, spiders are never "as big as Buicks," but expressing such an idea gets a certain feeling across in a fun way. (Refer to "Understatement" and "Hyperbole" in the handbook index for additional explanations and examples.)

Carefully read over the sentences below. Put an *H* in front of the sentence if it is an example of *hyperbole*, a *U* if it is an example of *understatement*. Then rewrite each example as its opposite. For instance, if the given sentence is an example of understatement, rewrite it as hyperbole. The first one is done for you.

___U___ My mom was perturbed when my baseball entered the living room through her plate-glass window.

> *My mom had a nuclear meltdown when my baseball crashed into*

> *the living room through her plate-glass window.*

___U___ The quaint old cabin looked a bit drafty.

> *The decrepit old shack looked about as drafty as Swiss cheese.*

_H_ My big husky pulled my arm out of its socket and went running down the street with it during our morning walk.

My big husky gave my arm a firm, 90-pound tug during our morning walk.

_H_ Every night, my hungry baby sister wakes the whole house with a wail that measures 6.8 on the Richter scale.

Every night, my hungry baby sister wakes us by caressing our ears with her determined crying.

_U_ The 2005 concept car was a bit small, seating one adult under 90 pounds.

The 2005 concept car was so tiny, only a squirrel could drive it.

THE NEXT STEP • On your own paper, write original examples of *hyperbole* and *understatement*. Then exchange your work with a classmate and rewrite each of your partner's examples as you did above. Share your results.

SENTENCE-COMBINING WORKSHOPS

Getting Started

Improving Your Writing Style

In talking about the writing process, writer Jane Yolen had this to say: "A story is never perfect when I write it down the first time, or the second time, or the fifth time. But it always gets better as I go over it and over it." In other words, with each change in the content and style of her work, she comes closer and closer to a finished product that is ready to publish.

The **Sentence-Combining Workshops** focus on the style and sound of sentences. In six of these workshops, you will practice combining ideas from short sentences into longer, more complex thoughts. In the last workshop you will learn about sentence expanding, a technique that will help you add more details to your sentences. The skills that you practice in this section will help you make your own writing smoother and clearer—whether you're working on your second, third, . . . or fifth revision.

Special Note: Your handbook has a lot of important things to say about sentence combining and sentence style. (Refer to "Sentence" in the index for this information.)

User's Checklist

Check your progress as you work on these **Sentence-Combining Workshops.**

<ul style="list-style:none">
<li>☐   **Combining Sentences with Key Words** • *He has a real knack with yarn.*</li>

<li>☐   **Sentence Combining with Basic Ideas** • *And Another Thing!*</li>

<li>☐   **Combining Sentences with Phrases** • *Transplanting Phrases*</li>

<li>☐   **Combining Sentences with Adverb Clauses** • *In the Beginning . . . And at the End*</li>

<li>☐   **Combining Sentences with Adjective Clauses** • *Relatively Speaking*</li>

<li>☐   **Sentence-Combining Review** • *Chunky vs. Creamy Style*</li>

<li>☐   **Sentence Expanding: A Special Challenge** • *Near the Breaking Point*</li>
</ul>

AFTER • WORDS   If you want to experiment with different stylistic techniques, refer to the list of exercises at the end of "Styling Sentences" in your handbook.

COMBINING SENTENCES WITH KEY WORDS

He has a real knack with yarn.

THE FIRST STEP • Imagine you have two pieces of yarn, and you lay them side by side. What do you end up with? You've got nothing more than two pieces of yarn lying side by side, right? But if you weave them together, you've got the start of something bigger, maybe a shawl or a scarf. Writing is sort of like that. As you weave and shape your thoughts into sentences and paragraphs, you eventually have the makings of something bigger, maybe a story or a report.

The following workshop introduces you to an effective way to combine or weave short, simple thoughts into longer, more complex sentences. Make use of what you learn here in your own writing.

> **Combine the sentences on the following page using the type of key words asked for in parentheses. Underline the key word you have used in each new, combined sentence. The key words can be *one-word adjectives, compound adjectives, participles,* or *adverbs.* Study the examples below before you begin. Also see your handbook for more information about combining sentences with key words. (Refer to "Sentence, Combining" in the index.)**

Examples:

Clyde's goldfish eats constantly. Clyde's goldfish is hungry. **(adjective)**

> *Clyde's <u>hungry</u> goldfish eats constantly.*
> (*Hungry* is an adjective.)

Tasha's dog begs for food at dinner. Tasha's dog slobbers. **(participle)**

> *Tasha's <u>slobbering</u> dog begs for food at dinner.*
(*Slobbers* has been rewritten as the participle *slobbering* in the combined sentence.)

I plan to go on a diet. I will go on the diet tomorrow. **(adverb)**

> *<u>Tomorrow</u> I plan to go on a diet.*
> (*Tomorrow* is an adverb.)

My mom loves coffee in the morning. She grinds it fresh. **(compound adjective)**

> *My mom loves <u>fresh-ground</u> coffee in the morning.*
> (*Grinds it fresh* has been rewritten as the compound adjective *fresh-ground*
> in the combined sentence.)

1. Aunt Agnes made liver and onions for dinner. She cooked dinner yesterday. **(adverb)**

   Aunt Agnes made liver and onions for dinner <u>yesterday</u>.

2. I like babies. I like them when they are fat. **(adjective)**

   I like <u>fat</u> babies.

3. The wolves circled the dark cabin. The wolves howled. **(participle)**

   The <u>howling</u> wolves circled the dark cabin.

4. During the emergency, we dialed 911. We dialed quickly. **(adverb)**

   During the emergency, we <u>quickly</u> dialed 911.

5. My shoes hurt my feet. My shoes are new. **(adjective)**

   My <u>new</u> shoes hurt my feet.

6. The basketball fan received the last ticket. The basketball fan smiled. **(participle)**

   The <u>smiling</u> basketball fan received the last ticket.

7. My sister's hair is scary looking. My sister's hair is pink. **(adjective)**

   My sister's <u>pink</u> hair is scary looking.

8. Glinda ate a doughnut. It was filled with jelly. **(compound adjective)**

   Glinda ate a <u>jelly-filled</u> doughnut.

SENTENCE COMBINING WITH BASIC IDEAS

And Another Thing!

THE FIRST STEP • The words *and, but, or, nor, for, so,* and *yet* are used to connect words, phrases, and clauses in writing. These connecting words are called **coordinate conjunctions**, and they are used often by all writers. Careful writers, however, don't *overuse* them! They don't want their writing to ramble on and on.

> **Combine the following sets of short sentences into longer ones, using the method asked for in parentheses. The first four are done for you. Study the answers and explanations carefully before you complete the rest of the activity. (Refer to "Series, words in a," "Compound, Sentence," and "Compound, Subject [Verb]" in your handbook index for additional help.)**

1. The dress is old. The dress is ripped. The dress is perfect for our play.

(Use a series of words.) *The dress is old, ripped, and perfect for our play.*

   (*Old, ripped, and perfect* is a series of adjectives modifying *dress*.)

2. It rained all day. Our picnic plans were ruined.

(Make a compound sentence.) *It rained all day, so our picnic plans were ruined.*

   (The two simple sentences are combined with the connecting word *so* preceded by a comma.)

3. Lemonade tastes great. Lemonade quenches your thirst.

(Use a compound verb.) *Lemonade tastes great and quenches your thirst.*

   (*Tastes and quenches* is a compound verb.)

4. Sam is a champion skateboarder. Sarah is a champion skateboarder.

(Use a compound subject.) *Sam and Sarah are champion skateboarders.*

   (*Sam and Sarah* is a compound subject.)

5. Earning money is important to Sarah. Gymnastics is important to her. Sketching is also important to her.

(Use a series of words.) _Earning money, gymnastics, and sketching are important to Sarah._

6. The kids want to build a clubhouse. They don't have enough money.

(Make a compound sentence.) _The kids want to build a clubhouse, but they don't have enough money._

7. Sarah sells magazines. Sarah baby-sits on the weekends.

(Use a compound verb.) _Sarah sells magazines and baby-sits on the weekends._

8. The team waited for the head coach, who was arguing with a referee. The assistant coaches also waited for the head coach.

(Use a compound subject.) _The team and the assistant coaches waited for the head coach, who was arguing with a referee._

THE NEXT STEP • Use your handbook to complete the following statement about *coordinate conjunctions*. (Refer to "Coordinate conjunctions" in the index for help.)

The words, phrases, or clauses joined by a coordinate conjunction must be _____equal_____ **or of the same** _____type_____.

Once you complete this statement, share your thoughts about it with a classmate.

COMBINING SENTENCES WITH PHRASES

Transplanting Phrases

THE FIRST STEP • Ideas from short sentences can be combined into longer units of thought by moving a **phrase** from one sentence to the other. It's almost like transplant surgery. To learn how to transplant phrases in your own writing, you'll need the help of your handbook. (Refer to "Phrase, Combining with" in the index.) After you carefully review this information, move on to the workshop that follows.

Combine each pair of simple sentences using the phrase asked for in parentheses. The first four are done for you. Study these examples carefully before you begin work on the rest of the workshop.

1. That spaghetti sauce tastes gross.
   It's cooking on the stove.
   (participial phrase)

   That spaghetti sauce _____ cooking on the stove _____ *tastes gross.*

2. I got a new coat yesterday.
   I got it at the department store.
   (prepositional phrase)

   I got a new coat _____ at the department store _____ *yesterday.*

3. Jesse studied for hours.
   He studied to get an A on the test.
   (infinitive phrase)

   Jesse studied for hours _____ to get an A on the test _____ .

4. Bruce was actually reading a book.
   Bruce is a self-proclaimed book hater.
   (appositive phrase)

   Bruce, _____ a self-proclaimed book hater _____ , *was actually reading a book.*

5. Marion turned into a prune.
   She was swimming all afternoon.
   (participial phrase)

   _____ Swimming all afternoon _____ , *Marion turned into a prune.*

6. That stray cat is adorable.
   He's sitting in the yard.
   (participial phrase)

   That stray cat _____*sitting in the yard*_____ *is adorable.*

7. Johanna won two medals last week.
   She's a first-rate gymnast.
   (appositive phrase)

   Johanna, _____*a first-rate gymnast*_____ *, won two medals last week.*

8. Manuel is studying.
   He's at the library.
   (prepositional phrase)

   Manuel is studying __*at the library*_____ .

9. Mike cheerfully volunteered.
   He volunteered to help his little brother with his math homework.
   (infinitive phrase)

   Mike cheerfully volunteered ___*to help his little brother with his math*___
   *homework*_____ .

10. Todd goes to the movies twice a week.
    He's the neighborhood movie freak.
    (appositive phrase)

    Todd, _____*the neighborhood movie freak*_____ ,

    goes to the movies twice a week.

THE NEXT STEP • In the space provided above, write one original sentence containing a *participial phrase*, another sentence containing an *infinitive phrase,* and, if you have room, still another one containing an *appositive phrase*. (Share your results.)

COMBINING SENTENCES WITH ADVERB CLAUSES

In the Beginning . . . And at the End

THE FIRST STEP • You can combine two simple sentences into a **complex sentence** using adverb clauses. An adverb clause is one that begins with a word like *after, although, before,* and *unless* (called *subordinate conjunctions*). Note how a subordinate conjunction is used to combine two simple ideas in the following example:

Jerome checked his wallet for money. He bought the best-selling thriller.
(two simple ideas)

Jerome checked his wallet for money <u>before</u> he bought the best-selling thriller.

(The subordinate conjunction *before* connects the two ideas.)

Note: If the group of words introduced by a subordinate conjunction comes at the beginning of a sentence, a comma is placed after it.

Combine the following sets of short sentences into complex sentences using the subordinate conjunctions given in parentheses. The first three have been done for you. Study them carefully before you complete the rest of the activity.

1. The rope-and-wood bridge collapsed.
   Joe stood and watched. **(as)**

   The rope-and-wood bridge collapsed <u>as</u> Joe stood and watched.

2. The first colonists looked to England for help.
   It had been their home. **(because)**

   The first colonists looked to England for help <u>because</u> it had been their home.

3. Maurice filled his bicycle tires with air. **(after)**
   He pedaled to the south side of town.

   <u>After</u> Maurice filled his bicycle tires with air, he pedaled to the south side of town.

4. Tim settled into his favorite fishing spot.
The sun came up. **(as)**

Tim settled into his favorite fishing spot as the sun came up.

5. Scotty stopped running.
He heard the policeman shout. **(when)**

Scotty stopped running when he heard the policeman shout.

6. Two feet of snow fell. **(although)**
Lisa made it home.

Although two feet of snow fell, Lisa made it home.

7. You're all set to go to camp.
You haven't registered properly. **(unless)**

You're all set to go to camp unless you haven't registered properly.

8. Brenda checked on the two children. **(after)**
She fell asleep.

After Brenda checked on the two children, she fell asleep.

THE NEXT STEP • Write freely for 5 minutes about what happened yesterday afternoon between the time you were dismissed from your last class and the time you sat down to dinner. Try to put in as much detail as you can. Then exchange your writing with a classmate. Note ideas in each other's work that could be combined using *adverb clauses*.

COMBINING SENTENCES WITH ADJECTIVE CLAUSES

Relatively Speaking

THE FIRST STEP • You can combine two simple sentences into a **complex sentence** using adjective clauses. An adjective clause is one that begins with a word like *who*, *which*, or *that* (called *relative pronouns*). Combining ideas with these words will help you cut down on unnecessary repetition in your writing. (Refer to "Complex sentence" [the first listing] in the handbook index for more information.)

Examples:

The radio station played unfamiliar songs.
The radio station was geared for an older audience.

(two simple ideas)

The radio station, <u>which</u> was geared for an older audience,
played unfamiliar songs.

(By combining the two ideas with *which*, the unnecessary repetition
of *radio station* is avoided.)

> **Combine the following pairs of simple sentences into one complex sentence. In each case, a relative pronoun, other key words, and punctuation marks have already been put into place. (The first one has been done for you.)**

1. The beady-eyed mailman delivers on Wednesdays.
   The beady-eyed mailman is my uncle.

   The beady-eyed mailman who _____*delivers on Wednesdays*_____ is
   _____*my uncle*_____ .

2. The waitress looks sad and weary.
   She works at the corner cafe.

   The waitress who _____*works at the corner cafe*_____ looks
   sad and weary _____ .

3. The pink Cadillac was dented by hail.
   The pink Cadillac was parked in the driveway.

   The pink Cadillac that _____*was parked in the driveway*_____

   was dented _____*by hail*_____ .

4. The statue was stolen.
   It stood by the birdbath in the garden.

   The statue that _stood by the birdbath in the garden_

   was _stolen_ .

5. Pluto is the most distant planet in our solar system.
   It takes 248 years to orbit the sun.

   Pluto, which _takes 248 years to orbit the sun_ ,

   is _the most distant planet in our solar system_ .

6. The extreme heat affected the runners.
   The runners were participating in the conference relays.

   The extreme heat _affected the runners_ who

   were _participating in the conference relays_ .

7. John's half-eaten apple is a Golden Delicious.
   The apple is now totally brown.

   John's half-eaten apple, which is now _totally brown_ ,

   is _a Golden Delicious_ .

THE NEXT STEP • Refer to "*Who/which/that*" in the handbook index and find out when you should use each of these words. Discuss the results of your research with a classmate.

SENTENCE-COMBINING REVIEW

Chunky vs. Creamy Style

❚ Combine the following sets of short sentences into single, longer ones. Combine each set using the method asked for in parentheses. (Refer to "Sentence, Combining" in the handbook index for help.)

Example:

Gus swallowed two peanut butter sandwiches whole. Then he sat down to dinner.

Use a subordinate conjunction:

***After** Gus swallowed two peanut butter sandwiches whole, he sat down to dinner.*

1. The dog is loud. The dog is smelly. The dog is messy.

(Use a series of words.) *The dog is loud, smelly, and messy.*

2. Katie goes swimming every day. Josh goes swimming every day.

(Use a compound subject.) *Katie and Josh go swimming every day.*

3. I thought I did well on the math test. I got a D-.

(Make a compound sentence.) *I thought I did well on the math test, but I got a D-.*

4. My mom always picked the weeds. They still took over her garden.

(Use a subordinate conjunction.) *Although my mom always picked the weeds, they still took over her garden.*

5. The clerk gruffly asked us to take a seat. The clerk scowled.

(Use a participle.) *The scowling clerk gruffly asked us to take a seat.*

Combine the following sets of simple sentences and then finish the story on your own paper. Key words and punctuation marks are included in each problem to help you with your work. (The first combined sentence is done for you.)

1. Rachel's heart was pounding. She stood watching the softball game.

   Rachel's heart was pounding as she stood watching the softball game.

2. This was the third game of the season.
   Rachel still hadn't gotten to play.

   *This was the third game of the season*_____ , and

   *Rachel still hadn't gotten to play*_____ .

3. She should have been sitting on the bench.
   She was too anxious to sit still.

   *She should have been sitting on the bench*_____ , but

   *she was too anxious to sit still*_____ .

4. Rachel was small for her age.
   She had been practicing hard and was eager to help her team win.

   Although *Rachel was small for her age*_____ ,

   she had *been practicing hard and was eager to help her team win*

   _____ .

5. The fifth inning started.
   Coach Suarez looked down the bench.
   He saw Rachel.

   When *the fifth inning started*_____ ,

   Coach Suarez *looked down the bench*_____ and

   *saw Rachel*_____ .

The coach also saw Sonja next to her.
He had to decide . . . (Finish on your own paper.)

THE NEXT STEP • Exchange stories with a classmate. Check each other's work for combined sentences like those you created above.

SENTENCE EXPANDING:
A SPECIAL CHALLENGE

Near the Breaking Point

THE FIRST STEP • You needn't pack specific facts and details into all of the sentences in a piece of writing. That would be overdoing it. But, it's also true that you will not hold a reader's attention if most of your sentences lack detail. Note the two sentences that follow.

John fell.

Stepping on the toy truck completely hidden from his view, John fell flat on his backside.

The basic idea is the same in both sentences (*John fell*), but the second sentence is *expanded* with more showing detail. It shows *why* and *how* John fell; it almost tells a little story of its own.

■ **Carefully note below the process of expanding a sentence.**

The basic sentence: *Karlene smiled.*

***When* did she smile?** *This morning, Karlene smiled.*

***How* did she smile?** *This morning, Karlene smiled slyly.*

***Why* did she smile?** *This morning, Karlene smiled slyly as her brother sat in the scrambled eggs.*

■ **Now you try it. Build the following basic idea into an expanded sentence.**

The basic sentence: *Sidney ran.*

When did he run?

All at once Sidney ran.

Where did he run (in what location), or *what* was his destination?

All at once Sidney ran away from the gang.

How did he run?

All at once Sidney ran helter-skelter away from the gang.

Why did he run?

All at once Sidney ran helter-skelter away from the gang who didn't

approve of trespassers on their turf.

Expanded Sentence Revisited

Carefully read and evaluate your newly expanded sentence. Decide if it contains too little, too much, or just enough detail. Rewrite it below if you think you can make it better. (Your sentence doesn't have to answer all of the questions asked above.) Share your results with a classmate.

Revised Expanded Sentence:

THE NEXT STEP • Write three basic ideas that could be starting points for additional expanded sentences. Exchange these ideas with a classmate for more sentence-expanding practice.

EDITING WORKSHOPS

Checking for Sentence and Usage Errors

It is a fact of life that we all have to obey certain rules. We have to stop at red lights, wear shoes and a shirt in restaurants, speak softly in libraries, pass or shoot after we've stopped dribbling, and so on. (I'll bet you could fill up a page or two with rules you have to obey.)

The **Editing Workshops** in this section deal with two basic rules of writing: *Use clear and complete sentences*, and *Use words correctly*. The opening set of workshops will help you learn about or review common sentence errors so that you will be better able to follow the first basic rule. Rambling sentences, sentence fragments, comma splices, and run-on sentences are covered here. Also included is an activity that will help you use transitions to tie your sentences together.

The next set of workshops will help you learn about common usage errors so that you will be better able to follow the second basic rule. All of the frequently misused pairs of words like *your* and *you're* are covered here.

User's Checklist

Check your progress as you work on these **Editing Workshops.**

☐ **Avoid Rambling Sentences** • *Summer Snapshot*

☐ **Correcting Sentence Fragments** • *Great Balls of Fire!*

☐ **Correcting Comma Splices/Run-Ons** • *My Favorite Martian*

☐ **Sentence Errors—A Review** • *Out of Control*

☐ **Editing for Smoothness, Clarity** • *Zip it!*

☐ **Using the Right Word 1** • *T-Shirts or Tuxedos*

☐ **Using the Right Word 2** • *Go fetch!*

☐ **Using the Right Word 3** • *Put it in writing!*

☐ **Using the Right Word 4** • *Two Left Feet*

☐ **Using the Right Word—Review** • *Dog Talk*

AFTER • WORDS Before you turn in a writing assignment, always have a trusted friend, classmate, or family member check your work for sentence and usage errors. It's hard to obey all of the rules without a little help.

AVOID RAMBLING SENTENCES
Summer Snapshot

THE FIRST STEP • If you have a little brother or sister, you know that small children can produce very long sentences. "Mommy" might be the first word they learn, but "and" is not far behind. Be careful not to use too many *and*'s, *but*'s, and *so*'s in your own writing. Otherwise your sentences might ramble on like those of an excited four-year-old. (See "Rambling sentences" in the handbook index for more information.)

Read the following paragraph aloud. Listen for sentences that seem to go on forever. Correct these sentences by taking out some (but not all) of the *and*'s, *but*'s, and *so*'s. Then fix the punctuation and capitalization as needed. (The first few rambling ideas have been corrected for you.) *Remember:* **Remove only the connecting words that make the sentences go on and on.**

We went up to my grandfather's cabin last weekend. It was fantastic. We went fishing on Saturday morning, and I caught a bass off the pier. ~~so~~ Dad said he'd have Mom cook the fish for lunch. Cleaning a fish is kind of gross because you have to cut it open, but Dad did most of that. ~~and~~ Then we went swimming at the swimming hole. My brother Tad and I took turns pushing each other out over the water in a tire swing. Tad would push me hard, and I'd jump off into the water. ~~and~~ Then he'd yell for me to swim back and push him. ~~and~~ We spent all afternoon swimming and pushing. On Sunday morning, Dad cooked pancakes and thick, crunchy bacon on the old wood-burning stove. ~~and~~ We ate like pigs. ~~and~~ Tad and I wanted to go swimming again, but then we decided to go for a hike instead. We looked for creepy bugs while we were in the woods and found slugs, centipedes, and caterpillars. ~~but~~ We also caught a few butterflies, but we let them go. We kept a couple of the caterpillars in a jar and looked at them all the way home in the car.

CORRECTING SENTENCE FRAGMENTS
Great Balls of Fire!

THE FIRST STEP • A **sentence fragment** is a piece of a sentence trying to pass itself off as a complete thought. At first glance, it might look like an acceptable sentence because it starts with a capital letter and ends with a period (or some other end punctuation mark). But looks are deceiving.

A sentence must have a subject and a verb, and it must also express a complete thought. A fragment occurs when a group of words is missing either a subject or a verb, or it doesn't express a complete thought. (Refer to "Fragment sentence" in the handbook index for more information.)

Put an *F* on the line before each group of words below that is a sentence fragment. Put an *S* on the line before each group of words that is a complete sentence. (The first few have been done for you.)

_S_ 1. Jupiter is the largest planet.

_F_ 2. Is the fifth planet from the sun. *(no subject)*

_F_ 3. Jupiter, made of gas and ice, a huge, red globe. *(no verb)*

_F_ 4. Jupiter so large that 1,300 Earths could fit inside it.

_S_ 5. Jupiter is a big ball of hot gas like the sun.

_F_ 6. Could have been a star if it had been a little bigger.

_F_ 7. This ball of hot gas, like a huge, raging storm.

_S_ 8. Jupiter has 16 satellites, or moons.

_F_ 9. Has rings around it like Saturn does.

_S_ 10. Jupiter was named after the Roman king of the gods.

THE NEXT STEP • On your own paper, correct each group of words you marked as a fragment so it expresses a complete thought. (Share your results.) *Remember:* Always check your writing assignments for fragments before you turn them in. Have a classmate check your writing as well.

CORRECTING COMMA SPLICES/RUN-ONS

My Favorite Martian

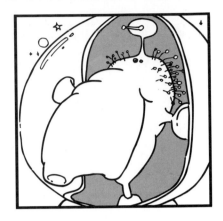

THE FIRST STEP • A **comma splice** occurs in writing when two simple sentences are incorrectly connected with a comma. A comma plus a connecting word, an end punctuation mark, or a semicolon should be used between two simple sentences. A **run-on sentence** occurs when two simple sentences are incorrectly joined without punctuation or a connecting word. (Refer to "Comma, Splice" and "Run-on sentence" in your handbook index for more information and examples.)

> In the groups of words below, place a *CS* in front of each comma splice, an *RO* in front of each run-on sentence, and a *C* in front of each correct sentence. Correct the sentence errors. (The first few have been done for you.)
> *Note:* Work on this workshop with a classmate if your teacher allows it.

_RO_   1. Mars is the fourth planet from the sun ⟨. It⟩ it is the one you can see most clearly from Earth.

_C_   2. Mars is only one-half the size of Earth.

_CS_   3. Mars shines with red and orange light, ⟨and⟩ it is often called the Red Planet.

_RO_   4. The Romans named Mars after their god of war ⟨because⟩ its red color reminded them of blood and war.

_RO_   5. Mars has seasons like those on Earth ⟨. Its⟩ its days are also about 24 hours long.

_C_   6. Mars has two moons called Phobos and Deimos.

_CS_   7. People used to believe that there were people on Mars, ⟨and⟩ they made up stories about Martians.

_C_   8. About a hundred years ago, scientists thought they saw water on Mars.

RO   9. In 1964 a spacecraft called *Mariner 4* went to Mars ~~it~~ *and* it took a lot of pictures.

CS   10. Scientists studied the pictures, *but* they found no signs of life.

C   11. The pictures did show craters like the ones on our moon.

RO   12. Someday astronauts will go to Mars *.T* they will live on the planet for a while and check for signs of life.

CS   13. They will be able to see if there is any plant life, *and* they can also check for any signs of water.

CS   14. Mars is very much colder than Earth *.T* the astronauts will need food and heated suits.

C   15. It will be great to learn more about Mars when astronauts finally do go there!

THE NEXT STEP • Let's say you want to know more about Mars and other planets in our solar system. Where could you turn for information? Certainly you could refer to a book about the planets in your school library. You could also turn to an encyclopedia or your science textbook. But before you refer to any of these sources, check the information on the planets in your handbook. The section called "Planet Profusion" contains a handy chart of interesting facts and figures. (Refer to "Planets" in the index.)

SENTENCE ERRORS—A REVIEW
Out of Control

THE FIRST STEP • Sentences have a way of running out of control. Your goal as a writer should be to avoid the errors that lead to "wayward" sentences. Three of the most common types of sentence errors are **run-on sentences, comma splices,** and **sentence fragments.** (Refer to the handbook for explanations and examples of these errors.)

Put an *RO* in front of any run-on sentences that follow, a *CS* in front of any comma splices, and an *F* in front of any fragments.

RO   Yesterday, Mark and I hiked into the woods we wanted to have a picnic lunch with a nice crowd of trees.

F   Some sandwiches and pop in a school backpack.

CS   We had to hike 2 1/2 miles to get to shade, the shortest trail in the park was 4 miles.

CS   It was hot on that trail, we were sweaty, cranky, and red faced.

RO   The woods were raining wood ticks they fell on our hair and climbed inside our clothes.

F   Totally grossed me out!

CS   The bugs drove me crazy, Mark called me a wimp.

F   Picked ticks out of my hair when we rested.

THE NEXT STEP • Rewrite this little story in complete sentences on your own paper. (Share your results.)

Special Challenge: What else might have happened on this outing? If you have any ideas, continue the story. Make sure to use complete sentences.

EDITING FOR SMOOTHNESS, CLARITY

Zip it!

THE FIRST STEP • **Transitions** or linking words like *finally, however,* and *also* help readers get from one end of your writing to the other in a smooth and logical manner. You have a lot of transitions to choose from to assist your readers along their way. (Refer to "Transitions" in your handbook index and see what we mean.)

■ **Use the following transitions to fill in the blanks below. (The first one has been done for you.)**

as soon as	finally	before
moreover	for instance	in fact

My parents and I get along pretty well. ___*However*___ , there are certain things

we disagree about. ___*For*___ ___*instance*___ , I think my curfew is unrea-

sonably early (7 p.m.). They won't budge an inch on the subject. I tried to win

them over one day, giving them many good reasons why I should be able to stay out

later. My best friend can stay out till 8 p.m. ___*In*___ ___*fact*___ ,

everyone I know can stay out later than I can. ___*Moreover*___ , I am very respon-

sible and would not get into trouble if I stayed out later. ___*Finally*___ , being

able to stay out later would make me more mature. ___*As*___

___*soon*___ ___*as*___ I finished my arguments, my father said he'd

make my curfew 5:30 p.m. if I didn't stop bugging him about it. ___*Before*___ ,

I talked about curfews all the time, but I keep my mouth shut these days.

THE NEXT STEP • Select five transitions listed in your handbook and use them in a brief paragraph about something funny, surprising, or unusual you've witnessed. (Share your results.)

USING THE RIGHT WORD 1
T-Shirts or Tuxedos

THE FIRST STEP · The words you use are like the clothes you wear. They must fit the occasion. Certain words and expressions you use freely among your peers are not acceptable in more formal settings. Your teachers, for example, expect you to use language that is appropriate for the classroom, not the type of in-group talk used among close friends. Your teachers also expect you to use language correctly in your writing. That is why you study usage, grammar, and punctuation in your language arts classes.

   One area in which all language learners must focus a good deal of their attention is errors in **usage**. These errors are commonly made when one word is confused with another. (*Good* is used instead of *well*; *there* is used instead of *their* or *they're*.) Whenever you review your writing, pay close attention to the pairs or sets of words that often confuse you. Also make sure to refer to "Using the Right Word" in your handbook whenever you have a usage question. (See "Usage and commonly mixed pairs" in the index.)

> **Carefully read the following story. If an underlined word is incorrect, cross it out and write the correct form above it. If the underlined word is correct, leave it alone. The first few underlined words have been corrected for you. (Work on this activity with a partner if your teacher allows it.)**

1. A few months ago, my mother read a book called *Diet for a Small Planet*.

   The book said it was better to eat ~~fewer~~ *less* meat and more vegetables. Mom was

   ~~all ready~~ *already* a vegetarian (someone who doesn't eat meat), and she wanted the rest

   of the family to choose the same course. Since Mom did most of the cooking,

   we knew we had to choose ~~among~~ *between* going vegetarian or starving altogether.

2. In order to ~~learn~~ *teach* us how to appreciate vegetables, Mom said we'd start a

   windowsill garden. We all went to the store to ~~by~~ *buy* supplies. "Just don't make

   me eat ~~beats~~ *beets*," I pleaded.

3. "Let's grow beans first," said Mom, "because they have ~~alot~~ *a lot* of protein." "That's

a ~~capitol~~ *capital* idea," replied Dad. "Beans grow quickly, so we won't have to <u>wait</u> for

weeks to get a sprout."

4. We planted a variety of seeds. I was ~~aloud~~ *allowed* to start ~~an~~ *a* tomato plant of my own,

~~too~~ *too*. It was my job ~~too~~ *to* keep the plants watered. I had to water the soil until

the ~~wholes~~ *holes* on the bottom of the pots started to leak. That's how we ~~new~~ *knew* if the

plants had enough water.

5. We <u>set</u> the pots next to the sliding glass door in the kitchen because <u>a lot</u> of

sunlight comes ~~threw~~ *through* there. Now all we could do was ~~weight~~ *wait*. All three of us,

on a <u>continual</u> basis, checked the pots for sprouts. In less than a ~~weak~~ *week*,

everything started to grow ~~alright~~ *all right*, except for the split pea seeds.

6. Now my dad and I are ~~real~~ *really* into vegetables. We grow all kinds in pots in our

kitchen and outside in a garden. Yesterday we cooked up some of our own

scarlet runner beans (<u>they're</u> poisonous unless cooked). ~~Its~~ *It's* great growing ~~you're~~ *your*

own food!

THE NEXT STEP • *Here's a special challenge:* Use the following pairs or sets of words correctly in sentences (use one set of words per sentence): *fewer, less; altogether, all together; bring, take;* and *it's, its*. Share your results.

Example:

"Visiting the <u>capitol</u> building is a <u>capital</u> idea," said Grandfather.
(The words "capitol" and "capital" are correctly used in this sentence.)

USING THE RIGHT WORD 2

Go fetch!

If the underlined word is incorrect, cross out the word and write the correct form above it. Do not change a word that is correct. (The first two underlined words are corrected for you.)

1. A brontosaur was a large, plant-eating dinosaur
   with ~~fore~~ *four* legs ~~who~~ *that* lived about 150 million years
   ago.

2. Brontosaurs traveled in herds across great ~~planes,~~ *plains* living on leaves and grasses.

3. Ginkgo trees were ~~there~~ *their* principal source of food.

4. Brontosaurs were probably ~~real~~ *really* quiet, like giraffes.

5. A healthy brontosaur's ~~wait~~ *weight* was about 30 tons. It took 1,000 pounds of food
   every day to satisfy ~~it's~~ *its* hunger.

6. Although scientists ~~wright~~ *write* book after book about dinosaurs, no one is really
   ~~quiet~~ *quite* sure what they were like.

7. Scientists have to infer information about brontosaurs and other dinosaurs from
   ~~there~~ *their* remains—bones and fossils.

8. But they don't know, for instance, what color brontosaurs were. Perhaps they
   were gray like elephants.

9. ~~Its~~ *It's* a mystery, ~~to,~~ *too* whether they could run ~~good~~ *well* or just plod along clumsily.

10. We'll probably never piece together enough information to answer all of our
    questions about brontosaurs ~~ore~~ *or* the other kinds of dinosaurs.

USING THE RIGHT WORD 3
Put it in writing!

If the underlined word is incorrect, cross out the word and write the correct form above it. Do not change any word that is correct. (The first two underlined words are corrected for you.)

1. Gina's party would be fun, but I was ~~vary~~ *very*

   concerned about Annie and Nathan's ~~personnel~~ *personal*

   problem.

2. My thoughts hadn't ~~aloud~~ *allowed* me a moment's ~~piece~~ *peace*, so I wrote a note to Erin.

3. During the video, in the ~~quite~~ *quiet* of the classroom, I ~~past~~ *passed* my note to Tom.

4. This is where it got quite out of control.

5. Tom thought the note was ~~fore~~ *for* Eric and gave it to him.

6. Eric ~~excepted~~ *accepted* it, ~~red~~ *read* it, and passed it on to show Scott.

7. Scott, ~~who's~~ *whose* eyesight must not be very ~~well~~ *good* in the dark, turned it in.

8. Mr. Kline read it and ~~complemented~~ *complimented* Scott on writing his notes so ~~good~~ *well*!

9. The note read, "Everybody today is thinking ~~sew~~ *so* much about Gina. They

   (Annie and Nathan) need to get along better. I hope ~~sum~~ *some* peace will come ~~real~~ *very*

   soon."

10. Mr. K.—apparently with ~~week~~ *weak* eyesight—thought it ~~red~~ *read*, "Everybody today is

    thinking about Ghana. The animals and native inhabitants need help. I hope

    peace will come soon."

11. I also learned that Mr. K. is ~~real~~ *really* nice because he leaned over and said to me, "~~You're~~ *Your*

    handwriting is improving." And then he smiled.

USING THE RIGHT WORD 4
Two Left Feet

If the underlined word is incorrect, cross out the word and write the correct form above it. Do not change a word that is correct.

1. As far as I'm concerned, ~~their~~ *there* is nothing worse ~~then~~ *than* gym class.

2. ~~Fore~~ *For* the kids who run and jump ~~good~~ *well*, I'm sure ~~its~~ *it's* great.   But for nonathletic types like me, gym class is torture.

3. ~~Beside~~ *Besides* looking like a real jerk in a gym uniform, I'm always picked last when it's time to ~~chose~~ *choose* teams.

4. The other kids never ~~leave~~ *let* me have the ball when we play basketball; they say I'm ~~to~~ *too* short to shoot a basket.

5. When we play softball, I can never hit the ball hard enough to get ~~passed~~ *past* first base.

6. Of ~~coarse,~~ *course* the worst part is trying not to look like an idiot.

7. I always feel as if ~~their~~ *there* is a ~~led~~ *lead* weight dragging behind me during gym class.

8. Whenever I ~~here~~ *hear* the teacher blow that ~~medal~~ *metal* whistle, I could ~~feint~~ *faint*.

9. I would ~~by~~ *buy* my way out of this class if the ~~principle~~ *principal* would let me.

10. I'm looking forward ~~too~~ *to* my senior year in high school because physical education is optional that year . . . or so I've heard.

USING THE RIGHT WORD–REVIEW

Dog Talk

In the following story, draw a line through any word incorrectly used, and write the correct form above it. Study these sentences carefully since no words are underlined. (The first two errors have been corrected for you.)

(1) When our neighbor's cocker spaniel had
knew *whole*
puppies, I ~~new~~ I'd get the pick of the ~~hole~~ litter.
two
(2) I narrowed it down to ~~too~~ blonde pups, and
chose
then I ~~choose~~ the one with little white paws and freckles.   (3) I named him
there *to* *know*
Snooze because ~~their~~ was no puppy that liked ~~too~~ sleep as much.   (4) I didn't ~~no~~
weeks
much about puppies, but Snooze was only two ~~weaks~~ old when I picked him out,

so I had time to learn.
some *a*
(5) My dad and I bought ~~sum~~ wood to build ~~an~~ doghouse.   Then my mom
teach
said she'd ~~learn~~ me how to train my dog to do tricks.   (6) We went to the
read
library and borrowed a book about dog obedience. We ~~red~~ about house-training a
compliments *teaching* *heel*
dog with ~~complements~~ (not punishment) and about ~~learning~~ it to ~~heal~~ and sit.
morning *passed*
(7) Every ~~mourning~~ I'd visit Snooze at my neighbor's house.   We ~~past~~ the time
to *already*
getting ~~too~~ know each other.   (8) By the time Snooze came home, he ~~all ready~~

knew how to heel and give me his paw to shake.
dear
(9) I think we were as ~~deer~~ to him as he was to us.   He always raised our
morale *seemed* *Except*
~~moral,~~ and he ~~seamed~~ to watch over us.   (10) ~~Accept~~ for all the blonde hair he
a
left on our beds, he was ~~an~~ great dog.

PROOFREADING WORKSHOPS

Using Capital Letters and Punctuation

Capital letters and punctuation marks make written communication possible. With a period, a question mark, or an exclamation point, you can signal that one of your ideas has come to an end. Then, by capitalizing the next word, you can signal that a new idea is about to begin. With a comma, you can, among other things, indicate a pause or a break in the middle of a longer idea. You get the picture, right? These handy markers are as important to writing as road signs are to car travel.

The seven **Proofreading Workshops** in this section provide a review of the common uses of capital letters and punctuation marks. As you complete your work, you will learn how helpful "The Yellow Pages" in the handbook can be when you proofread. All of the different rules for capital letters, punctuation, grammar, and usage are included there. (This section is easy to find because it is color coded.)

Remember: When you proofread the final copy of your writing, always make sure that the proper markers are in place, directing the flow of your ideas.

Getting Started

User's Checklist

Check your progress as you work on these **Proofreading Workshops.**

☐ **Reviewing Caps & Abbreviations** • *That, my dear friend, is a dog!*

☐ **End Punctuation** • *I need to rest my brain.*

☐ **Punctuating Dialogue** • *A Shot in the Arm*

☐ **Using Commas** • *Don't forget the salt.*

☐ **More About Using Commas** • *Let's get serious . . . about commas.*

☐ **Using Other Forms of Punctuation** • *For Those Special Occasions . . .*

☐ **Punctuation Review** • *Million-Dollar Cleanup*

AFTER • WORDS No one expects you to know *all* of the punctuation and capitalization rules. But everyone expects you to know and follow the basic rules of mechanics. Otherwise your writing will be too hard to follow.

REVIEWING CAPS & ABBREVIATIONS
That, my dear friend, is a dog!

THE FIRST STEP • When a sculptor creates a face out of a lump of clay, close attention is paid to every detail. The shape of the face has to be carefully molded, and each of the face's features has to be sculpted in just the right way. Writers are a lot like sculptors since they also pay close attention to every detail. This includes carefully looking over a final draft, making sure every period and capital letter is in its proper place.

Carefully read each sentence below. Put a line through any word or letter that is capitalized or abbreviated incorrectly. Make corrections above each mistake. The first few sentences have been done for you. (Work on this activity with a partner if your teacher allows it.)

Hint: Go through once and fix everything you're sure about. Then use your handbook to help you with the tougher spots. (Refer to "Capitalization" and "Abbreviations" in the handbook index for help.)

1. mr. glick bought a st. bernard puppy.
    M G   Saint B

2. he gave the puppy to ms. plumpcheeks, who lived on mississippi st.
    H   M P   M   Street

3. Ms Plumpcheeks told Mr. Glick that her Mother likes puppies, too.
    .   m

4. They decided to go visit her mother in the South.

5. They took the puppy, which they had named barrelneck, and headed for
    B
georgia.
G

6. mother plumpcheeks kissed Barrelneck and gave him some Spaghetti and
    M P   s
Meatballs.
m

7. "mother," cried Ms. Plumpcheeks, "spaghetti is not good for Dogs!"
    M   d

8. "sure it is," said Mother plumpcheeks. "I eat it all the time."
    S   P

9. Mr. Glick told Ms. Plumpcheeks that he liked her funny Mother.
                                                    m

10. They decided to take Barrelneck to ~~d~~isney ~~w~~orld.
    (D) (W)

11. ~~t~~he man selling Disney World ~~T~~ickets told them that rides weren't good
    (T) (t)

    for dogs.

12. "Yes they are," said Mother Plumpcheeks. "I go on rides all the time."

13. Barrelneck and Mother Plumpcheeks rode a ~~R~~oller ~~C~~oaster.
    (r) (c)

14. Later Barrelneck began reading a book called ~~dog~~ ~~day~~ ~~afternoon~~.
    (D) (D) (A)

15. ~~p~~eople thought it was strange to see a dog reading a ~~N~~ovel.
    (P) (n)

16. "~~h~~e can't read ~~H~~istory books," said Mr. Glick, "~~B~~ecause he never eats his
    (H) (h) (b)

    vegetables."

17. Then Mr. Glick, Ms. Plumpcheeks, Mother Plumpcheeks, and Barrelneck went

    swimming in the Atlantic ~~o~~cean.
    (O)

18. A man named Samuel Smart, ~~m.d.~~, told Mr. Glick that swimming wasn't
    (M.D.)

    good for dogs.

19. "~~i~~ know it's so because I graduated from ~~h~~arvard ~~u~~niversity," said Dr. Smart.
    (I) (H) (U)

20. They all told Dr⊙ Samuel Smart to buzz off.

21. Traveling ~~N~~orth on their way home, they planned trips to other parts of
    (n)

    the ~~U.S.~~
    United States⊙

END PUNCTUATION

I need to rest my brain.

THE FIRST STEP • Periods, exclamation points, and question marks usually signal the *end* of a sentence. Commas, on the other hand, signal *pauses* within sentences. If you keep these points in mind, end punctuation marks (and commas) are not that difficult to master.

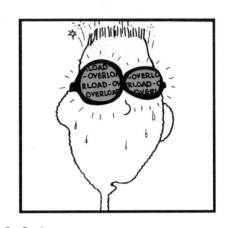

> **Put periods, question marks, and exclamation points where they are needed in the following paragraphs. Also supply the needed capital letters at the beginnings of sentences. The first two sentences have been marked for you. (Refer to your handbook for help.)**

you know, of course, that people need to sleep have you ever asked yourself why it is often said that if you work hard during the day, you'll sleep well during the night

how wrong that thinking is scientists now feel that the need for sleep has little to do with your physical state it's your brain that needs sleep it will not function normally for long without sleep it is now known that people need to dream in order to stay "brain healthy"

scientists have found that everyone dreams if people do not dream, their brains will begin to malfunction if you go without dreaming, you will become very irritable after a while, you may even suffer memory loss the effects of dreamlessness may last for weeks or months how about that

why is dreaming so necessary scientists are not sure of the

answer. During sleep the brain really doesn't rest. It is very active all night long. For some reason, the brain needs the special kind of activity it gets while you sleep.

How can you help your brain function properly? The next time you think about staying up late to watch TV or do homework, do some good dreaming instead.

Share the results of your work with a classmate. Discuss any differences in each other's answers. Then refer to "Exclamation point" in the handbook index. Once you turn to that section, look specifically at the "Caution" at the bottom of the first column. Read this information carefully. You might be one of those writers who sometimes goes overboard with exclamation points.

THE NEXT STEP • See your handbook to learn more about your brain. Find out about left-brain and right-brain thinking and about different phases of thinking. (Refer to "Thinking, Using your brain" in the index.) In the space provided above identify two things that you learned from reading this brief section. Share your results.

PUNCTUATING DIALOGUE
A Shot in the Arm

THE FIRST STEP • Carrying on a conversation is usually pretty easy. You just open your mouth and talk. Then another person says something, and presto—you have a conversation. A conversation in writing is not such an easy matter. And why is that? There are certain rules for punctuating dialogue (written conversations) that must be followed. Review these rules in your handbook and see what we mean. (Refer to "Dialogue, Punctuation" in the handbook index.)

Punctuate the following examples of dialogue with quotation marks, commas, and end marks. The first three have been done for you.

Note: **Make good use of what you learned about punctuating dialogue in your handbook as you work through each of these sentences.**

1. "I'm bored," said Clara. "Let's go shopping."
   (A *period* comes after Clara because that's the end of a completed sentence.)
   "O yeah," joked Keith, "I'd just love to get a new dress."
   (A *comma* comes after Keith because what follows completes the sentence.)
   "Would you like a new address, Keith?" Clara asked her brother.
   (The *question mark* is placed inside the quotation marks because the quote is the question.)

2. "Hey, there's a bee in your ear!" yelled Carlyle. Several students started

   waving their arms.

   "Everyone be quiet and take your seats," ordered Mr. Beech.

3. "Do you want to go to the movies on Friday?" asked Bela. "I've got two passes."

   "Well," replied Bronson, "I don't know if I can. My mother wants me to paint the

   garage."

   ✳ Each time the speaker changes as you write dialogue, you indent.

THE NEXT STEP • Share the results of your work with a classmate. Then re-create a conversation you recently had with a friend, classmate, teacher, etc. (Ten to twelve lines is enough.) Make sure to punctuate the conversation correctly.

USING COMMAS
Don't forget the salt.

THE FIRST STEP • **Commas** are given a lot of attention in your handbook. And they deserve it. They are to written language what salt is to food. Few pieces of writing would be complete without commas, just as few recipes would be complete without salt.

Commas are often used to signal pauses or to separate certain words or word groups so readers don't become confused. Note how they are used in the following example sentences.

After I drank the entire quart of orange juice, I lay down and "died."
(The comma after *juice* signals a pause after the opening group of words.)

I like strawberry jam, cream cheese, and green-olive sandwiches.
(The commas separate a series of words.)

Carefully read the model paragraph that follows and add commas where you think they are really needed. Do not refer to your handbook for help. (Commas have already been added in the first few sentences.)

I have a computer that I use for producing final drafts, but I can't actually write on it. I turn it on, listen to it boot up, put my fingers on the keyboard, and then... nothing. On the other hand, writing on paper makes me feel as if I can conquer the whole world. When I see the ink flowing onto the page, I know I'm making my mark. The words are like clay in my hands, and I can work them over until they're just right. I might change a word once, twice, or even three times before I am satisfied. In the opposite way, words on a computer screen seem written in stone. They stare at me with impersonal eyes, and I can't bear to work with them.

THE NEXT STEP • Exchange your work with a classmate, and check each other's work. If you have questions, now you may refer to the handbook. Then ask your teacher for the right answers.

MORE ABOUT USING COMMAS
Let's get serious . . . about commas.

THE FIRST STEP • Without realizing it, you were introduced to four very important uses of commas in the previous workshop. An explanation for each of these uses follows.

A. Commas were used between two independent clauses (a compound sentence):

I have a computer that I use for producing final drafts, but I can't actually write on it.

B. Commas were used to separate items in a series:

I might change a word once, twice, or even three times before I am satisfied.

C. Commas were used to separate long introductory phrases or clauses from the rest of the sentence:

When I see the ink flowing onto the page, I know I'm making my mark.
(an introductory clause)

D. Commas were used to set off phrases that interrupted the main thought:

On the other hand, writing on paper makes me feel as if I can conquer the whole world.

Note: For more information about these uses, refer to the comma section in your handbook.

The Matching Game

Identify the rule from above that applies to the commas used in each of the following sentences. For each answer, use the letter (A, B, C, or D) that corresponds to the comma rule. For the last five sentences, you must also supply commas.

Example:

__*B*__ I like shopping, reading, and playing Monopoly. (***B*** is the correct answer because the commas in this sentence separate items in a series.)

1. __*A*__ I would love to go to the movies, but I have a ton of homework to do.

2. __*D*__ My history teacher, on the other hand, loves to take piles of work home with her.

3. __*B*__ Pick up your laundry, do the dishes, and stop your whining.

4. __C__ Because I forgot to plug in the heater, all of the fish in our aquarium died.

5. __A__ My mother often tells me I'm pretty, yet I try to hide behind my hair.

6. __C__ Although Mario takes very good care of his teeth, he has three cavities.

7. __C__ When I see the first spring flowers, I can't help but feel like smiling.

8. __C__ In the rural schools of the past, kids in different grades sat together in one room.

9. __B__ Lawrence could finally relax after taking a shower, rushing through breakfast, and running to the bus stop.

10. __D__ Jackie watched three movies, believe it or not, before she developed a major headache.

Now it's your turn.

Write original sentences according to the directions provided below. (Make sure to use commas correctly in your sentences.) Share your results.

Write a compound sentence using the connecting word *but*.

I'm not really hungry, but I can't stop eating these crackers.

Write a sentence that includes a series of words or phrases.

I have to go to the doctor, change my clothes, and dash off to the party.

Write a sentence that includes a long introductory phrase or clause.

After eating pounds of Bing cherries, I always get a stomachache.

Write a sentence that includes a phrase that interrupts the main thought of the sentence.

Liver and onions, on the other hand, aren't nearly as tempting.

USING OTHER FORMS OF PUNCTUATION
For Those Special Occasions . . .

THE FIRST STEP • A writer can generally get by with a few basic punctuation marks: *periods, commas, apostrophes,* and *question marks.* But there are certain occasions when he or she may need to use more specialized marks of punctuation. Which ones are we referring to? Read on and find out.

Review the rules in your handbook about using *semicolons* and *colons.* Then punctuate the following sentences correctly. The first two are done for you. (Work on the following exercises with a classmate if your teacher allows it.)

1. Amber and Catlyn look like sisters; however, they are just friends.

2. There are five foods I cannot stand: brussels sprouts, liver, peas, hot dogs, and bologna.

3. My dog is the cutest pet in the world; she is all fluffy and white with a black patch around one eye.

4. I wanted to name my dog Madonna; however, I was overruled by my mother, who named her Helga.

5. When I asked my father if I could go to the concert, I got the typical response: "No."

Review the rules in your handbook for using *hyphens* and *dashes.* Then punctuate the following sentences. (The first two are done for you.)

1. The teacher gave another assignment to the work-weary students.
   (*Work-weary* is a hyphenated adjective.)

2. I know what I want for a present—new downhill skis.
   (A dash is used here to emphasize *new downhill skis.*)

3. I'm in the mood for a six-topping, large pizza.

4. Someone should invent self-polishing shoes.

5. I pleaded with my mother—really begged—and she finally agreed.

6. My parents have been married for twenty-two years.

> **Carefully read the paragraph below, paying special attention to the underlined words. Put a line through any of these words that contain *apostrophe* errors and write the correct form above it. The first two underlined words have been checked for you. (Refer to "Apostrophe" in the handbook index for help.)**

Hint: Five of the underlined words (including the one corrected for you) contain apostrophe errors.

(correct)

When I was little, I used to bake cookies at my grandmother's house all

the time. My favorite kind was chocolate chip, but we also baked a lot of

grandpa's

peanut-butter cookies. Peanut-butter cookies were my ~~grandpas'~~ favorite.

Whenever it rained, my grandmother would call over to my house and say,

(correct)

"Looks like it's a good day for baking." I'd put on my raincoat, borrow my

brother's   *(correct)*   *bike's*

~~brothers'~~ bike, and ride over to my grandparents' house. (My ~~bikes'~~ tires always

(correct)

seemed to be flat.) Once there, I'd immediately turn on the oven and keep

its   *Grandpa's*

checking ~~it's~~ temperature while Grandma cracked the eggs. ~~Grandpas'~~ eyes

looked a little disappointed when he saw we were making chocolate-

(correct)

chip cookies. Maybe someday I'll bake all of my relatives' favorite cookies.

THE NEXT STEP • Write a paragraph about a pleasant memory involving a grandparent or some other adult. Any little memory will do. (Use the paragraph above as a model.) Before you share your results with a classmate, check your writing for punctuation errors.

PUNCTUATION REVIEW

Million-Dollar Cleanup

Proofread the paragraphs below. Draw a line through any mark of punctuation or capital letter that is used incorrectly; add any needed punctuation or capital letters. The first few errors have been corrected for you. (Work on this review with a classmate if your teacher allows it. Also refer to your handbook for help.)

1 Imagine yourself sitting in your living

2 room, and you're watching TV. All of a sudden, oil starts to gush through

3 the windows. Pretty soon your whole house is covered with oil. In addi-

4 tion, black, sticky oil is all over you. *It's* Its in your mouth, in your ears, and

5 in your hair. You can't breathe, without getting it in your nose, and

6 *there's* ~~theres~~ no clean place in the house where you can go to get away from the

7 stuff.

8 In March 1989, this is just what happened to the fish, birds, and

9 other animals that call Alaska their home. An ~~Oil~~ ~~Tanker~~ called the

10 Exxon ~~valdez~~ hit a reef in Prince William Sound. The *ship's* ~~ships'~~ side had a

11 huge hole ripped in it, and the oil inside began spilling out. By the time

12 the spill was stopped, 10 million gallons of crude oil had escaped into the

13 sound.

14 The massive oil slick then headed for shore. Fish were poisoned, and

15 seals were left with nothing to eat. Birds who tried to fish for food were

16 covered with terrible, black guck. They couldn't preen themselves clean,

17 and they couldn't fly to clean water with their feathers stuck together.

18 Even if the birds could have gotten to clean water ; it wouldn't have done

19 them any good ; oil ~~doesnt~~ *doesn't* just rinse off.

20   Some scientists figured it would take a billion dollars to clean up the

     (.O) optional

21 oil spill ; ~~others think~~ , the affected area will never return to normal.   The

  costs

22 ~~cost's~~ are so high that some of the mess will probably just be forgotten

23 and left there.

24   Unfortunately , the wildlife may never be able to exist along the

25 affected shoreline .

Compare your work with a classmate's (or with another team's) before you turn it in. Discuss any differences. And make sure to double-check your work by reviewing the rules for punctuation in your handbook.

THE NEXT STEP • Write a descriptive paragraph about the oil spill from a seal's point of view. Here's a possible starting point:

I was basking on the beach when all of a sudden . . .

PART III
Language and Learning Workshops

LANGUAGE WORKSHOPS

A "Word's Worth" of Activities

Our language is made up of thousands of words, each one with its own special meaning, feeling, and sound. We use many of these words easily and effectively. For example, we don't need to be taught how to ask our mother for advice, or how to ask our teacher if we may get a drink of water, or how to ask our friends what they plan to do this weekend. We become effective language users simply by listening, imitating, and experimenting.

The workshops in this section are designed to build on what you already know about language. For example, you'll be asked to classify words according to the eight parts of speech. You'll also be asked to address special features of words like the singular and plural forms of nouns and the principal parts of irregular verbs. And most importantly, you'll be asked to work with words in new and creative ways. All in all, you're sure to get your "word's worth" in these **Language Workshops**.

Special Note: "The Yellow Pages" in your handbook is your complete guide for using the language. How do you find this section? Look for the pages that are . . . yellow.

User's Checklist

Check your progress as you work on these **Language Workshops.**

☐ **Nouns: A Quick Review** • *Let me introduce you.*

☐ **Common and Proper Nouns** • *Is that proper?*

☐ **A Closer Look at Nouns** • *Noun Play*

☐ **Verbs: A Quick Review** • *Swing, shimmy, shuffle!*

☐ **Working with Verb Tenses** • *A Tense Time*

☐ **Using Irregular Verbs** • *Driving You Crazy*

☐ **Subject-Verb Agreement** • *Sign on the dotted line.*

☐ **Adjectives: A Quick Review** • *Roughing It*

☐ **Using Colorful Adjectives** • *An "Eggstraordinary" Idea*

☐ **Adjectives: A Closer Look** • *Words have feelings, too.*

☐ **Types of Adverbs** • *Falling into Place*

☐ **Pronouns: A Quick Review** • *I'm your new substitute.*

☐ **Identifying Prepositional Phrases** • *Prepositional Locomotion*

☐ **Interjections: A Quick Review** • *Yech! A Pickled Frog*

☐ **Working with Conjunctions** • *The Conjunction Connection*

☐ **Parts of Speech Review** • *Pieces of Eight*

☐ **Parts of Speech Review** • *Last one in is a rotten egg!*

AFTER • WORDS | Your language is too valuable to take for granted. Instead, become a student of the language and constantly listen and learn new things about it.

NOUNS: A QUICK REVIEW

Let me introduce you.

THE FIRST STEP • Nouns name the people, places, things, or ideas we use in our writing and speaking. Note the nouns (underlined) in the following sentence:

> Sally met her new classmates
>   in the hallway.

Sally names a girl, *classmates* names the people who have gathered around her, and *hallway* names the place where they stand. *Sally* is also the subject of the example sentence. (The subject is the part of a sentence that is doing something or about which something is said.)

▌ Underline the nouns used as simple subjects in the sentences that follow. **Tell whether each subject (noun) is a *person, place, thing,* or *idea* in the space provided. (Refer to "Subject, Of a sentence" in the handbook index for help.)**

Example: ____*idea*____ The <u>thought</u> of introducing herself made Sally feel queasy.

____*person*____ 1. The <u>students</u> stared at the nervous girl.

____*idea*____ 2. Her <u>nervousness</u> was obvious to everyone.

____*thing*____ 3. The first-hour <u>bell</u> scared Sally.

____*person*____ 4. The <u>teachers</u> told all the students to get to their first-hour classes.

____*person*____ 5. <u>Sally</u> had no idea which way to go.

____*place*____ 6. <u>McKinley School</u> was so much larger than her old school.

____*person*____ 7. Two <u>girls</u> walked up to Sally, smiled, and offered to help.

____*person*____ 8. <u>Sally</u> breathed a sigh of relief and thanked the girls.

What's your number?

Underline all of the nouns in the sentences that follow. Write *S* above each singular noun and *P* above each plural noun. (The number of nouns in each sentence is given in parentheses.)
Note: **Refer to "Noun, Number" in the handbook index for information about singular and plural nouns.**

Example: Big <u>celebrations</u> (P) have been held every <u>year</u> (S) on the
<u>Fourth</u> (S) of July. (3)

1. Long ago, one <u>celebration</u> (S) was always held in the <u>field</u> (S) behind the <u>Bunde</u> (S) <u>Methodist Church</u> (S) in <u>Minnesota</u> (S). (4)

2. That <u>church</u> (S) is in the <u>country</u> (S), next to the <u>highway</u> (S), about three <u>miles</u> (P) from <u>town</u> (S). (5)

3. There were <u>games</u> (P) and <u>contests</u> (P) with <u>prizes</u> (P) all <u>day</u> (S). (4)

4. The <u>women</u> (P) from the <u>Ladies Aid Society</u> (S) were competing to pound a <u>handful</u> (S) of huge <u>spikes</u> (P) into a thick <u>beam</u> (S). (5)

5. Suitcase <u>relays</u> (P) for the <u>men</u> (P) always made the <u>people</u> (P) laugh. (3)

6. The clothesline <u>relay</u> (S) for the <u>men</u> (P) entertained everybody. (2)

7. The <u>women</u> (P) were especially amused to watch the <u>men</u> (P) racing in <u>teams</u> (P) to hang <u>laundry</u> (S) on the <u>lines</u> (P). (5)

8. <u>Shirts</u> (P) hanging by their <u>cuffs</u> (P) and <u>gloves</u> (P) pinned down <u>finger</u> (S) by <u>finger</u> (S) looked strange. (5)

THE NEXT STEP • In your handbook, read about using specific nouns in writing. (Refer to "Noun, Specific" in the index.) Then create a "Choosing Specific Nouns" chart for a person, a place, a thing, and an idea. Remember to start with very general nouns and gradually make them more specific. (Work on this activity with a partner if your teacher allows it.)

COMMON AND PROPER NOUNS
Is that proper?

Underline each noun in the sentences below. (The number of nouns in each sentence is in parentheses.) Write *C* above each *common noun*. Write *P* above each *proper noun*. *Note:* See your handbook for help if you don't know the difference between a common noun and a proper noun.

Example:

            P   C

        Jim bought his car from a

           C   C

        company that rents autos. (4)

     C   C   P

1. A company that rents cars, such as Hertz or

   P

   Avis, must care for them. (4)

         C   C   C

2. The engine had received good care and regular service. (3)

       C   P   C   C

3. This car, a 1990 Ford Escort, never had had a good coat of wax, however. (4)

           C   C   C   C

4. Most rental cars stand in the outdoors, winter and summer. (4)

  P   C   P   P

5. Jim waxed it for the first time on a Thursday in July. (4)

             C   P   C   C

6. He has no idea when his Escort will receive its next coat of wax. (4)

Title-Down Poetry

Apply your knowledge of common and proper nouns in two title-down poems. The title for one of your poems should be a *common noun*, and the title for your second should be a *proper noun*. Refer to "Title-down poetry" in your handbook index for a model. (Use your own paper for your work.)

THE NEXT STEP • Share the results of your work with a classmate. Select each other's best poem for a "title-down" display in your classroom.

A CLOSER LOOK AT NOUNS
Noun Play

THE FIRST STEP • Experienced writers appreciate the value of **specific nouns** in their writing. Specific nouns help them create clear images or pictures for their readers. Can you recognize award-winning, specific nouns when you see them? Let's find out. Carefully read the two columns of nouns that follow. Decide which column contains specific nouns.

shelter	pup tent
poultry	duck
animal	wombat
campground	Camp Runamuck
lake	Mud Lake

Did you choose the second column? Good! These nouns are more specific—which means they are easier to "see." You can help your readers see more in your own writing by using specific nouns. (Refer to "Noun, Specific" in your handbook index for more information and examples.)

Top Ten

On your own paper, create a list of interesting or important nouns. (List at least 10 words.) Have a good reason for including each of your choices. How will you "find" these words? Some suggestions follow.

It might be the sound of certain nouns that attracts you. (I like the way *mozzarella cheese* rolls off my tongue.) Maybe the feeling a noun gives you is important. (*Willow* gives me a good feeling.) Then again, maybe a specific name is important to you. (*Burnley* is important to me because it's the name of my mother's hometown.)

Note: Look in a dictionary, a thesaurus, and your handbook for award-winning nouns. Also, take note of appealing nouns as you read books, magazines, and advertisements.

Answers will vary.

THE NEXT STEP • Share your work with a classmate. Discuss which words you like in each other's list. Use one of your favorite nouns as the starting point for a clustering activity. (Refer to "Clustering" in the handbook index for guidelines and a model.)

VERBS: A QUICK REVIEW

Swing, shimmy, shuffle!

THE FIRST STEP • *Swing, shimmy,* and *shuffle* are lively, active words. They are fun to say and fun to use in your writing. For example, a form of the word *swing* makes the following idea come alive for the reader:

> Joe expertly <u>swung</u> Debbie
> into the air at the last dance.

All of these lively words have one important thing in common: they can all be used as **verbs**. Action verbs give life and energy to our language.

Note: Not all verbs are action packed. Words like *is, are, was,* and *were* are called **linking verbs** because they "link" subjects to nouns or adjectives.

> Joe and Debby are good dancers.
> (*Are* links the subject *Joe and Debby* to *dancers.*)

Underline the verbs with two lines in each of the following sentences. Label each action verb (like *swing* or *shimmy*) with an *A* and each linking verb (like *is* or *was*) with an *L*. See your handbook for a complete list of linking verbs. (Refer to "Verb, Linking" in the index. Once you turn to that section, the list is at the bottom of the page.)

Example: The students <u>entered</u> the dance through the gym door. *A*

The decorations <u>were</u> colorful streamers of crepe paper. *L*

1. Our dance <u>began</u> right after school. *A*

2. The theme of our last dance <u>was</u> "Friends Forever." *L*

3. Most of the students <u>attended</u> the dance. *A*

4. Our disc jockey <u>played</u> a lot of oldies. *A*

5. Most of us <u>were</u> very nervous at the beginning of the dance. *L*

6. One of the chaperons <u>arranged</u> us in pairs to dance. *A*

7. Larry and Rick <u>hid</u> from the "matchmaker." *A*

8. Jackie <u>danced</u> with Robert, a real hunk. *A*

Auxiliary Verbs

Auxiliary or **helping verbs** come before main verbs. See your handbook for an explanation of auxiliary verbs plus a list of the most common ones. (Refer to "Auxiliary verbs" in the index.)

▌ **In each of the following sentences, underline the verbs with two lines. All but two sentences contain auxiliary or helping verbs.**

Examples: The dance <u>was enjoyed</u> by almost everyone.

The organizers <u>could have sold</u> at least 50 more tickets.

1. However, the gymnasium at Fillmorton Recreation Center <u>had become</u> a disaster area.

2. Three students <u>had been selected</u> as the cleanup committee.

3. They <u>were moving</u> slowly through the debris on the gym floor.

4. They <u>found</u> Moe Epstein's baseball cap.

5. He <u>may have lost</u> it during his dance with Sasha Seabury.

6. Earlier they <u>had discovered</u> Rachel Sveum's retainer under a heap of streamers.

7. She probably <u>lost</u> it during the swing contest.

8. That <u>may have been</u> the highlight of the dance.

THE NEXT STEP • Submit three vivid, action-packed verbs (like *swing, shimmy,* and *shuffle*) for a classroom exchange. Once you select or receive your trio of verbs, use one of these words as the subject of a *concrete poem*. (Refer to "Concrete poetry" in the handbook index for a model.)

WORKING WITH VERB TENSES

A Tense Time

THE FIRST STEP • We depend on a watch or clock for the time—except when we are reading or writing, that is. Then we must depend on the **tenses** of verbs to help us keep track of time. Verbs don't tell us if it's 1:30 in the morning or 3:05 in the afternoon. That's clock time. Verbs refer to time in a different way.

The **simple tenses** of verbs indicate whether an action takes place in the present, past, or future. The **perfect tenses** of verbs indicate special segments of time—such as when an action beginning in the past continues into the present. (Refer to "Tense of verbs" in the handbook index for explanations and examples.)

Now let's experiment with the different tenses. For each of the verbs that follow, write sentences expressing the tenses, or "times," asked for. (The first one has been done for you.)
Note: If you're not sure how to form these verbs in certain cases, see your handbook for help. (Refer to "Irregular verb" in the index.)

throw

I always **throw** *potato peelings to the ducks.*

(present)

I **threw** *the potato peelings to the ducks.*

(past)

I **have thrown** *potato peelings to the ducks.*

(present perfect)

bring

I **brought** *potato salad to the picnic.*

(past)

I **will bring** *potato salad to the picnic.*

(future)

I **had brought** *potato salad to the picnic.*

(past perfect)

write

I **write** in my journal.

(present)

I **wrote** in my journal.

(past)

I **had written** in my journal.

(past perfect)

take

I **take** my dog to the park.

(present)

I **will take** my dog to the park.

(future)

I **have taken** my dog to the park.

(present perfect)

Answers will vary.

(   )

(   )

(   )

THE NEXT STEP • Create another tense-writing frame for a verb of your own choosing. (Use the space provided above.) Exchange your work with a classmate and complete each other's frame.

USING IRREGULAR VERBS
Driving You Crazy

THE FIRST STEP • Let's suppose you've been hired as an editor and proofreader for your favorite magazine. You start reading through the first stack of copy that's piled on your desk. Suddenly you break out in a cold sweat. Every sentence seems to contain an **irregular verb,** and you hate irregular verbs. Remembering the different forms of verbs like *burst, bring,* and *shake* drives you crazy.

What are you going to do?

Here's a suggestion: Refer to the chart of irregular verbs in your handbook. It will answer all of your questions about these troublesome words . . . and help you keep your job. (See "Irregular verb" in the index.) You'll also benefit from the following activity, which addresses many of the words listed in the chart.

■ **Study these irregular verbs. Read them quietly to yourself several times.**

Present Tense	Past Tense	Past Participle
break	broke	broken
drive	drove	driven
eat	ate	eaten
fall	fell	fallen
give	gave	given

Note that these verbs have a certain rhythm that helps them stick in your mind. Now try some more.

Present Tense	Past Tense	Past Participle
catch	caught	caught
fly	flew	flown
rise	rose	risen
teach	taught	taught
write	wrote	written

Special Note: The principal parts of most verbs are formed by adding "ed" to the main verb (*squish, squished, has squished*). The principal parts of irregular verbs like those above follow no set pattern (*bite, bit, has bitten*). You use the principal parts of verbs to form the different tenses.

After carefully studying the chart of irregular verbs in the handbook, fill in the blank spaces below. (Have your handbook closed as you do your work. Refer to it only after completing your work.) Share your results with a classmate.

Present Tense	Past Tense	Past Participle
begin	began	begun
bring	brought	brought
burst	burst	burst
do	did	done
draw	drew	drawn
freeze	froze	frozen
go	went	gone
grow	grew	grown
see	saw	seen
shake	shook	shaken
sing	sang	sung
take	took	taken
throw	threw	thrown
weave	wove	woven

THE NEXT STEP • Write five sentences in which you purposely misuse some of the irregular verbs covered in this activity. (On the back of your paper, write each sentence correctly.) Submit your work for a class pool of "irregular" sentences that can be used for additional review work.

SUBJECT-VERB AGREEMENT
Sign on the dotted line.

THE FIRST STEP • Here are some definite signs of agreement: a nod of the head, a handshake, and a signature on a contract. Do you know of any others? We know of one, and it has to do with writing and speaking. A singular subject (*one Gila monster*) matched with a singular verb (*snickers*) is a definite sign of agreement. In the same way, a plural subject (*three Gila monsters*) matched with a plural verb (*snicker*) is another sign of agreement.

Subjects and verbs matched together must **agree** in number. That is, they must both be singular or plural. The activity that follows focuses on this important sign of agreement.

> **Put a check next to each sentence in which the subject and verb do not agree. In each sentence, the subject is underlined with one line and the verb with two lines. For those sentences you check, correct the subject-verb agreement errors. (The first four have been done for you.)**
> *Note:* **Refer to "Subject-verb agreement" in the handbook index for help.**

_____ 1. My friends go with me every year to the state fair.
       (Both the subject and verb are plural, so they agree.)

✔ 2. Carlos and I ~~rides~~ *ride* the rocket cars instead.
       (Compound subjects connected by "and" require plural verbs. "Rides" is singular.)

_____ 3. Everyone enjoys the music in the grandstand area.
       (Indefinite pronouns like "everyone" require singular verbs. "Enjoys" is a singular verb, so the subject and verb agree.)

✔ 4. Neither Alfredo nor Jim ~~like~~ *likes* amusement rides.
       (With compound subjects connected by "or" or "nor," the verb must agree with the subject nearest the verb. "Jim" is singular and "like" is plural.)

_____ 5. One of my friends goes immediately to see the sideshows.

✔ 6. Cotton candy and caramel corn ~~is~~ *are* my favorite snacks.

✔ 7. Carlos and I ~~saves~~ *save* our money for the rides.

_____ 8. The double Ferris wheel or the roller coaster is my favorite ride.

✔ 9. John, as well as my other friends, ~~love~~ *loves* the bumper cars.

_____ 10. My sister and Mary always ride the tilt-a-whirl.

✔ 11. Neither Julie nor Sally ~~visit~~ *visits* the animal barns.

_____ 12. Nobody but me likes to watch the pig races.

✔ 13. We all ~~loves~~ *love* the fair more than any other summertime activity.

THE NEXT STEP • This activity focused on a special *agreement* rule. For this follow-up activity, let's turn the tables and focus on something completely different. Write about a time when you *disagreed* with a friend, brother or sister, teacher, etc., about something. (Use your own paper.)

Note: Don't forget that subjects and verbs must agree in all types of writing—even when you are writing about "disagreeable" topics.

ADJECTIVES: A QUICK REVIEW

Roughing It

THE FIRST STEP • Your best writing starts with a good writing topic. You must have a good story to tell (or some interesting facts to present). Then you must tell your story well. Specific nouns and vivid, action-packed verbs can add a great deal to your writing. **Adjectives**, which modify nouns or pronouns, can also help you tell a good story. See your handbook for more on this part of speech. (Refer to "Adjective" in the index.)

> **Underline the adjectives in the following sentences. (The number of adjectives in each sentence is indicated in parentheses.)**

Note: Possessive pronouns like *his, her,* or *their* function as adjectives. The articles *a, an,* and *the* should not be considered adjectives in this activity.

Example: Steve participated in <u>two</u> <u>school</u> activities. (2)

1. Steve played on the <u>seventh-grade</u> <u>soccer</u> team. (2)

2. He also played <u>first</u> cornet in the <u>jazz</u> band. (2)

3. Steve was <u>excited</u> about the <u>upcoming</u> weekend. (2)

4. On <u>Friday</u> night <u>his</u> parents were going to let him pitch <u>their</u> <u>umbrella</u> tent in

   the backyard. (4)

5. He had invited Dave and Greg and <u>three</u> <u>additional</u> "leaders" from <u>his</u> crowd of

   friends. (3)

6. <u>That</u> night, they ran an <u>extension</u> cord from the <u>nearby</u> house and watched mov-

   ies on a VCR until midnight. (3)

7. Dave said, "Shelly and <u>her</u> <u>best</u> friends are sleeping in a <u>small</u> <u>Winnebago</u>

   camper at <u>her</u> house." (5)

8. At 12:30 the <u>six</u> guys sneaked over there and rocked the camper. (1)

9. The <u>aluminum</u> camper was <u>dark</u> and <u>empty</u>, so they went home. (3)

10. A note taped to one of the <u>tent</u> flaps said, "Sorry we missed you at the camper.

See you <u>first</u> hour on Monday." (2)

11. Later Greg threw <u>some</u> firecrackers from behind a <u>nearby</u> bush. (2)

12. Luckily for Steve none of <u>his</u> <u>family</u> members or <u>next-door</u> neighbors woke up. (3)

13. For almost a week, Steve felt <u>good</u> about the weekend. (1)

14. Then Dave wore a <u>screaming</u> <u>Hawaiian</u> shirt to school, and suddenly the <u>camp-</u>

<u>ing</u> experience was forgotten. (3)

THE NEXT STEP • Write a word cinquain poem like the one below for an idea or a feeling like *love, hate, freedom,* or *shyness.* See your handbook for writing guidelines. (Refer to "Cinquain" in the index.)

Example: Freedom
Sweet, priceless
Raises our spirits
Like a fresh breeze
Elbowroom

Note: The second line in a word cinquain contains two *adjectives.*

USING COLORFUL ADJECTIVES
An "Eggstraordinary" Idea

THE FIRST STEP • Whenever possible, use vivid, **colorful adjectives** to describe the nouns in your writing. Colorful adjectives are seldom the first ones that come to mind. At times, you'll need to dig deep to find just the right word to modify a certain noun. (Refer to "Adjective, Colorful" in the handbook index for more information.)

| Write two colorful adjectives that could be used instead of the overused adjective underlined in each sentence. (Use a thesaurus for this exercise if you think it would help you.)

Example: Double Bubble gum had a <u>funny</u> first name: "Blibber Blubber."

_____*curious*_____   _____*playful*_____

1. Harvey Kennedy had a <u>good</u> idea for an invention—the shoelace. He earned over $2,000,000 for his idea.

_____*fantastic*_____   _____*profitable*_____

2. Walter Hunt made a <u>bad</u> decision when he sold his safety-pin patent for $400. He never received any more for this item, which is now used in every household.

_____*lousy*_____   _____*unfortunate*_____

3. Hyman Lipman had a <u>neat</u> idea when he combined a pencil with an eraser. He sold his patent for $100,000 in 1858.

_____*creative*_____   _____*inventive*_____

4. One man earned money in a <u>different</u> way. He allowed an advertising company to completely paint his Volkswagen Beetle with ads.

_____*weird*_____   _____*unusual*_____

THE NEXT STEP • Decide which new adjective works best in each sentence. Circle your answer. Afterward share your work with a classmate.

ADJECTIVES: A CLOSER LOOK

Words have feelings, too.

THE FIRST STEP • When you choose an **adjective** to modify a certain noun, make sure it adds color to the noun in question and that it expresses the right feeling. (Refer to "Connotation" in the handbook index for more information about the "feelings" of words.)

Fill in each blank beneath the paragraph with one of the two words listed. Choose the word that BEST expresses the right *meaning* and *feeling*. (The two italicized words in the first sentence set the tone for the rest of the paragraph.)

My world is overflowing with *impatient* and *thoughtless* people. Sadly, many of these ___1___ people seem to be in the local shopping malls every time I go there. I can't count how often I've been bumped by ___2___ shoppers, snapped at by ___3___ clerks, and pestered by ___4___ children running up and down aisles. Many people seem to think that shopping is a competition, to be won. While a shopping trip used to be an enjoyable, ___5___ time, lately it's more likely to end up being an ___6___ afternoon full of ___7___ experiences. The way things have been going lately, I think I'd rather stay home and clean my bedroom than have to make even one more shopping trip. Well, almost.

1. _____impolite_____ (weird, impolite)

2. _____rude_____ (rude, nervous)

3. _____grouchy_____ (angry, grouchy)

4. _____wild_____ (complaining, wild)

5. _____relaxing_____ (relaxing, comforting)

6. _____exhausting_____ (exhausting, sickening)

7. _____unpleasant_____ (unpleasant, terrifying)

TYPES OF ADVERBS
Falling into Place

THE FIRST STEP • Words like *loudly, really, very,* and *never* are classified as **adverbs**. They are used to modify verbs, adjectives, or other adverbs. Adverbs fall into four different types or classes: adverbs of *time, place, manner,* and *degree.* See a discussion of these different types in your handbook. (Refer to "Adverb" in the index.)

In the chart below, arrange the following list of adverbs according to the four different types. There are five adverbs per category. (A few of the words have already been "charted" for you.)

today	really	lazily	there	soon
away	carefully	daily	nervously	scarcely
hurriedly	forward	here	very	everywhere
almost	tomorrow	hardly	before	brilliantly

Charting Adverbs

Time (answers *when*)	Place (answers *where*)	Manner (answers *how*)	Degree (answers *to what extent*)
today	away	hurriedly	almost
tomorrow	forward	carefully	really
daily	here	lazily	hardly
before	there	nervously	very
soon	everywhere	brilliantly	scarcely

Special Challenge: Add one more adverb per category.

Falling into Action

▐ **Write one sentence using an example of each type of adverb listed below. (Use the adverbs you charted on the previous page in your sentences.)**

adverb of time

Tomorrow I'll drive for 13 hours straight.

adverb of place

Your sneakers are here.

adverb of manner

He read the poem brilliantly.

adverb of degree

I could hardly believe my ears.

Special Challenge: Really lay it on thick by using three or more of the adverbs from the chart in one sentence. (Write your sentence in the space below.)

I try daily to do my homework very carefully.

THE NEXT STEP • Use adverbs in a fun way by creating at least one *Tom Swifty*. Two examples follow:

"Look at that punctured tire," my dad said flatly.

"Stay down," the sergeant whispered lowly.

In both examples, the underlined adverbs turn the statements into little jokes, or Tom Swifties.

PRONOUNS: A QUICK REVIEW

I'm your new substitute.

THE FIRST STEP • Which idea interests you more? *They stared at him.* (or) *The students stared at Mr. Simpson.*

The first sentence offers a reader nothing more than a vague reference to a group *(they)* and a male *(him)*. *They* and *him* are **pronouns**. The second sentence—the one with the nouns *students* and *Mr. Simpson*—presents a clearer picture. By their very nature, pronouns are more general and less interesting than nouns.

So why do we use pronouns? They allow us to communicate clearly and smoothly. The following sentences reveal the importance of pronouns in our language.

> ***Sentence without Pronouns:*** Mr. Simpson thought that Mr. Simpson should write Mr. Simpson's name on the board.
>
> *Discussion:* This example sounds silly and awkward with the repetition of the noun *Mr. Simpson*.
>
> ***Sentence with Pronouns:*** Mr. Simpson thought that he should write his name on the board.
>
> *Discussion:* Substituting the pronouns *he* and *his* for *Mr. Simpson* makes this sentence easier to understand.

Most of the pronouns you use are **personal pronouns** *(I, we, they, he, her,* etc.), but there are six other types as well. Your handbook has explanations and examples for all seven types of pronouns. (Refer to "Pronoun" in the handbook index.)

> **Underline the PERSONAL PRONOUNS in the following sentences. The first one has been done for you. (The number of personal pronouns in each sentence is given in the parentheses.)**

1. My husband and I asked the elderly man to plant some trees for us. (3)

2. He dug two ash saplings out of his grove; they had grown there wild. (3)

3. In early spring, he came with them, their roots neatly balled in burlap. (3)

4. I watched as he skillfully planted those trees, his hands knowing exactly what

   to do. (3)

5. Their branches were full of leaf buds. (1)

6. "When you transplant a tree," he said, "you must leave the taproot as long as

possible." (3)

7. With his feet he firmly tamped down the soil around the roots. (2)

8. As he put his tools away, we asked him in for a cup of coffee. (4)

Antecedents

The word that the pronoun replaces is called the **antecedent**. If the antecedent is singular, the pronoun must be singular; if it is plural, the pronoun must be plural. (Refer to "Antecedent" and "Pronoun, Problems" in the handbook index for more information.)

Underline the correct pronoun in parentheses. Then draw an arrow to its antecedent. (Use _him or her, his or hers_, etc., when either a male or female could be referred to by the antecedent.)

Examples: The players won **(his/their)** matches.

A soldier may one day become an officer if **(he or she/they)** is dedicated.

1. Both magazines offered **(its/their)** customers a good deal.

2. The boss will hire anyone unless **(he or she/they)** can't serve on weekends. (_Anyone_ is a singular antecedent.)

3. Paula and Rosa brought samples of **(her/their)** winning recipe.

4. The club decided to raise **(its/their)** membership dues.

5. Not everyone should include weight lifting in **(his or her/their)** exercise program. (_Everyone_ is a singular antecedent.)

THE NEXT STEP • Define _pronoun_ in a sentence. Don't refer to the definition provided in the handbook until you have written your own version. You can, however, refer to "Definition, Guidelines for writing" in the index for help.

IDENTIFYING PREPOSITIONAL PHRASES

Prepositional Locomotion

THE FIRST STEP • A **preposition** is like a train engine. It has to pull something before it is useful. What does a preposition pull? A preposition pulls adjectives, adverbs, and noun or pronoun objects. A prepositional train (actually a *prepositional phrase*) is a preposition and all of the related words it pulls.

Example Trains:

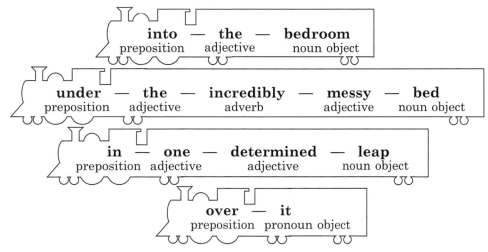

Note: The words *a, an,* and *the* are special types of adjectives called articles.

"Training" Yourself

Find the list of prepositions in your handbook. (Refer to "Preposition" in the index.) Make three prepositional trains of your own.

Special Challenge: **Label the parts in your trains.**

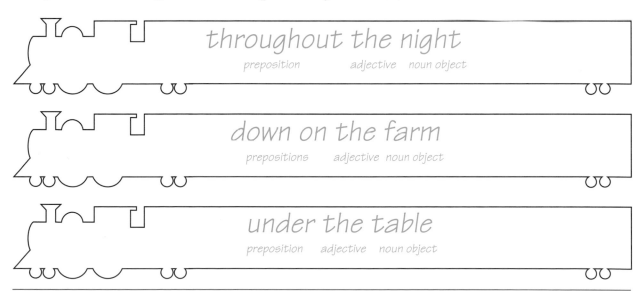

■ Use each of your prepositional trains in a sentence. (Use the space below for your work.)

> Lawrence burst <u>into the bedroom</u> and dove <u>under the incredibly messy bed.</u> (Two phrases are used in this example.)

1. _I watched for the meteor shower throughout the night._

2. _We went strawberry picking down on the farm._

3. _My dog begs for food under the table._

It's time for a contest.

■ In the space provided below, change the preposition as many times as possible in the following sentence. (Use your own paper if you run out of room.)

> Freezer Breezer swam <u>alongside of</u> the whales.

> Freezer Breezer swam <u>under</u> the whales.

(Some prepositions like *alongside of* consist of two words.)

Freezer Breezer swam over the whales.

Freezer Breezer swam beneath the whales.

Freezer Breezer swam behind the whales.

Freezer Breezer swam between the whales.

Freezer Breezer swam over to the whales.

Freezer Breezer swam around the whales.

THE NEXT STEP • Exchange your work with a classmate, and see who was able to use the most prepositions. (Refer to your handbook if you need help checking your partner's work.)

INTERJECTIONS: A QUICK REVIEW

Yech! A Pickled Frog

THE FIRST STEP • An **interjection** is a word(s) that expresses strong emotion or surprise. Interjections are especially useful when you are writing dialogue for a play or story. Either an exclamation point or a comma is used to separate an interjection from the rest of the sentence. Notice the interjections (underlined) in the following examples:

*Yech! Why do we have
to study pickled frogs?*

Hmm, I think I'll leave mine in the jar.

Good grief, Robin!

▌ **Underline each interjection in the narrative that follows. Supply an interjection when a space is provided.**

1. "Wow, Batman! Look at that!" screamed Robin.

2. "Good grief, Robin, what do you see through the telescope?"

3. "Holy cow, someone's driving off in a truck containing the Bat Boat, Bat Copter,

   Bat Plane, Bat Cycles, and Bat Mobile."

4. "We've no time to lose, Boy Wonder. Yipes! Get on your Bat Skates and let's

   roll after him."

5. "Oh, Mr. Wayne and Mr. Grayson," called Alfred the butler, "I have a message

   for you."

6. "___*Holy bad timing*___, Alfred, quickly tell us what it is!"

7. "Oh bosh, Robin, don't get so excited," replied old Alfred.

8. "What is it, Alfred?" asked Batman. "Creepy criminals! I'm excited, too."

9. "Well," answered Alfred, "I just wanted to say that Chief O'Hara wants to talk to you."

10. "_____Jeepers_____, Batman, see what he wants!" exploded Robin.

11. "Holy Ann Landers, Robin, that's good advice," retorted Batman.

12. "Well, I don't like to do this to you and Robin," said O'Hara in a stern voice, "but as chief of police, I'm holding all your vehicles and placing you both under arrest."

13. "_____Holy speed trap_____! Why are you taking my wheels?" exclaimed Batman.

Holy conclusions, Batman!

Continue the conversation on the lines below. Include at least three additional interjections. (Use your own paper if you need more space.)

"Heck, you drive like you've got bats in your belfry," cried Chief O'Hara.

"Aha!" chirped Robin. "I told you to drive slower, Batman."

"Sorry sidekick, Robin, don't be a backseat Bat Mobile driver," said Batman.

"Well, if you promise to wear your seat belts, I'll let you off with a warning," remarked Chief O'Hara.

THE NEXT STEP • Exchange conversations with a classmate. Note how your partner used interjections in his or her work.

WORKING WITH CONJUNCTIONS

The Conjunction Connection

THE FIRST STEP • Suppose you want to go from Chicago to Crosby, North Dakota. (Don't ask us why.) Your uncle drives you to the airport. You fly to Minneapolis, where you change planes and fly to Grand Forks, North Dakota. Again, you change planes and fly to Minot, North Dakota. You then catch a bus to Crosby. You have made many connections.

    A reader must also make many connections in a piece of writing, moving along from one idea to the next. To ensure that readers have a smooth trip, writers often connect ideas with **conjunctions**. Read on and see how much you know about these connecting words.

> **Review the list of conjunctions in your handbook. (Refer to "Conjunction" in the index. Once you turn to that section, the list is at the bottom of the page.) Did you have any idea there were so many? Practice using conjunctions by combining the following pairs of brief sentences into longer, smoother-reading ones. The first two have been done for you. Try to use a different connecting word (underlined) in each of your new sentences.**

1. Tasha loves creamed asparagus on toast. Her older brother Michael gags at the sight of this meal.

   Tasha loves creamed asparagus on toast, <u>but</u> her older brother

   Michael gags at the sight of this meal.

2. My little sister's swimming pool was "bleeding." I applied a big Band-Aid.

   <u>Because</u> my little sister's swimming pool was "bleeding," I applied a

   big Band-Aid.

(Connecting words called *subordinate conjunctions* can be used at the beginning of sentences. *Because* is a subordinate conjunction.)

3. Lucille tried on many bathing suits. Not one of them fit her right.

   Lucille tried on many bathing suits, yet not one of them fit her

   right.

4. Father thought he saw a mermaid. Fred got the big seining net.

Father thought he saw a mermaid, so Fred got the big seining net.

5. Hagar the Horrible is a ruler of men. His wife and daughter rule over him at home.

Hagar the Horrible is a ruler of men, yet his wife and daughter rule over him at home.

6. My dog Oscar's belly almost drags on the ground. I can't bear to put him on a diet.

Although my dog Oscar's belly almost drags on the ground, I can't bear to put him on a diet.

7. Turn left at this corner. You'll end up in a deep pit.

Turn left at this corner, and you'll end up in a deep pit.

THE NEXT STEP • Exchange papers with a classmate, and see what conjunctions your partner used in his or her sentences. Then write sentences using the following **correlative conjunctions:** *either, or; neither, nor;* and *both, and.* (Refer to "Correlative conjunction" in the index for help.)

PARTS OF SPEECH REVIEW
Pieces of Eight

THE FIRST STEP • If you could attach a monetary value to each of the eight parts of speech, which one would be worth the *least* amount of money? And which part of speech would be next in line in terms of its measly monetary value? Think about these two questions as you work through the following review activities. Ask a classmate what he or she thinks. Then, as a class, discuss this problem and see if you can come up with an answer.

Each "coin" contains a list of words representing one of the eight parts of speech. Identify the part of speech for each list of words on the blank space provided within each coin.

pirates
treasure
Long John Silver
map

_____noun_____

buried
shuffle
limp
speak

_____verb_____

we
they
hers
ours

_____pronoun_____

loudly
quietly
never
really

_____adverb_____

huge
heavy
shiny
smaller

_____adjective_____

by
near
over
under

_____preposition_____

Ahoy!
Wow!
Gross!
Hey!

_____interjection_____

and
but
or
because

_____conjunction_____

PARTS OF SPEECH REVIEW

Last one in is a rotten egg!

Pair up with a classmate and, as a team, identify the part of speech for each underlined word. There are four examples of each part of speech, except for the interjection, which has one example. (A few words have been labeled for you.)

                                      adverb   *preposition*

Last Saturday, the public pool <u>finally</u> opened <u>for</u> the year. My friend Sharla and

pronoun   *adjective*

<u>I</u> had been waiting for what seemed like months. Come to think of it, it had been <u>two</u>

                        verb

months. Anyway, we <u>were</u> there bright and early even though it was only about 75

                               adjective   *noun*   *adverb*

degrees outside. Sharla was wearing a <u>purple</u> and gold striped <u>bikini</u>. I had <u>earnestly</u>

                                   conjunction

begged my mom to let me have a bikini, too, <u>but</u> she said that young ladies shouldn't let

         noun

their <u>belly buttons</u> show.

                         pronoun   *adverb*

    "Who do <u>you</u> think you are," she asked, with her eyebrows <u>practically</u> pulled up

              preposition

over the top <u>of</u> her head, "Madonna?"

                                                             interjection

    The whole neighborhood showed up within an hour. <u>Well</u>, there might have been

conjunction   *verb*   *adjective*   *conjunction*

one <u>or</u> two kids missing. Sharla <u>looked</u> like a big, <u>blue-lipped</u> goose bump in purple <u>and</u>

gold because the water was so cold. We had a great time, though. Carl and Burton,

              preposition   *pronoun*

two boys <u>from</u> the eighth grade, did belly flops off the low-dive until <u>they</u> were covered

          noun   *adjective*

with red <u>blotches</u>. I won the underwater swimming contest. There was only one <u>bad</u>

      noun   *preposition*

moment. <u>Beaufort</u> showed up <u>with</u> a bag of sand, which he started hurling at people

                           verb

after yelling, "Look out! I'm <u>throwing</u> a beach party."

                           adverb *conjunction*   *verb*

    I walked home <u>quickly</u> <u>because</u> I had the chills. I <u>was</u> glad my mom hadn't let

pronoun

<u>me</u> have a bikini. Sharla was picking sand out of her belly button all the way to her

front door.

READING AND LEARNING STRATEGIES

There's fun reading . . . and then there's study-reading.

It's one thing to read and enjoy a good book, and it's quite another thing to study-read for facts, details, and general information. With a good book, you find a comfortable chair, kick off your shoes (unless, of course, you're in school), and snuggle into the story. A more careful approach must be taken when you study-read. You have to pay close attention to all of the important facts and details presented in the material, and you also have to make sure that you understand and remember them. We've designed the **Reading Strategies** primarily with this second type of reading in mind.

Each activity in this section (except for one) addresses a different strategy for study-reading. Know-want-learn (KWL), question & answer, and stop 'n' write are three of them. Your work here will prepare you to tackle even the most challenging reading assignments.

Special Note: See your handbook for more information on study-reading. (Refer to "Study-Reading" in the index.)

Getting Started

User's Checklist

Check your progress as you work on these **Reading and Learning Strategies.**

☐ **Know-Want-Learn (KWL)** • *Wha-da-ya-know?*

☐ **Question & Answer** • *This is too easy!*

☐ **Locating the Main Idea** • *Clues*

☐ **Locating the Main Ideas in a Chapter** • *Head-Sum*

☐ **Using Charts and Diagrams** • *Charting a Course*

☐ **Categorizing** • *That reminds me . . .*

☐ **Stop 'n' Write** • *Getting "Unstuck"*

☐ **Responding to Characters** • *Bio-Rama*

☐ **Using Charts** • *Picture This!*

AFTER • WORDS	It's your responsibility to put these strategies into practice once you learn how to use them. If a particular strategy really seems to work for you, apply it to your next reading assignment.

KNOW-WANT-LEARN (KWL)

READING STRATEGY

One of the best reading strategies you can use is **KWL**. *You can use KWL whenever you read, but especially when you begin a new chapter or area of study. KWL will help you under-stand what you know about a topic for a classroom report as well as what you want to discover. Read on to see how KWL works.*

Wha-da-ya-know?

Turn to the "Writing a Summary" section in your handbook. (See "Summary" in your index.) Find the short essay about acid rain on the second page of this section. Then follow the KWL directions given in the following chart: (Complete your chart with a classmate if your teacher allows it.)

K What do I already KNOW about the topic? (List two or three points before you begin reading.)	W What do I WANT to learn? (List two or three points.)	L What did I LEARN from the reading? (List two or three points.)

AFTER •
WORDS

Review your **L** list after the reading to discover if you have answered all of your questions in the **W** column. Also add any new questions to the **W** list. Share the results of your work with another classmate or group. For additional practice, use KWL for your next reading assignment.

QUESTION & ANSWER

<table>
<tr><td>

READING STRATEGY

*A study-reading strategy that is quick and simple to use is the **Question & Answer** strategy. By simply listing questions and answers for each page (or paragraph), you end up with a complete picture of the reading material.*

</td><td>

This is too easy!

To use the **Question & Answer** strategy, do the following:

■ Beginning with the first page of your study material, enter the page number on a chart similar to the one below.

■ Then, as you read, think of at least one question you could answer from the information on that page.

■ In the third column, answer each question.

■ Continue to ask and answer questions until you've completed the reading.

 TIP Try to come up with questions you think might be on a quiz as well as questions that get at the main idea of the reading.

■ Use this *question & answer* strategy as you read a chapter from one of your books (or from a book assigned by your teacher).

</td></tr>
</table>

Question & Answer Chart

Page Numbers	Questions	Answers

AFTER • WORDS	Use your chart as a study aid by covering the answer column. Also exchange your work with a classmate and see how many of your partner's questions you can answer.

LOCATING THE MAIN IDEA

READING STRATEGY

The **Clues** *strategy described on this page will help you unlock the basic meaning of whatever you are reading by looking closely at key clues. Read on and find out how.*

Clues

A detective doesn't expect to find easy answers when setting out to solve a crime. She or he will begin by searching for clues, often tiny things the rest of us would never notice. By studying and following certain clues, a good detective can usually solve a crime. Approaching reading material like a detective might help you solve the mystery of its meaning. For example, to *find the main idea* in reading assignments (paragraphs, short articles, sections in chapters, etc.), look for the following clues:

C L U E S

1. nouns and names that are repeated
2. words that are **boldfaced**, underlined, or *italicized*
3. the subject of the first sentence
4. the topic sentences (those sentences that describe the topic of each paragraph—often the first sentence in a paragraph)
- **Put together** all of your clues and decide what the main idea of the reading assignment is.

■ **Using a paragraph from one of your textbooks (or a paragraph your teacher gives you), fill in the following blank spaces.**

1. These nouns are repeated often (include synonyms):

_____

_____

_____

_____

2. These words are **boldfaced**, underlined, or *italicized*:

_____

_____

_____

3. The subject of the first sentence is _____

_____

4. I think this is the sentence that best announces the topic of this paragraph:

_____

_____

_____

_____

■ After considering all the clues, I believe this is the main idea of the paragraph:

_____

_____

_____

_____

_____

**AFTER •
WORDS** Now use the **clues** method for another short reading assignment. (With practice, you will be able to detect and make sense of reading clues in your head, rather than having to put everything on paper.)

LOCATING THE MAIN IDEAS IN A CHAPTER

READING STRATEGY

*To find the main ideas in a chapter, use the **Head-Sum** strategy. By simply studying the chapter headings and reading the chapter summary, you should be able to locate the main ideas in a chapter.*

Head-Sum

▌ Select a chapter from one of your school books (or use the one your teacher assigns) and follow this reading strategy. Use the spaces below to list the chapter headings:

1. _____

2. _____

3. _____

4. _____

5. _____

6. _____

TIP Study the chapter headings. Do they all have some connection to the chapter title? Taken together, are they a list of the main ideas in this chapter?

▌ **List below the events, people, places, objects, and ideas mentioned in the summary. (If no summary is given, look for the events, people, places, etc., talked about in the topic sentences of each paragraph.) Check this list against the list of chapter headings. Do you find the same things in both lists? Are these the main ideas?**

_____

_____

_____

_____

AFTER • WORDS Now read the entire chapter, not just the headings and summary. Each time you come to a main idea included in your list, put a check by it. If you find new main ideas, add them to your list. Finally, check one of the following: The **head-sum** strategy gave me *all* ( ), *most* ( ), *some* ( ) of the main ideas in this chapter.

USING CHARTS AND DIAGRAMS

READING STRATEGY

When you gather information, it is a good idea to organize it in some way. This process of gathering and organizing is called **Synthesizing.** *As we synthesize information, we are helping our brains form a pattern that can be stored and remembered more easily. (See "Synthesizing Information" in the "Thinking and Writing" section of your handbook for more information.)*

Charting a Course

Here's your chance to gather and organize something from scratch. On your own paper, "chart" the following pieces of information for the two continents in the Western Hemisphere—North America and South America. (The map section in your handbook contains the information you need for your chart.)

- The percent of earth's land
- The total square kilometers
- The longest river
- A fact or figure of your own choosing
- Another fact or figure of your own choosing
- (Keep going if you wish.)

 TIP Use the "chart starter" below if you need a starting point for your own creation. And don't forget to compare your results when you finish.

	North America	South America
Percent of Earth's Land	16.3%	12.0%
Total Sq. Kilometers	24,258,000	17,823,000
Longest River	Mississippi-Missouri	Amazon

AFTER • WORDS Find another useful "pool of information" in your handbook that you can "chart." Bring your idea to class, along with possible ways to put the information into chart form.

CATEGORIZING

READING STRATEGY
Another way to remember what you have read is to **Categorize** *the information. By brainstorming for words and ideas and then categorizing them, you can make things easier to understand and remember.*

That reminds me . . .

■ **BRAINSTORMING:**

PLANTS

perennial	lettuce	chlorophyll
cucumbers	grass	hybrid
pollination	photosynthesis	broccoli

To use this categorizing strategy, simply list as many words and ideas as you can on a particular topic. Once you have collected a dozen or so related words (see sample list above), you must then select the categories these words will fit into. In the sample below, the categories for plants turn out to be *green, flowering,* and *eatable.* All of the words fit under one of these categories.

■ **CATEGORIZING:**

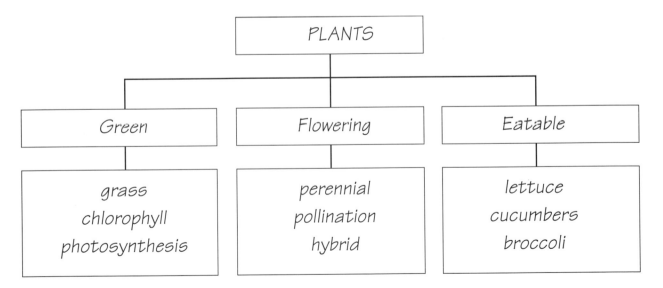

 TIP Not all the words you come up with when you brainstorm will fit neatly into the categories you choose. Some will probably be left over. You can put these leftovers in a category of their own.

Now you try it! Get together with your partner or group and decide on a topic to brainstorm about. (Again, try to use a topic you are studying in school.) Brainstorm until you have a dozen or more words and phrases. Look your list over carefully and think of different categories these words could fit into. (See the directions on the previous page for help.)

AFTER •
WORDS
Use this **categorizing** strategy the next time you need to organize or study a fairly large group of words or ideas. (This strategy works especially well with science topics.)

STOP 'N' WRITE

READING STRATEGY

It's very important for readers to know what to do when they get stuck, when they don't understand what they are reading. One of the best strategies for better understanding is to simply **Stop 'n' Write**.

Getting "Unstuck"

When you stop 'n' write, you need to summarize in your own words what you have just read—and then try to figure out exactly what you do or do not understand. Here are the steps you can follow when you need to stop 'n' write:

✔ Write down everything you know about what you've read.

✔ Write down the questions you have—what you don't understand.

✔ Scan the page(s) you are reading for familiar ideas.

✔ Try to get an overall idea of the topic and what you already understand.

✔ Make a quick list (or map) of as many details as you can that support the overall idea.

✔ Read ahead, adding details as you go.

✔ Continue to stop 'n' write even after you think you understand what you're reading. It's an excellent way to keep yourself on track.

Using one of your textbooks (or whatever your teacher recommends), do a stop 'n' write. Find a page near the end of the book that looks especially difficult and begin reading. Following the suggestions above, stop 'n' write as soon as you finish the first paragraph (or two).

AFTER • WORDS Use the **stop 'n' write** strategy whenever you read difficult or complicated material. Share your writings with your classmates and learn from one another.

RESPONDING TO CHARACTERS

READING STRATEGY

One of the many strategies you can use when you read stories is **Character Re-creation**. *This strategy gives you a closer look at the characters and allows you to become personally involved in the story.*

Bio-Rama

Let's suppose your teacher has access to new technology that makes it possible to re-create a true-to-life, holographic image of a fictional or historical character. With this technology in mind, the following assignment is made:

Think of a memorable character from the world of literature or history and present a true-to-life image of this person in a bio-rama. A bio-rama is like a three-dimensional snapshot of an important scene in a character's life. (Think in terms of the life-size dioramas you see at historical and wax museums.)

Wow! That's quite an assignment, even with the help of your teacher's marvelous "character maker." To get you started on this project, we've designed the following questions for you to answer. (Do your writing on your own paper.)
Note: **Work on these questions with a partner if your teacher allows it.**

1. Which character or historical figure will you re-create?

2. In which important scene or event will you place this individual?

3. What will he or she be wearing?

4. Will the character be standing, sitting, smiling, frowning, etc.?

5. What else will you need to include in your bio-rama?

6. What will your bio-rama look like when it is finished? (Draw a picture or plan of it.)

AFTER • WORDS
Write a brief script for your **bio-rama**: *Provide* background information, *describe* the character, *discuss* the scene depicted in the bio-rama, *explain* what happened before and after this scene, and so on.

USING CHARTS

Picture This!

Charts are a popular way to make a point. They provide a picture of information. One place to find a lot of charts is in newspapers. They use charts to show how much crime there is, how the economy is doing, how students performed on standardized tests, and so on. This activity will help you better understand one very common type of chart called a table.

The following table was created using information from the "Plant Profusion" section of your handbook. Study the table; then answer the questions on your own paper.

	Venus	Earth	Mars	Jupiter
No. of Satellites	0	1	2	16
Distance to Sun*	67.23	92.96	141.7	483.7

*in millions of miles

1. How many rows does this table have? _____2_____

2. How many columns? _____4_____

3. How many different things does the table tell you about each planet? _____2_____

4. Of the planets shown, which is closest to the sun? _____Venus_____

Now create a table of your own. You'll find the information you need in the "Index to World Maps" and the "Topographic Tally Table" in your handbook. Find the latitude, longitude, and area of the islands of Greenland and Madagascar. Create a table that shows all the information. *Tip:* Start by making two **columns**, one labeled Greenland, one labeled Madagascar. Put the latitude, longtiude, and area of each in **rows**.

■ In the "Reading Charts" section of your handbook, find the model of a line graph. Study it. Then answer the following questions.

1. How many CD's and cassettes did Kenny have in 1991? _____ *10* _____

2. How many did he have in 1993? _____ *50* _____

3. Write a sentence that describes what the graph shows. _____ *The graph shows how*
   Kenny's music collection grew during three years. _____

■ Now try your hand at a line graph. Start with the grid below. You'll find the data for your graph in the "Historical Time Line" in your handbook. Look up the population for each year and place a dot on the correct spot on the graph (it won't be exact!). The first dot is drawn for you. After you've done this for each year, draw a line connecting the dots. You just made a line graph.

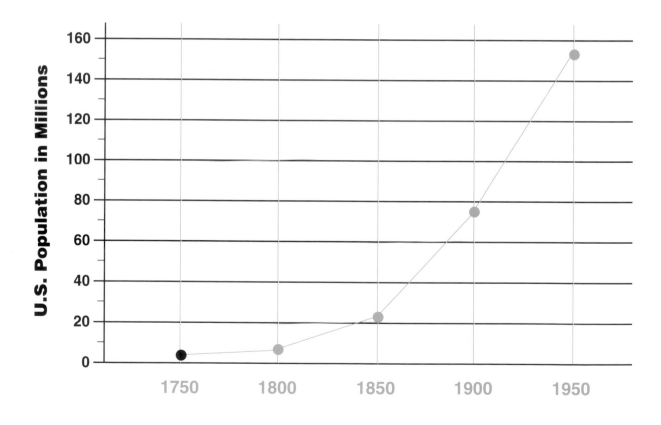

| AFTER • WORDS | Find some information in one of your textbooks to make into a table or line graph. *Remember:* A line graph shows how something changed over a period of time. A table can show almost any kind of information. |

TALKING AND LISTENING ACTIVITIES

"We interrupt this program for a special announcement."

Whenever an important news item was broadcast on television, my mother would always say, "Listen." She wasn't asking us to listen, really, but rather to stop talking so she could listen. With that one word, she was trying to control distractions, tune into the speaker's message, and concentrate on the news item.

I learned about some very important news events this way—the Kennedy assassination, the Vietnam War, the moon landings—but I also learned respect for both the listener and the speaker.

In this set of activities, you'll work on developing both your listening and speaking skills, "tuning in" to your full potential as an effective communicator.

Special Note: Refer to the "Speaking and Listening to Learn" section in your handbook for information on preparing speeches, reading out loud, listening, and interviewing.

Getting Started

User's Checklist

Check your progress as you work on these **Talking and Listening Activities.**

☐ **Group Listening and Information Gathering**
   • *World's Fair 2000*

☐ **Thinking and Listening** • *It sounds like . . .*

☐ **Recalling Details** • *You took what?*

☐ **Interviewing a Classmate** • *What's my line?*

☐ **Acting and Observing** • *Instant Improv*

☐ **Surveying Listening Skills** • *Listening Logjam*

☐ **Group Discussions** • *Take me to your leader.*

☐ **Recalling and Sharing Memories** • *A Pleasant State of Mine*

AFTER • WORDS *Remember:* Your language is a "whole language" made up of five interconnected parts: *reading, writing, speaking, listening,* and *thinking.* Give a fair amount of attention to all five parts and become a real student of your language.

GROUP LISTENING AND INFORMATION GATHERING

World's Fair 2000

If two heads are better than one for thinking up new ideas, then a whole group of wild, wacky, creative "noggins" churning out ideas should be awesome. Put your heads together in the following activity: It's your job to create ideas for the World's Fair 2000. That means you need to come up with ideas for exhibits, amusement rides, displays, and concession stands. Before you begin, study the following rules for brainstorming:

❑ One person is chosen to write down all the ideas.
❑ ALL ideas are welcomed.
❑ Ideas may be expanded by others.
❑ Criticism of ideas is not permitted.
❑ Ideas can be revised to make them clearer.
❑ All group members must contribute at least one idea.

Examples:

Bic's Voice-Activated Computer Pen Display
"Laser-plane" Ride
Polaroid Instant 3-D Photo Booth
Hologram Hall of Celebrities

After brainstorming for 10 or 15 minutes, it's time to work separately. Choose one idea that really interests you, and write a sentence to be used on the sign explaining your attraction.

Example: Bic's Voice-Activated Computer Pen . . . The amazing pen of the future that writes your words down on paper AS YOU SPEAK!

THE NEXT STEP • Develop a plan for this idea and share it with the class. Design the booth, exhibit, display, etc. Show how it would work. Tell about the interesting details. Be prepared to answer questions about your exhibit.

THINKING AND LISTENING
It sounds like . . .

One of the most popular party games is charades. A player of this game panto-mimes clues (using actions but no words) to other players who try to guess the titles of songs, movies, television shows, or books. How do you communicate a song title to other people without talking?

1. First, give a clue for the category of your title (pretend to sing if it's a song).
2. Next, indicate the number of words in the title (hold up four fingers).
3. Finally, act out the words or the concept ("Walk Like an Egyptian").

 TIP Listening to the responses of the other players is the most important part of the game. Often, in charades, the presenter is so busy thinking of clues that he or she doesn't "listen" to responses that might easily lead to the correct answer.

Privately list some possible titles that could be acted out in a game of charades. Work together with a small group and try to guess each other's titles. As you act out clues, listen closely to the responses. "Shake off" those that will not lead to the correct answer and "jump on" those that will.

Songs   Movies

_____   _____

_____   _____

_____   _____

Television Shows   Books

_____   _____

_____   _____

_____   _____

Special Note: Your teacher or fellow classmates may have some additional hints on how to deliver charade clues. (For example, pulling on your ear means "It sounds like . . .")

THE NEXT STEP • How about "Team Challenge Charades"? Divide the class into two teams and see which team guesses the title first. Then hang on! It will get pretty intense.

RECALLING DETAILS
You took what?

Details, details, details! How do you learn to listen for details? Here's one answer to that question—word games. Yes, word games. People use memory word games (and have done so for hundreds of years) as an effective and fun way to remember details. So let the games begin!

Game 1: *I Went on a Trip*

Complete the statement "I went on a trip, and I took along . . ." by adding an item onto the end of the phrase. Choose a word that starts with each letter of the alphabet. The first word should start with *A*, the second word should start with *B*, then *C*, and so on. Your teacher will select a student speaking order, and each student, in order, must repeat the previous examples before adding another item to the end.

Example: Student #1:
"I went on a trip, and I took along **a**luminum cans."

Student #2:
"I went on a trip, and I took along **a**luminum cans and **b**oard games."

Student #3:
"I went on a trip, and I took along **a**luminum cans, **b**oard games, and **c**ash."

Student #4:
"I went on a trip, and I took along **a**luminum cans, **b**oard games, **c**ash, and **d**_____ ."

Special Note: Look at each person as they speak and associate that person with his or her item to help in remembering the details.

Game 2: *Certain Things You Shouldn't Bring to School*

Complete the following statement by adding an item onto the end of the phrase: "There are certain things you shouldn't bring to school, like . . . ." For this game, choose words that represent the rainbow colors. To remember the rainbow colors and their order, use the name ROY G. BIV—red, orange, yellow, green, blue, indigo, and violet. (Pink may be substituted for indigo.) The first item should be an item that is typically red; the second, typically orange; etc.

Example: Student #1:

"There are certain things you shouldn't bring to school, like **fire hydrants**." (red object)

Student #2:

"There are certain things you shouldn't bring to school, like **fire hydrants** and **basketballs**." (orange object)

Student #3:

"There are certain things you shouldn't bring to school, like **fire hydrants**, **basketballs**, and **yield signs**." (yellow object)

Remember: Pink may be substituted for indigo.

Game 3: *When I Visited Aunt Gladys*

Complete the statement "When I visited Aunt Gladys, I brought her . . ." by adding an item onto the end of the phrase. As in game #1, start with the letter *A* and choose words that begin with each letter of the alphabet. But here's a twist! Make each item an animal.

Example: Student #1:

"When I visited Aunt Gladys, I brought her an **aardvark**."

Student #2:

"When I visited Aunt Gladys, I brought her an **aardvark** and a **buffalo**."

Student #3:

"When I visited Aunt Gladys, I brought her an **aardvark**, a **buffalo**, and a **camel**."

THE NEXT STEP • Develop your own word game. Think of different statements to which a list of items can be added.

INTERVIEWING A CLASSMATE
What's my line?

You are too young to remember this, but there used to be a great TV game show called *What's My Line?* Contestants would ask "yes" or "no" questions of a mystery guest and then try to guess his or her line of work. For instance, if a fireman were the mystery guest, the players might ask questions like, "Do you work for the public?" "Is your line of work dangerous?" "Do you climb ladders in your line of work?" And then finally, "Are you a fireman?"

Pick a Profession

So, what's your line? Yes, we know you're a student. But if you could be anything you wanted to be, what would you be? Pick a profession, but don't tell anyone in your class what you "are." In the space below, list duties and general activities associated with your profession, just to get you "into character." *Hint:* Try to come up with something unusual (an astronaut), but not completely off the wall.

_____

_____

_____

_____

_____

_____

THE NEXT STEP • You and your classmates take turns being mystery guests. As a mystery guest, you should sit in the front of your classroom and answer questions related to your line of work. (*Note:* The questions asked should be able to be answered with a "yes" or "no.") Go around the room and let each student ask one question until the mystery guest's line of work is figured out.

ACTING AND OBSERVING
Instant Improv

Improvisation is the act of creating spontaneously (making things up as you go along). Creating something on the spot is an exciting challenge for anyone. As you come up with new ideas, you also discover things about yourself. As writer W. H. Auden once said, "Words will tell you things you never thought or felt before."

"Instant Improv" is an activity that will help you explore and create through words. A scene is set, a situation established, and whatever happens, happens.

> **Get together in a group of four (a fifth person can be used to record what happens). Choose one of the "Instant Improv" examples below and act out a 2- or 3-minute skit based on the opening scene. Take a few minutes before your improvisation to organize your team and write the first few lines of dialogue. (*Important Note:* Don't write more than those first few lines, though. Make up the rest as you go!)**

Setting the Scene . . .

Scene #1: Their first day on the job, four employees are sitting around a table taking a break in the back room of a large variety store. They each work in different departments of the store.

Scene #2: You're ducks flying south for the winter. You've been flying for days; there's snow blowing behind you and freezing rain in front of you.

Scene #3: Three kids (a 16-year-old, an 11-year-old, and a 9-year-old) are sitting in the living room of their house. They hear a noise in the basement. Their parents are out to dinner.

Scene #4: A bowler has just knocked down six pins. You are the four pins still standing on the lane.

Scene #5: Four teachers are in the teachers' lounge right after school on a particularly hot day in the month of May.

Scene #6: Four writers are sitting around a conference table trying to come up with ideas for a new television show. The show will be called *Harrigan*. The writers have to come up with the rest.

THE NEXT STEP • Jot down something you liked in each performance. Discuss the results of your improvisations at the end of the class period.

SURVEYING LISTENING SKILLS
Listening Logjam

     Have you ever been told to pay attention or hurry up, or you may miss the boat? Well, I actually missed the boat once because I hadn't been listening. I met my friend at the boat dock—two hours late!—because I hadn't listened when he told me the specific meeting time. Another time, I forgot I had a science test and did poorly because I hadn't listened carefully enough in class. So what can poor listeners do to improve their listening skills? Read on.

     First of all, it's important to understand that listening is an active process. You need to listen ACT-ively. You need to give your **A** – *attention*, **C** – *concentration*, and **T** – *thinking* to each listening task. ACT now and improve your listening skills. (Refer to "Listening skills" in the index of your handbook for more information.)

Study your own listening habits for a day. Keep a listening log of a typical day in your life. Record your listening activities on the chart provided. Write ACT next to the times you felt you really listened, or write DAZE (daydreamed), PTL (pretended to listen), or QUIT (gave up, felt it was too difficult). Be prepared to share your results with a classmate or the class.

Listening Log

Student _____   Date _____

Example:

Time Period	Activity	Listening Code	Comments
6:00-6:30	Getting ready	ACT	Listened to mom
6:30-7:00	Eating breakfast	PTL	Nodded while sister talked
7:00-7:30	Going to school	DAZE	Stared out window
7:30-8:00	Milling around	ACT/DAZE	Listened to friends off and on
8:00-8:45	English class	ACT/QUIT	Listened/didn't understand

Listening Log

Student _____   Date _____

**LISTENING
CODE:**

ACT – Actively listened   **PTL** – Pretended to listen
DAZE – Daydreamed from time to time   **QUIT** – Gave up listening

Time Period	Activity	Listening Code	Comments

GROUP DISCUSSIONS

Take me to your leader.

 We've all been involved in discussions in class and with friends. Sometimes discussions can get a little bit crazy with everyone talking at once and no one really listening. But it doesn't have to be that way. If you (and your classmates) know how a good discussion works, you can make future discussions better. How? Let's discuss it—together. (Refer to "Group skills" in the index of your handbook.)

▉ **Read the introduction at the top of the "Group Skills" section. Then answer the following questions:**

❑ What does "collaborative" mean? *It means "to work together."*

❑ What five skills will help you work and learn better in groups? *listening, observing, cooperating, responding, and clarifying*

❑ What is meant by "people skills"? *These are skills that help people work together successfully in groups.*

▉ **Get together in a small group of three to five students to read about and discuss one of the five group skills. (Your teacher will tell you which skill to read about.) List on the lines below what you learned about this group skill.**

Next, report to the class the important points from your reading. Keep track of what each group reports on the lines below.

Skills for Listening: _____

_____

_____

_____

Skills for Observing: _____

_____

_____

_____

Skills for Cooperating: _____

_____

_____

_____

Skills for Responding: _____

_____

_____

_____

Skills for Clarifying: _____

_____

_____

_____

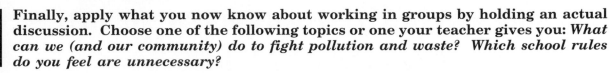

Finally, apply what you now know about working in groups by holding an actual discussion. Choose one of the following topics or one your teacher gives you: *What can we (and our community) do to fight pollution and waste? Which school rules do you feel are unnecessary?*

Use the "Personal Checklist" below to measure how well you were able to apply what you now know about group skills.

Group Skills: Personal Checklist	Most of the time	Half of the time	Once in a while
Listening			
I listened carefully.			
I interrupted properly.			
I responded to interruptions correctly.			
Observing			
I noticed body language.			
I offered words of encouragement.			
Cooperating			
I offered compliments or thanks.			
I used no put-downs.			
I did not disturb others.			
Responding			
I responded to put-downs properly.			
I stopped to think before responding.			
I disagreed properly.			
I learned from disagreements.			
I used "I" statements.			
Clarifying			
I offered to explain or clarify.			
I asked for clarification.			
I helped the group reach a decision.			

RECALLING AND SHARING MEMORIES
A Pleasant State of Mine

Trips taken to visit people, to see events, or to vacation in different places are often remembered as the fondest days of childhood. Any one of these trips—whether it be to a state capital, to Grandma's, to a ball game or concert—can be a good choice for a writing or speaking topic.

Describe a trip you have taken. First, sketch on the top of a piece of paper a scene or symbolic reference of your trip. (Examples: a tent as a symbol of a camp-out or a drawing of a city skyline as a symbol of an urban visit) Next, plan and deliver a 2- to 3-minute speech around your sketch. Be prepared to answer questions about your trip.

Questions to consider:
- ❑ When did the trip take place?
- ❑ What was the purpose of the trip?
- ❑ Who went along on the trip?
- ❑ How did you get there, and how long did it take?
- ❑ What do you remember most about the place you stayed or the place you visited? (Make a list.)
- ❑ How was this trip more important (memorable) than others?
- ❑ What do you remember about the people?

THE NEXT STEP • At the end of your speech, locate the place you went to on a map and label it with your name and the name of the location. As each student labels the map, it will become an interesting record of places visited by you and your classmates.

THINKING WORKSHOPS

Hmm . . . what do you think?

Let's suppose Melissa's trying to figure out why her older sister and her sister's boyfriend argue all of the time. And let's suppose Yolanda is interested in the history of her new neighborhood, and Lawrence is planning a report about trends in the '90s.

How could each of these individuals start looking for information and answers? If they had access to a SourceBook, the **Thinking Workshops** would be a perfect starting point. A workshop called "The Bickersons" would help Melissa analyze arguments. One called "Back and Forth from My House" would help Yolanda investigate her neighborhood. And finally, one called "Culture Vultures" would help Lawrence form some understanding about current trends.

But that's not all that is included in this section. It contains 14 thoughtful and fun-filled workshops, each one focusing on one of five important thinking skills: *solving a problem, making a decision, forming an understanding, evaluating information,* or *building an argument.*

Special Note: See your handbook for everything you will need to know about the thinking process. (Refer to "Thinking" in the index.)

Getting Started

User's Checklist

Check your progress as you work on these **Thinking Workshops.**

■ **Solving Problems**

☐ **Brainstorming and Persuading** • *Missing!*

☐ **Creating and Explaining** • *The World According to . . .*

■ **Forming Understanding**

☐ **Seeing Things Differently** • *Wacky Glasses*

☐ **Analyzing and Naming** • *How a Blorpalizer Works*

☐ **Analyzing and Synthesizing** • *The Nobel Prize for Being You*

☐ **Observing and Interpreting** • *Culture Vultures*

☐ **Investigating and Interviewing** • *Back and Forth from My House*

■ **Making Decisions**

☐ **Comparing and Contrasting** • *Captain Wahoo's Advice Column of the Air*

☐ **Deciding and Organizing** • *Once in a Lifetime!*

■ **Evaluating Information**

☐ **Judging and Qualifying** • *True Owl and False Fox*

☐ **Questioning and Analyzing** • *Job Interview*

■ **Building Arguments**

☐ **Pretending and Persuading** • *Pineapples and Bananas*

☐ **Comparing and Arguing** • *Tug-of-War*

☐ **Analyzing a Process** • *The Bickersons*

AFTER • WORDS

Our hope is that you will be more aware of your thinking process after working through these workshops, and that you will apply what you learn to solving problems, building arguments, making decisions, and on and on.

BRAINSTORMING AND PERSUADING

Missing!

When a child suddenly disappears, possibly kidnapped, possibly lost, the parents of that child are not the only ones who are frightened. The whole community grows concerned. They want to protect their own children. They want to solve the mystery. And most of all, they want to see the missing child returned.

How can parents and police bring a missing child to the community's attention? That's a challenge we would like to give you. Somebody had the bright idea of putting a missing child's picture on a milk carton. That puts the message right in our hands, right before our eyes, over our breakfast cereal.

Get together with three or four others and brainstorm until you come up with a surprising *new* way to advertise a reward for finding a missing child. Be creative!

TIP

The best ideas are often ones that make us slap our heads and say, "Of course, why didn't I think of that?" Think of familiar places where you sit, stand, and walk each day. Think of objects you often hold or places where many people often gather. Think of different means of communication, such as newspapers, books, magazines, songs, computers, films, television, skywriting, etc.

THINKING IT OVER • Make a mock-up (a model) of your idea and share it with several people if you can. Use their reactions as a guide for revision.

CREATING AND EXPLAINING

The World According to . . .

The king has ordered you to answer some of his most pressing questions. If you please the king with your explanations, he will reward you with fame and fortune. If you disappoint him, however, he might banish you forever.

This royal order presents you with a great challenge since little or nothing is known about how and why things happen. For example, the king wants to know, and no one *does* know, why plants stop growing and producing each fall. (The fact that the earth's axis tilts away from the sun at that time of year won't be discovered for hundreds of years.)

Identify five (or more) things that the king might want explained. *Note:* **Consider other common occurrences in nature.**

1. _____

_____

2. _____

_____

3. _____

_____

4. _____

_____

5. _____

_____

THINKING IT OVER • On your own paper, write your explanation for one of the ideas from your list. Write your explanation as a story with a beginning, a middle, and an end. Don't be afraid to make your explanation creative. The king likes to be entertained.

SEEING THINGS DIFFERENTLY

Wacky Glasses

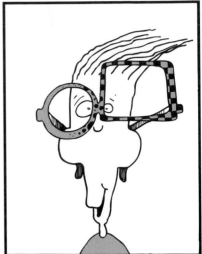

Sometimes, to see things more clearly, you have to put on different glasses. If ordinary glasses don't work, try wacky ones. The ordinary question is "Who are you?" Through wacky glasses, the question might be . . .

- ■ If you were translated into a different language, what language would you be?
- ■ If you were a car, what model would you be?
- ■ If you were a month, which month would you be?
- ■ If you were a sport, what sport would you be?

Make up more questions like these and answer them. Each time you come up with an answer, give a reason for choosing it.

VARIATIONS

- Play a game called "Wacky Glasses" with a friend. In this game, each person must make up at least 10 wacky questions, writing each question on one side of a card (10 cards in all). On the other side of the cards, write the answers you think your partner will give. Finally, take turns holding up one card at a time, showing your partner the question only. Ask him or her to answer, and give yourself a point for each answer you guessed correctly. The first person to reach 5 points wins. (Make up your own rules if you wish.)

- Use scissors, tape, glue, and whatever other materials you need and create a pair of "Wacky Glasses" inspired by one of your questions. For example, if your question is "If you were a car . . . ," create a pair of glasses with a frame in the shape of a car and lenses where the wheels would be. When you wear your glasses, ask people the question that inspired the design. Compare the answers you receive.

ANALYZING AND NAMING

How a Blorpalizer Works

Find an old toy or tool with moving parts—a plastic cash register, an Etch-A-Sketch, a mechanical pencil sharpener, etc.—and study it. Figure out how it's made and how it works.

❑ For better understanding, give each part a special nonsense name, such as "jingamathig" or "fratwad."

❑ For each part, fill in the following sentence frame (or a frame of your own choosing):

"The *(name the part)* _____

is shaped like _____

so that it can _____."

When you have described all the parts, give the whole thing a nonsense name and write a full, clear paragraph titled "How a Blorpalizer (or whatever you've named it) Works."

HANDBOOK HELPER

For help in designing a paragraph of this kind, check out the hints in *Write Source 2000*. Refer to "Explanation, describing" in the index.

THINKING IT OVER • Here are some extra twists you might want to give your project: (1) draw a simple diagram of each part, label it, and attach the whole diagram to your paragraph; (2) write a simple set of directions for assembling your "Blorpalizer," as if you were going to include the directions in a package.

ANALYZING AND SYNTHESIZING

The Nobel Prize for Being You

You are amazing. Wonderful. What a personality! You have a sense of humor different from Mikhail Gorbachev's. You are a more loyal friend than Lassie and have a heart as big as Mother Teresa's. Is it any wonder then that you have just won the Nobel prize for being you?

Create two documents in connection with your Nobel prize. Let the first document be a NOMINATION letter written by the person who knows you best. Let the second be the script for your ACCEPTANCE speech, which you will give at the annual award ceremony in Stockholm, Sweden. In your speech, give credit to anyone or anything deserving attention for being important in shaping your life.

THINKING IT OVER • If you have the time and the drawing materials, draw a picture of a trophy that is specially designed for you and no one else. Write on it the special inscription that announces your award.

OBSERVING AND INTERPRETING
Culture Vultures

In the late '60s it was bell-bottom pants, granny glasses, and sideburns. In the '70s, we saw earth shoes, water beds, houseplants, and encounter groups. In the '80s, there came break dancing, BMX bikes, punk looks and preppy looks, video games, and more. What are the trends in the '90s? And what do the trends mean?

Think of the latest styles in pants, shirts, haircuts, music, toys, school supplies, bicycles, fast food, etc. Choose one trend you think is especially interesting. Then ask four people why they think so many people follow that trend. The first person should be your own age, the second person about 10 years older, the third person 30 years older, and the fourth person 60 years older. Collect all the comments you've heard about the meaning of the trend. **Describe the trend** and write down your own interpretation here:

THINKING IT OVER • To figure out the meaning of a trend, you need to ask many questions. For example, you might ask, "What is this trend a reaction *to* or *against*?" Use the following phrases as hints to help you form other helpful questions: past, present, and future; different ages; different sexes; parts of the country; advertising; feelings; beginnings and endings.

INVESTIGATING AND INTERVIEWING

Back and Forth from My House

We usually take for granted the houses, apartments, and neighborhoods where we live. But they have not been there from the beginning of time. And they may not be there until the end of time. Are you curious about how your neighborhood once was and how it will be?

Find out who has lived in your neighborhood longer than anybody else. Go talk to that person, if you can, or to any other older person who might know about how your neighborhood was built. Ask what the land was like before the streets were put in and the houses built. Write a description of your neighborhood's history based on the best information you can gather.

THINKING IT OVER • To find more information, go to your public library (ask the librarian for help) or call the local newspaper to see if they have any pictures on file. If a church, school, or other older institution is located in your neighborhood, ask someone there if they have a record of when the building was constructed.

COMPARING AND CONTRASTING

Captain Wahoo's Advice Column of the Air

Suppose you have your own TV show called *Captain Wahoo's Advice Column of the Air.* You're Captain Wahoo. One of your young viewers sends you this letter:

Dear Capt. Wahoo,

Lots of times I want to get something out of my mom and dad or my teachers, like money or new shoes or help with my home- work and some junk. And, like, it never works, you know? So, like, what should I do? Should I act, like, really weird? Or should I sweet-talk them, like, totally all out? Maybe I should try bribery. What do you think? Or should I maybe threaten to embarrass them in public sometime if I don't get my way? You're one of my all-time favorite dudes, I mean it. So answer, OK? I'm sick of getting stiffed by everybody.

-- B.W. from Sacramento

Choose a partner and together write out your answer to this letter in the form of a made-for-TV skit. In your skit, have two parts, one demonstrating "DOs" and the other demonstrating "DON'Ts." (In other words, one part should show a good way of getting your elders to help you out, and the other part should show a bad way.)

THINKING IT OVER • If you can, put on your skit in front of a small audience. Afterward, ask them to describe the message they got from the skit. Talk with the audience about how *they* would answer B.W.'s letter.

DECIDING AND ORGANIZING

Once in a Lifetime!

It's time for a family celebration! Your grandmother will be 100 years old on her next birthday, which is about two months from now. You have been asked by your family to help plan a stupendous celebration—a truly happy and meaningful one for your grandmother. Since she is so old, most of her friends have already died, and she lives in a retirement center near your home. She often tells you about her life and what it was like when she was your age. You like your grandmother, and you want this birthday to be especially meaningful for her. Consider these questions:

What special things can you plan that will bring back pleasant memories for your grandmother—memories about simple things as well as a few lifetime highlights?

Whom will you invite?

What gifts will be appropriate? How could you learn what elderly people like and need?

Decide what you will do for your grandmother to make this birthday special; then put together a special invitation to send to all of your grandmother's friends and relatives.

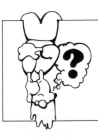

THINKING IT OVER • Which do you think would be more valued by the elderly—gifts you purchase or gifts you make or put together yourself? Is it more important to them to have lots of family or lots of "things"?

JUDGING AND QUALIFYING
True Owl and False Fox

Suppose one day you crawl under your bed and there discover a staircase leading down to a secret passage. You follow the passage toward a patch of light. As you approach the light, you see that it is a shaft of sunlight falling through leaves of a tree. On a low bough of the tree sits a fat, old, tufted owl arguing with a sharp-nosed fox on the ground below. From the shadows, you realize that the two creatures are arguing about *you*. Fascinated, you eavesdrop. The owl is saying things about you that you *believe* are true. The fox is saying things about you that you *doubt* are true.

Write down the conversation you hear between the owl and the fox. Make it a lively one. Remember to keep both the owl and the fox in character. (Continue this conversation on your own paper.)

OWL: *But I know that _____ studies almost every night.*

FOX: *That may be, but . . .*

OWL:

THINKING IT OVER • The purpose of recording this conversation is to become more aware of who you are. It helps to be able to sort out what is true from what is not true. In order to get even more out of this project, pretend that after listening for a while, you step into the conversation, introduce yourself, and try to correct the two speakers. Use words like *sometimes, not always, seldom, often,* and the like to describe more accurately the real truth.

QUESTIONING AND ANALYZING

Job Interview

Every morning as she left for school, Jackie saw Mrs. Burlap leave for work in her white Grand Am. She knew Mrs. Burlap was a nurse, but she didn't know anything about "the Mr." She never saw him. He might live in a foreign country, for all she knew. Or maybe the Burlaps were divorced. Or maybe he was sick . . . or, gulp, dead.

But one day, during parent-teacher conferences, when Jackie was home, she saw the real Mr. Burlap watering his lawn in stockinged feet. Because she had a "Job Interview" assignment to do for school, she went up to Mr. Burlap, introduced herself, and interviewed him about what he did for a living. She had prepared good questions, and she found out what kind of job he had, how he had gotten it, what kind of education and experience he had needed, what he did on the job every day, what his goals were, and how he felt about his work. (By the way, Mr. Burlap was a writer. That's why he wore socks in the yard.)

Visit an adult who lives near you and is willing to be interviewed. Find out what he or she does for a living. For a good interview, you must ask good questions. Here are some prompts to help you think up a few.

1. Make up some questions about what the job is called, who it is done for, and what exactly has to be done—just the facts.
2. Make up some questions about what it takes to be qualified for this job.
3. Make up some questions about the good things this job may do for individual people and for society.
4. Make up some questions about feelings and attitudes.
5. Make up some more questions about the job. Ask about things that interest you and about things that would interest others.

HANDBOOK HELPER You can become a better interviewer by reading all about interviewing in *Write Source 2000*.

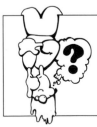

THINKING IT OVER • Be sure to take notes during your interview. When you are through, while you still remember what you heard, quickly write a first-draft report on the interview. Include all the most interesting things the interviewee said.

PRETENDING AND PERSUADING

Pineapples and Bananas

Do you know anyone who has a job that needs doing that you could volunteer to do for free? You could, for example, mow a lawn, search for a lost cat, baby-sit, shop for food, wash a car, hand out papers, or collect recyclable cans. Choose one. Then . . .

Pretend there is a talking banana on one shoulder urging you to do the job. On the other shoulder is a talking pineapple urging you not to do the job. Write out a long, heated debate between the banana and the pineapple. Let each one try its best to persuade the other.

TIP
If it would be more fun, let two friends play the roles of banana and pineapple and argue it out. Afterward, write out the debate, using their ideas (and a few of your own).

My Volunteer Job: _____

The Debate:

THINKING IT OVER • Did the debate cover all the important points or issues? What would you "get" out of doing this job? How would others (including your community) benefit?

COMPARING AND ARGUING

Tug-of-War

Having brothers and sisters isn't all bad. After all, if they're older than you, they can climb on the roof to get the ball you threw up there. And if they're younger, you can trade them three nickels for a quarter, and they'll think they got a good deal.

On the other hand, having brothers and sisters isn't all that good. If they're older, they'll make you clean their rooms to keep them from telling your parents that you were the one who put superglue in the stapler. If they're younger, they'll cough right in your eye.

Which is better, to *have* brothers and sisters or *not* to have them?

Let's have a tug-of-war.

On the left side, list all the reasons *for* having brothers and sisters (the "pro" side). On the right side, list all the reasons *against* having them (the "con" side). Whichever list is longer is the list with the most "muscle." That side wins!

PRO   CON

_____   _____

_____   _____

_____   _____

_____   _____

_____   _____

_____   _____

THINKING IT OVER • On the lines below, write what you believe is the strongest point in your argument for (or against) having brothers and sisters.

_____

_____

ANALYZING A PROCESS

The Bickersons

Arguments can be playful—or they can be ugly. Some arguments go on and on; the arguers pause only to eat and sleep. Some are quiet, hissy little affairs, while others are raucous pot-bangers. Some even end wth loud words and hurt feelings. The best ones end with both parties increasing their respect for each other.

Remember a specific argument, either one you were in or one you overheard. Write a PLAY SCRIPT or DIALOGUE in which you re-create the argument in as much detail as you can. Let your play script reveal the following:
  (1) Who are the people who are arguing?
  (2) What is the argument about?
  (3) What starts the argument?
  (4) What keeps the argument going?
  (5) What ends it?

TIP If it bothers you to talk about yourself and your own family, write your play script about a family of chipmunks or cartoon characters. Also, if you need help writing a play script, you'll find it in *Write Source 2000.* Refer to "Plays, writing" and "Dialogue, Writing" in the index.

THINKING IT OVER • For a special challenge that will help you see the argument from a new angle, rewrite the play script, adding a new character. Think of the *wisest* person you've ever met. Put this person into your play and see how his or her actions and words change the course of the argument.

VOCABULARY AND WORD PLAY ACTIVITIES

Let's get serious about play!

Because we ask you to play with words in **Vocabulary and Word Play** doesn't mean that the language is not important to us. We know that exploring and experimenting with words makes you a better language user. Translation: Working through the activities in this section will help you use the language more effectively in your writing and speaking.

In the first part of this section, you will be asked to develop a "word poem," write new slogans for bumper stickers, develop an eye-catching poster, and engage in other playful activities. In the vocabulary activities, you'll *learn about* and *work with* the most important prefixes, suffixes, and roots in our language. The end result? Whenever you come across words you're unsure of, you'll have a strategy for figuring out what they mean.

Special Note: The "Improving Vocabulary" chapter in the handbook contains lists of important prefixes, suffixes, and roots. Make good use of these lists when you work on these activities and when you develop your thoughts in other writing and speaking assignments.

Getting Started

User's Checklist

Check your progress as you work on these **Vocabulary and Word Play Activities.**

☐ **Writing Poetry** • *A Vision of Poetry*

☐ **Playing with Poetry** • *Poetry for Everyone!*

☐ **Writing Slogans** • *WARNING: Littering causes warts.*

☐ **Developing Posters** • *What a Rip-Off!*

☐ **Creating Character Names** • *What a Character!*

☐ **Parts of Speech** • *A Strange Invitation*

☐ **Using Prefixes and Roots** • *Building Words*

☐ **Using Word Parts** • *Are you a "structologist"?*

AFTER • WORDS

Become a student of your language. What do we mean by that? Keep your eyes and ears open for new and interesting words, well-put ideas, and eye-opening conversations. Make use of what you see and hear in your own work.

WRITING POETRY

A Vision of Poetry

The writers of your handbook talk a lot about using vivid language, "showing" language. They say that your writing should show rather than tell. It should paint a picture in the minds of your readers. Well, there is a kind of poetry that does just that. It's called typographical or concrete poetry. It actually shows and tells at the same time. (Look at the example below.)

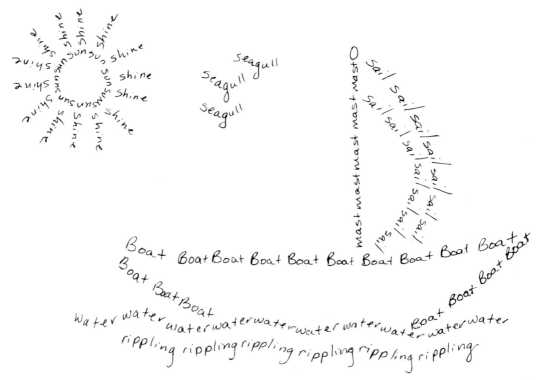

On your own paper, write a typographical poem about yourself. It can show your face (a self-portrait), it can show you doing something you enjoy, it can depict your favorite sport, or . . . surprise us.

AFTER WORDS Share your poem with your classmates (and friends and family). Do a larger version of it using colored paper, special lettering, a frame . . .

PLAYING WITH POETRY

Poetry for Everyone!

Poetry has been around for a long time. You might think poetry is found only in English textbooks, but, in fact, poetry is all around you. There is poetry in TV commercials, in Hallmark cards, in popular songs on the radio. Anytime words are arranged creatively to take on rhythm or rhyme—or simply arranged to express an idea in a striking way—that's poetry.

> Bug,
> Small, Creepy
> Hides, Slithers, Crawls
> Seen, Hunted
> Smushed

The pattern of this "word poem" follows:

1st line: Name of the subject

2nd line: Two words to describe the subject

3rd line: Three words describing action of the subject

4th line: Two words to describe the subject

5th line: Another name for, or description of, the subject

This pattern is simple and fairly easy to follow. Try writing a poem in this pattern about yourself. And then try writing a second one about a friend, a relative, or someone you admire. (Do this on your own paper.)

1st line:

2nd line:

3rd line:

4th line:

5th line:

AFTER • WORDS   Exchange the poem about yourself with a classmate. Discuss whether the poems capture anything "true" about yourselves. Make suggestions for how they might be improved. Also check to see that the poems follow the pattern given.

WRITING SLOGANS

WARNING: Littering causes warts.

The title above probably wouldn't be picked as the slogan for a citywide cleanup campaign because it treats a serious problem too lightly. However, *Warning: Littering Causes Warts* would be more fun to see on a bumper sticker than a serious slogan like *Warning: Littering Is a Crime.*

A Slogan Sampler

Slogans are brief, attention-getting statements used in advertising and promotional campaigns. They can be written in many different ways.

- Sometimes they will be crazy and surprising statements like the title of this activity, *Warning: Littering Causes Warts.*

- Sometimes they will be serious and dramatic like the second slogan above, *Warning: Littering Is a Crime!*

- At other times, they will be rhyming ideas like *Give a Hoot; Don't Pollute.*

- In addition, some new slogans will play on other more familiar slogans. A slogan like *Have You Kicked a Soccer Ball Today?* plays on this popular slogan: *Have You Hugged Your Kids Today?*

- And still other slogans are simply creative ways of saying something. For example, *We're into More Than Monkey Business* could be a creative slogan for a zoo.

Slogans for Sale

■ **Write bumper-sticker slogans for two of the situations listed below.**

❑ The grand opening of your city's remodeled airport

❑ A fund-raising project for new band uniforms

❑ A neighborhood campaign against crime

❑ A promotion for an upcoming concert

Mayberry Maces Muggers

AFTER • WORDS Suppose you were a slogan writer sometime in the distant past. Write "timely" slogans for advertising or promotional campaigns for that period in history.

DEVELOPING POSTERS

What a Rip-Off!

Another popular form of word play we see around us every day is the poster. Posters play with words to get our attention and convince us to go somewhere, buy something, or change our attitude in some way. See how well you do when you play with words on a poster of your own.

Design a poster in which you warn your friends, your classmates, or the general public about a product you bought recently that was, for some reason, a big disappointment. Include words, pictures, graphics, and colors that make your poster eye-catching and dramatic. (Use the space below for sketching out your poster idea.) Put your final poster on a large piece of paper or poster board.

Responses will vary.

TIP Look closely at the posters hanging in your classrooms and in your bedroom (as well as billboards and advertisements) for design ideas.

AFTER • WORDS Hang your poster in a place where lots of people will see it. Maybe you can stop them from making the same mistake you did.

CREATING CHARACTER NAMES
What a Character!

All writers try to create interesting characters for their stories. Some also come up with interesting names for their characters. Sometimes these names help describe the character for the reader. Names such as Hans Solo (a loner) or Luke Skywalker (a dreamer) from the *Star Wars* movies are very descriptive. Mr. Sowerberry (an undertaker) and the Artful Dodger (a young pickpocket) from Charles Dickens' *Oliver Twist* are names that tell us a lot about the characters' personalities. Other character names from fiction include the following:

- Mrs. Whatsit, an unearthly visitor, from *A Wrinkle in Time* by Madeleine L'Engle
- Long John Silver, a pirate, from *Treasure Island* by Robert Louis Stevenson
- True Son, a boy caught between cultures, from *The Light in the Forest* by Conrad Richter

Create your own descriptive names for each character described below. Try to come up with two or three for each character. (See the examples below.) Work with a partner if your teacher allows it.

1. a boy who can magically fly

   Jamie McFly, Glider, Copter Coogan

2. a 7-foot-tall high-school basketball player

   Stretch VonFrame, Arthur Beanpole, Lengthy Shadow

3. twin sisters who are very different

   Sillie and Seria Polapart, Topsy and Turvy Contrary

4. three dogs that journey 100 miles back to their home

   Jason, Achilles, and Hercules; Lassie, Lewis, and Clark

5. an adventurer who discovers lost treasures around the world

   Ace Von Fortune, Eric Goldseeker, Lucky Venture

AFTER • WORDS	Exchange your names with other students in class and ask them to match the names with the right description. Then continue to think of character names for future writings. Keep the list in your writing notebook.

PARTS OF SPEECH
A Strange Invitation

▍ You'll need to team up with at least one other classmate to play the following word game. Below is a list of parts of speech. One partner must ask the other to give an example of each part of speech listed and write it in the blank provided. (Try to come up with the most vivid or unusual words you can think of.)

Noun (proper) *Responses will vary.*

Noun (proper) _____

Adjective _____

Adjective _____

Adjective _____

Adverb _____

Noun _____

Noun _____

Verb (present) _____

Adjective _____

Verb (present) _____

Noun (-ing ending) _____

■ **Now fill in the blanks below with the words from your list.**

The parents of _____ and _____ would like
        noun   *noun*

to invite you to a(n) _____ wedding. The wedding will be held on
                    adjective

a(n) _____ Saturday in June. It will be a _____
        adjective   *adjective*

affair, so guests should dress _____ . It will not be catered, so
                              adverb

please bring a _____ to share with our _____ .
              noun   *noun*

Guests will also be expected to _____ to the music all night long.
                               verb

We've rented a(n) _____ band that will _____
                adjective   *verb*

until the band members drop from exhaustion. We and our children look forward to

_____ you. R.S.V.P.
noun (-ing ending)

| **AFTER • WORDS** | Together with your partner(s), make up your own passage with blanks and a parts-needed list. Then exchange passages with other classmates. The fun goes on and on. |

USING PREFIXES AND ROOTS
Building Words

Words are the Lego's of language. People pick them out, fit them together, and, in that way, build language. As you know, words themselves can also be built by fitting word parts together. (Refer to the lists of prefixes and roots in your handbook.)

Create and define as many words as you can from the list of prefixes and roots given below. (You may add endings and other letters as needed.) Then write a definition for each word. Finally, look for your words in the dictionary and compare the dictionary definitions with your own. Work with a classmate if your teacher allows it.

Prefixes: re, sub, intro, pre, super, post
Roots: cide, fract, ject, scrib (script), tract, vid (vis)

	Word	My Definition
1.	reject	Answers will vary.
2.	subtract	
3.	video	
4.	subject	
5.	prescribe	
6.	retract	
7.	fraction	
8.	postscript	

AFTER • WORDS Share your words with your classmates when you are finished. Chances are they came up with some words you didn't and vice versa.

USING WORD PARTS
Are you a "structologist"?

A chocolate cake isn't just a chocolate cake. It is really chocolate, flour, eggs, sugar, and more. When you eat a piece of cake, you probably don't think about all of its ingredients. Yet, a cake wouldn't be cake without all the parts that go into making it.

The same thing is true for many words in the English language. We use words every day without giving much thought to what goes into them. But words are made from a combination of prefixes, suffixes, and roots. The more you know about word parts, the more you will know about words. The more you know about words, the more you will know about your language.

> **Refer to the lists of prefixes, suffixes, and roots in your handbook for this word-building activity. Begin by filling in the blanks with the meanings of the following prefixes, suffixes, and roots.**

Prefixes:

inter _____ *between*

de _____ *from, down*

re _____ *back, again*

un _____ *not, release*

sub _____ *under*

mono _____ *one*

Suffixes:

able _____ *able, can do*

ure _____ *state of, act, process, rank*

ion _____ *act of, state of, result of*

ology _____ *study, science, theory*

ate _____ *cause, make*

ism _____ *system, manner, condition, characteristic*

Roots:

graph (gram) _____*write, written*_____

ject _____*throw*_____

hydr _____*water*_____

ten _____*hold*_____

struct _____*build*_____

chron _____*time*_____

log _____*word, study, speech*_____

■ **Using the word parts you have just learned, fill in the blanks below so that each word has a complete definition.**

1. **interjection:** *n.* the act of putting (throwing) something _____*between*_____ one thing and another

2. **monogram:** *n.* a combination of symbols or writing that marks something as

   belonging to _____*one*_____ person or family

3. **chronology:** *n.* the study or science of measuring _____*time*_____

4. **dehydration:** *n.* the act or process of removing _____*water*_____ from a substance

5. **untenable:** *adj.* not able to defend or _____*hold*_____ onto

6. **substructure:** *n.* state of being built _____*under*_____ another structure

| AFTER • WORDS | Make up as many other words as you can using the prefixes, suffixes, and roots above. Then share your words with a classmate and see how many he or she can figure out. |

PART IV
Writing and Learning Minilessons

Covering the important areas

of writing, language, and learning

included in *Write Source 2000*

MINILESSONS

Learning Bytes

We like to think that our **Minilessons** offer learning opportunities that are just the right size. They don't stuff you with seven courses of rules to remember and worksheets to complete, yet they don't necessarily leave you hungry for more information, either. It's learning in miniature, "byte-sized" learning, one important concept at a time.

One minilesson asks you to write run-on sentences for a classroom exchange. Another minilesson has you write a business letter to the employees of your company. And still another one has you punctuate a short list of titles.

Special Note: We offer a minilesson for nearly every important idea in your handbook. Read through your "User's Checklist" and see for yourself. Also read through some of the minilessons themselves. You've never seen learning like this before.

User's Checklist

Check your progress as you work on these **Minilessons**.

- ❏ **Writing Titles** • *Teenage Mutant Ninja Myrtle*
- ❏ **Clustering** • *Fanning Out*
- ❏ **Finding a Subject** • *Unless what?*
- ❏ **Exercises in Style** • *Why We Hiccup*
- ❏ **Punctuating Run-Ons** • *Stop that sentence!*
- ❏ **Using Index to Yellow Pages** • *How to Write Good*
- ❏ **Subject/Verb Agreement** • *Sergio y Maria*
- ❏ **Prewriting: Listing** • *My Room, No, My Bottom Drawer!*
- ❏ **Writing a Biography** • *My Partner, 'Tis of Thee*
- ❏ **Letter Format** • *The block starts here.*
- ❏ **Punctuating Salutations** • *Quiz Bowl*
- ❏ **Short Story Sampler** • *Once Upon a Coffin*
- ❏ **Writing Dialogue** • *Biting Dialogue*
- ❏ **Using the Reference Section** • *Hitting the Stacks*
- ❏ **Basic Writing and Thinking Moves** • *Let's do lunch.*
- ❏ **Creative Thinking** • *"What if . . . ?"*

❑ **Using Your Brain** • *What a Gas*

❑ **Reading to Others** • *3 x 3*

❑ **Listening Skills** • *Listen up.*

❑ **Commas and Periods**
• *Oranges and Bananas*

❑ **Using Periods** • *Stop it!*

❑ **Quoting and Reporting**
• *The Lemon-Lime Latitudes*

❑ **Using Semicolons**
• *A little dab'll do ya.*

❑ **Using Commas** • *Wanna come over?*

❑ **Using Colons** • *Feeling Listless*

❑ **Using Hyphens** • *Breaking up is hard to do.*

❑ **Dividing Words with Hyphens** • *OK, break it up.*

❑ **Punctuating Titles** • *Press on.*

❑ **Capitalization** • *Last Monday*

❑ **Capitalizing** • *Secret Message*

❑ **Capitalization** • *Shopping with the Biggies*

❑ **Forming Plurals** • *Seeing Double*

❑ **Acronyms and Initialisms**
• *Short Stuff*

❑ **Writing Numbers**
• *Numbers Game*

❑ **Writing Numbers**
• *Digital Readout*

❑ **Spelling** • *E Before I*

❑ **Spelling** • *"You spell what I spell?" "Nope. Got a code."*

❑ **Usage: Mixed Pairs**
• *Al(l)right, Al(l)ready*

❑ **Usage: Can and May**
• *Two Confused*

❑ **Independent and Dependent Clauses** • *Seeing Spots*

❑ **Kinds of Sentences**
• *Slime on Parade*

❑ **Nouns: Number and Gender**
• *Check out those nouns.*

❑ **Person of a Pronoun**
• *Nice Doggy*

❑ **Number of Verbs** • *Then don't shut your eyes.*

❑ **Active and Passive Verbs**
• *I get a kick out of this.*

❑ **Using Tables** • *Food from the Table*

❑ **Word Problems** • *Have I got problems.*

❑ **Journal Writing** • *Travel Log*

❑ **Using Metaphors** • *It's a monkey world.*

❑ **Parallelism** • *Get your ducks in a row.*

❑ **Understanding Vocabulary**
• *Before I say another word . . .*

❑ **Managing Your Time** • *Job Buster*

❑ **Reading Tables** • *Table-able*

❑ **Using Time Lines** • *Lewis and Clark Rap*

❑ **Using Time Lines** • *Dig into History*

AFTER • WORDS   Write minilessons of your own about writing and language learning to share with members of your writing group or the entire class.

MINILESSONS

| **A** | *Teenage Mutant Ninja Myrtle* . . . . Writing Titles |

■ In section **025** you will find some brief but valuable advice on writing titles. For practice,
  SUPPOSE a famous composer composed a symphony in your honor; give it an interesting
    one-word title.
  SUPPOSE a famous movie director made a horror movie loosely based on your life. What
    would you call it?
  SUPPOSE a famous writer wrote a biography of your life and used a well-known saying
    or quotation for the title. What would that title be?

| **B** | *Fanning Out* . . . . Clustering |

■ CHOOSE one of the topics from the "Essentials of Life Checklist" in section **036**.
  USE that topic word as the "nucleus word" for a cluster that you create.
  FOLLOW the directions for clustering in section **035**.
  At the end of your clustering, CHOOSE the one word you've written that would make the
    most interesting topic for writing.
  If you have 5-10 minutes, WRITE FREELY about your topic.

| **C** | *Unless what?* . . . . Finding a Subject |

■ Read the paragraph on "Free Writing" under "Selecting a Writing Subject" (**035**).
  WRITE the word "Unless" on a piece of paper and finish writing the sentence any way you
    can.
  CONTINUE writing, going wherever your fertile mind takes you.
  After 5-8 minutes, STOP and WRITE the single most important thought that has occurred
    to you during that time, whether you've written it yet or not.

| **D** | *Why We Hiccup* . . . . Exercises in Style |

■ Under "Writing Topics" (**040**), notice the subjects under the heading "Explaining . . .
  The causes of. . . ."
  CHOOSE one of the topics.
  PRETEND you are a kindergartner and write an explanation for the causes of whatever
    topic you've chosen.
  Now SWITCH. PRETEND you are an 80-year-old man or woman; EXPLAIN the causes of
    the same thing from that point of view.

A   *Stop that sentence!* .... **Punctuating Run-Ons**

■ READ the definition of a "Run-On" sentence (**091**).
  WRITE two sentences about giving a *very* unusual gift to someone you like—but don't separate the sentences with any punctuation or capitalization. (In other words, write a "run-on.")
  SWITCH papers with a partner and challenge your partner to put in a period and a capital letter where they belong.

B   *How to Write Good* .... **Using Index to Yellow Pages**

■ SUPPOSE a man from Turkey lived with your family for a while, trying to learn English.
  SUPPOSE he showed you a letter he was writing to his children back in Turkey, and in it he gave them the following advice:

How to Write Good

094-097   Subject and verb always has to agree.

099   Being bad grammar, the writer will not use dangling modifiers.

790   Prepositions should not be used to end sentences with.

091   Avoid run-on sentences they are hard to read.

126   Avoid cliches like the plague.

As you must have noticed, each of these sentences breaks its own rule. Fortunately, you have a copy of *Write Source 2000*. For each sentence, FIND a topic number in the handbook where the man from Turkey will find clear guidelines relating to that sentence. For example, where would you find guidelines on subject/verb agreement or avoiding dangling modifiers?
  USE the index to find your way around the book.
  WRITE the topic numbers in the space before each sentence.

| **A** | *Sergio y Maria* . . . . | **Subject/Verb Agreement** |

■ Sergio and Maria are brother and sister. They live in a tiny southern California house with no backyard and one bathroom for six people. Here are some sentences about their world. But I'm having trouble with the verbs. I'm not sure the subjects and the verbs in my sentences agree in number because these sentences have unusual word order—subjects come after the verbs, etc.

I hear you have a copy of *Write Source 2000*. Could you please look up "Agreement, Subject/verb" in the index and then tell me exactly what topic number I can turn to to find answers to my questions? Fill in the verbs, too. Thanks.

1. There on their bedroom window _____*were*_____ thick iron bars to keep the

   children from falling out. (Should I say "was" or "were"? Topic #: _*095*_)

2. Neither Sergio nor his brothers _____*dare*_____ play outside when the older

   boys are hanging out at the street corner. (Should I say "dare" or "dares"?

   Topic #: _*094*_)

3. _____*Were*_____ those Maria's stockings or her mother's hanging out to dry?

   (Should I say "Was" or "Were"? Topic #: _*095*_)

4. One of Maria's mother's front teeth _____*has*_____ a gleaming gold cap on it.

   (Should I say "has" or "have"? Topic #: _*096*_)

| **B** | *My Room, No, My Bottom Drawer!* . . . . | **Prewriting: Listing** |

■ Survey the "Personal Writing Sampler" (**149**) and choose one type of memory to write about.

NOTICE the instructions for "Listing" under "Selecting a Writing Subject" (**036**).

LIST as many thoughts and details as you can in connection with the memory you chose.

READ your list and pull together several of the most interesting items.

WRITE DOWN a *new* and *sharper* focus for your personal writing.

A *My Partner, 'Tis of Thee* . . . . **Writing a Biography**

■ Brush up on techniques of interviewing (see section **405-407**).
STUDY the directions for writing a "Bio-Poem" (**158**).
CHOOSE a partner from the class.
INTERVIEW your partner until you have found out enough information to complete a bio-poem.
WRITE a bio-poem about your partner and give it to him or her as a gift.

B *The block starts here.* . . . . **Letter Format**

■ For one crazy moment, dream that you are president of your own company. You've noticed recently that all your employees use "Semiblock Form" when they write business letters. You'd like to give your company correspondence a bit more up-to-date look, so you write a letter of instruction to your employees. On your gleaming marble desktop is your favorite handbook, *Write Source 2000*.
LOOK up "Business letter" in the index and under that FIND "Form." TURN to the diagrams of "Full-block" and "Semiblock" form. STUDY them and the sample letters on the following pages of "The Business Letter" section.
WRITE a letter to your employees telling them that in the future, all letters must be in "Full-block" form.
In your letter, EXPLAIN the key differences between "Full-block" and "Semiblock" form.
PUT your own letter in correct "Full-block" form so that it *shows* as well as *tells* how to do it.

C *Quiz Bowl* . . . . **Punctuating Salutations**

■ Quick! You're in a junior-high "Quiz Bowl." The question is "What is the proper punctuation after the salutation in a business letter?" Nobody has gotten the answer right yet. But you've sneaked a copy of *Write Source 2000* in under the table. LOOK UP "Salutation."
    BEEP!
    The answer is _____colon_____ .
    HONK! Too bad. The answer is correct. But you've been disqualified for cheating.

A *Once Upon a Coffin* . . . . Short Story Sampler

■ Survey the section on "Story Writing" (**237-252**), especially the section on "A Short Story Sampler" (**247-252**).

FORM a circle with your class or a large group. (This can be fun at a party!)

SET OUT to write a horror story.

WRITE the first sentence of your story on a piece of paper as everyone else does the same.

PASS your paper to the person next to you.

WRITE a second sentence on the sheet your neighbor passes to you. *Remember:* You're trying to write a horror story. Try to catch the spirit of your partner's story and keep it going.

CONTINUE adding sentences and passing papers until your own sheet goes all around the circle and comes back to you.

DO THE SAME for a mystery, a fantasy, a science fiction story, a myth, or a fable.

B *Biting Dialogue* . . . . Writing Dialogue

■ The short stretch of dialogue in **256** is a good example of dialogue that neatly blends the writer's comments with the speakers' words. READ it slowly. NOTICE how much didn't need to be said.

Here is some dialogue that isn't so well written. READ it slowly:

> "This is a conure," Nikki said to Rosco. "Conures don't bite. Here, let him sit on your finger."
>
> "You're lying," Rosco said. "Birds like that always bite me."
>
> "Billy!" said the conure, saying his own name.
>
> "Don't be a wimp," Nikki said to Rosco. "If you move slowly," Nikki said, "he won't be frightened. Here," she said, setting the bird on Rosco's wrist, "let him sit on your wrist."
>
> "Ow!" Rosco yelled at Nikki. Just as Rosco had feared, Billy had bitten him. A drop of blood was oozing out where the beak had punctured the skin. "See?" said Rosco. "He bites . . . and you lie." Rosco was angry.
>
> "Well, you've been a creep to me," Nikki said to Rosco.
>
> "Billy!" said the bird, as he had been taught.
>
> "Some sister you are," said Rosco to his sister Nikki. He was upset.

GO BACK over this dialogue and scratch out *every word* that isn't absolutely necessary— the "he saids" and "she saids" and any words that say the obvious. READ the slimmed-down dialogue and appreciate its new power.

A   *Hitting the Stacks* .... **Using the Reference Section**

■ Read through the section listing reference books of special interest to young people (**298**).
SELECT a book that you haven't heard of before.
GO to the library and find out how to use the book—what to look for in it, how to save
    time using it, etc.
WRITE a note summarizing your discoveries about the book.
GIVE the note to a neighbor in your class.

B   *Let's do lunch.* ...... **Basic Writing and Thinking Moves**

■ The chart in **310** is so full of information that you might overlook it unless you have
a reason to study it. Okay. I'll give you a reason. Your lunch. Lunches are full of
fascinating things: apples, blue corn chips, cold pizza. . . . If you don't think about
yours, you won't know how fascinating it is.

  ❑ CHOOSE one item from your lunch.
  ❑ CHOOSE *four* of the major thinking "moves" listed down the center of **310.**
  ❑ CHOOSE one minor move under each of the four major ones.

APPLY each of those four minor moves to your subject. WRITE DOWN the thoughts that
    result.
For even more interesting results, do this with a friend. Using the same lunch item, ASK
    your friend to choose four major thinking moves other than the ones you chose. When
    you are through, COMPARE your writings.

C   *"What if . . . ?"* .... **Creative Thinking**

■ Read the "What if . . .?" questions in section **334** and notice how they force you to think
creative thoughts.
THINK UP and WRITE DOWN three more good "What if . . . ?" questions to add to the
    list.
ANSWER any one of the questions in writing . . . creatively!

A *What a Gas* . . . . **Using Your Brain**

■ USE the table in section **358** and the information in section **359** to get a good "feel" for the difference between so-called "right-brain" and "left-brain" thinking.
DECIDE which of the following short descriptions is more "right brain" and which is more "left brain":

left brain 1. Duane used a long pipe made of steel to pry open the lid over the long-abandoned sewage pit next to the barn. Gas must have been building up in the pocket of air since the lid popped off easily and released a cloud of fumes that nearly overwhelmed us because it was so thick and foul.

right brain 2. Pop! This 80-pound steel plate sprang up at a touch as if the sewer gas beneath it were a warty, purple monster with a frisbee on its back. But gag me with a shovel! The smell of that monster's breath was like dozens of corpses chewing on Limburger cheese. I stumbled away from there with no sense of direction.

B *3 x 3* . . . . **Reading to Others**

■ After you read the notes on "Reading to Others," **400**,
CHOOSE a short poem from one of your books.
STUDY the poem until you understand its meaning and its tone.
JOIN a group of three people (including yourself) and read the poem aloud to the others in three ways:
       (1) Very slowly, loudly, expressively
       (2) Quickly, softly, flatly (not expressively)
       (3) Slowly, softly, with extreme expression

C *Listen up.* . . . . **Listening Skills**

■ In sections **402-404** you will find sound advice on how to improve your listening ability.
Now, to practice listening,
HAVE one person in your class or writing group tell the others about the last time he or she was really excited.
JOT down notes on important ideas as the speaker speaks.
At the end, SUMMARIZE what the speaker has said in no more than two sentences.
Finally, WRITE down questions that you think were not answered well in the speaker's story.
COMPARE your written responses to those of others.

A Oranges and Bananas .... Commas and Periods

■ REVIEW the rules for using periods and commas (**459-463**; **468-482**).

PRETEND you were just elected president of the United States, and you have written a short acceptance speech.

GIVE your short speech in front of a group, but whenever you should use a period, say "orange," and whenever you should use a comma, say "banana." (With a little practice *banana* it should be easy *orange*)

B Stop it! .... Using Periods

■ Study the rules in "The Yellow Pages" for using periods (**459-463**).

WRITE a sentence about something that came to a dead stop—a train, a game, a popcorn popper, or whatever.

In your sentence, SHOW all four uses of the period: after an initial, as a decimal point, at the end of a sentence, and after an abbreviation. (Be inventive!)

C The Lemon-Lime Latitudes ...... Quoting and Reporting

■ READ topic **472** in *Write Source 2000* to find out the difference between a direct quotation and an indirect one. (The first example in **472** is direct quoting; the second is indirect reporting.)

After you have read and understood **472**, FOLLOW these instructions:

1. REWRITE the following in the form of an **indirect** quotation:

Sondra raised her hand and said, "I read in the *Atlantic Monthly* about what they call the 'lemon-lime latitudes.' " *Sondra raised her hand and said she had read in the Atlantic Monthly about "lemon-lime latitudes."*

2. REWRITE the following in the form of a **direct** quotation:

As Sondra described them, the "lemon-lime latitudes" are areas chiefly in the Midwest, West, and Northwest where sales of lemon-lime soda are above the national average. *"The 'lemon-lime latitudes' are areas chiefly in the Midwest, West, and Northwest where sales of lemon-lime soda are above the national average," Sondra explained.*

A | A little dab'll do ya. . . . . Using Semicolons

■ SUPPOSE you are a fly working for the Student Punctuation Evaluation Commission (SPEC). Your job is to change sentences from comma-spliced sentences to correctly punctuated ones by dropping one dot—a flyspeck—in just the right spot, thus turning a comma into a semicolon (**477** and **484**). Here's your assignment. Fix these sentences with three "flyspecks":

I'm tired of driving, from now on, I walk.
Running strengthens your heart, however, it can weaken your knees.
Confide in me, please, what have you decided?

B | Wanna come over? . . . . Using Commas

■ READ and UNDERSTAND the following sentence:

She asked her only friend, living nearby, if she could spend the night.

TAKE OUT the commas and READ the sentence again.
TELL someone how you think the meaning of the sentence is changed when the commas are left out.

C | Feeling Listless . . . . Using Colons

■ WRITE a grammatically correct sentence containing a colon; after the colon, LIST all the different ways a colon can be used.
(Sections **488-493** should be a big help to you hcrc.)

D | Breaking up is hard to do. . . . . Using Hyphens

■ USE a dictionary (or sections **568-573**) to figure out where the following words should be hyphenated if they had to be broken at the end of a line (see the rules in **499**):

H a z-a r d-o u s

Y e l-l o w

P r e-v i-o u s

H o p-i n g

E m-b a r-r a s s

N u-c l e-a r

A *OK, break it up.* . . . . **Dividing Words with Hyphens**

■ It was a severe recession. So severe that we ran out of typing paper. We had to do all of our writing on little rolls of adding-machine tape. Fine, except for one problem: where do we place the hyphens? On skinny paper, practically every word has to be broken in the middle. If you don't know the rules for hyphenation . . . you'll mess up.

Fortunately for us, we had *Write Source 2000.* In **499**, we found six useful rules for hyphenation. I learned my lessons. I'll prove it. Here's what you should do with the following words:

	Hyphenate? (Yes or No)	Show Hyphenation
committee	*yes*	*com-mit-tee*
wouldn't	*no*	
grimaced	*yes*	*gri-maced*
sufficient	*yes*	*suf-fi-cient*
trough	*no*	

B *Press on.* . . . . **Punctuating Titles**

■ Our librarian, Ms. Sharif, gave us a box of press-on letters and told us to post a sign on the bulletin board announcing new materials in our library—books, articles, newspapers, movies, records, etc.—that she thought kids would like. The problem was that the box contained only three pairs of quotation marks. We weren't sure which titles took quotation marks and which ones had to be underlined.

"You'll have to find that out for yourselves," Ms. Sharif said. "Here's a copy of *Write Source 2000.* Look up the answers in here." Lucky for us, we found the answers in **517** and **529**.

SHOW which three of the following titles would get the quotation marks (write "Q") and which should be underlined (write "U"):

Q Kid in the Park (short poem)

U The New York Times (newspaper)

U The Effect of Gamma Rays on Man-in-the-Moon Marigolds (full-length play)

Q Blue Suede Shoes (song)

U All Things Wise and Wonderful (novel)

Q Are We Running Out of Fish? (magazine article)

| **A** | *Last Monday* .... **Capitalization** |

■ MAKE two lists. In the first, LIST all the words in the following paragraph that *should not* be capitalized but are. In the second, LIST all the words that *should* be capitalized but are not.
USE sections **533-546** for rules to guide you.

Last monday, on Labor day, the *Philadelphia Inquirer* reported that dr. Regina Sandvold, the scandinavian Mayor of the Eastern Missouri town of Pitfall, ordered a loaf of Wonder bread to be placed in every Hotel room in the area during the Republican national convention in honor of the invention of the Sandwich by the fourth earl of Sandwich in approximately 1740 A.D. She was taken to the Local hospital for psychiatric observation.

List #1	List #2
mayor	Monday
eastern	Day
hotel	Dr.
sandwich	Scandinavian
local	National
	Convention

| **B** | *Secret Message* .... **Capitalizing** |

■ In *Write Source 2000*, **533-546,** you will find rules to help you capitalize correctly. Be sure to notice the table under **541.**

STUDY the rules. Now look at the following sentences. **Is the <u>underlined</u> word in each sentence supposed to be capitalized?** Yes or no? If the answer is yes, CHOOSE the number from the "Yes" column at the left of the sentence. Then GO to the key below, FIND the letter that matches the number, and WRITE that letter in the proper blank space of the puzzle message, starting from the left. Follow the same procedure if the answer is no. Can you read the secret message? If not, ask a friend to help you.

YES	NO	
⑦	13	<u>Aunt</u> Gretchen is a part-time disc jockey.
⑮	1	The Pacific <u>northwest</u> is prospering.
14	⑮	Our balloon landed somewhere <u>northwest</u> of Dayton.
25	④	This <u>Winter</u> was so cold we froze our hibiscus.
⑩	5	"Stop it," she shouted. "<u>You</u> have no right to be here!"
1	⑮	I'm in danger of flunking <u>Mathematics.</u>
②	20	His <u>Western</u> attire was inappropriate for a wedding.

SECRET MESSAGE: <u>g</u> <u>o</u> <u>o</u> <u>d</u> <u>j</u> <u>o</u> <u>b</u>

Key:

a	b	c	d	e	f	g	h	i	j	k	l	m	n	o	p	q	r	s	t	u	v	w	x	y	z
1	2	3	4	5	6	7	8	9	10	11	12	13	14	15	16	17	18	19	20	21	22	23	24	25	26

A *Shopping with the Biggies* .... Capitalization

■ Study the rules for capitalization (**533-546**).
LIST three or four quite different famous people.
For each famous person, SUPPOSE that he or she went shopping for food, brand-name
  clothes, etc.
WRITE each person's shopping list *without* any capital letters.
TRADE papers with a partner and capitalize correctly.
CHECK your partner's work.

B *Seeing Double* .... Forming Plurals

■ WRITE a sentence in which you use at least five of the following words:

fox *foxes* tomato *tomatoes* banjo *banjos* plateful *platefuls*

loaf *loaves* fly *flies* goose *geese* child *children*

Now SUPPOSE you entered a "looking-glass world" in which there were two of everything—two me's, two you's, two of this book, two of these instructions, etc., etc. WRITE
your sentence again, but this time write everything using the plural form.
FORM the plurals correctly, using sections **547-554** to help you.

C *Short Stuff* .... Acronyms and Initialisms

■ GO to the index of *Write Source 2000* and find a section that explains the uses of
abbreviations. (NOTE that when you turn to the section, you will find two terms:
"Acronyms" and "Initialism.")
USE this section to find out the meaning of the following familiar acronyms and initialisms.
  WRITE DOWN the complete, unabbreviated form:

CIA - Central Intelligence Agency
PLO - Palestine Liberation Organization
radar - radio detecting and ranging
VISTA - Volunteers in Service to America

CARE - Cooperative for American
     Relief Everywhere
IRA - Irish Republican Army

Special Challenge: For an extra challenge, find the meanings of these acronyms and
  initialisms, which are not in the book:

IRS - Internal Revenue Service
NASA - National Aeronautics and
     Space Administration
NATO - North Atlantic Treaty
     Organization
UNICEF - United Nations International
     Children's Emergency Fund
OAS - Organization of American States

DMZ - demilitarized zone
NOW - National Organization
     for Women
GOP - Grand Old Party
FBI - Federal Bureau of
     Investigation
laser - light amplification by
     stimulated emission of radiation

| A | *Numbers Game* .... | **Writing Numbers** |

■ ARE the numbers in these sentences written correctly?

1. ***1973 was the year of the last really big oil crisis.***
   No: (reword) The last really big oil crisis was in 1973. (or) Nineteen seventy-three was the year of the last really big oil crisis.
2. ***Between six and thirteen ninth graders will receive special awards.*** *Yes.*
3. ***I'd say five and a half percent would be a standard interest rate.***
   No: 5 ¹/₂ percent or 5.5 percent
4. ***Chapter 12 contains the key to the whole plot.*** *Yes.*
5. ***He guessed nearly one and a half million beans and was way off.***
   No: 1.5 million

After your first response, CHECK your answers against the guidelines in sections **558-562**.

| B | *Digital Readout* .... | **Writing Numbers** |

■ Study the rules for writing numbers correctly (**558-562**).
REWRITE the following sentence correctly:
8 or nine of the twenty-6 seniors, or about 2 point six percent of the entire high-school population, had pledged to read 200 200-page books by July Four, Two Thousand.
TRADE papers with a partner and check your revisions.

Eight or nine of the twenty-six seniors, or about 2.6 percent of the entire high-school population, had pledged to read two hundred 200-page books by July 4, 2000.

| C | *E Before I* .... | **Spelling** |

■ Study the exceptions to the "i before e" rule in **564**.
COMPOSE your own sentence containing all of these exceptions: *height, counterfeit, their, foreign,* and *heir.* (Good luck!)

| D | *"You spell what I spell?"* *"Nope. Got a code."* .... | **Spelling** |

■ Turn to the "Yellow Pages Guide to Improved Spelling" (**568-573**).
RUN DOWN the lists of spelling words and PICK OUT 10 words that are hard for you to spell (*cupboard, harass, vacuum, etc.*).
LIST your 10 words.
WRITE a sentence for each one of your 10 words, using and spelling the word correctly.
CHOOSE a partner and give your partner a spelling test on your 10 words. CORRECT your partner's answers.

A   Al(l)right, Al(l)ready .... Usage: Mixed Pairs

■ Kelly and Earvin submitted such good stories to their school's literary contest that the judge refused at first to decide between them. But then the judge decided to give each story a very careful proofreading. The person with the more correct paper would win. Here's what the judge found:

> Earvin wrote, in one sentence, "All right, everyone, my mind is already made up."
> Kelly wrote, "It was Popo's frog, alright, quite flattened and all ready dead."
> Find out from *Write Source 2000*, **580-581**, who should get the prize.

> Earvin? ✔   or Kelly? _____   (Check one)

B   Two Confused .... Usage: Can and May

■ USE the index of *Write Source 2000* to locate guidelines for the proper use of the words "can" and "may."

Based on what you find there, DECIDE which word belongs in the following sentences. WRITE the word "can" or "may" in each blank.

1. ___*May*___ our group please go through the fossil wing of the museum?

2. If everyone carries an extra load, we ___*can*___ take up the slack for our injured guide.

3. According to the rule book, the third-base coach ___*may*___ stand here.

4. With the correct training, anyone ___*can*___ be a flame swallower.

C   Seeing Spots ..... Independent and Dependent Clauses

■ Study the guidelines for independent and dependent clauses (**710**).
Study the Braille alphabet in **799**.
WRITE a complex sentence (a sentence with one independent clause and at least one dependent clause) in *Braille*.

Special Challenge: Translate your sentence into Morse code (**800**), or cuneiform (**801**).

A   *Slime on Parade* .... **Kinds of Sentences**

■ In sections **715-718** you will find descriptions of the four basic types of sentences: declarative (statements), interrogative (questions), imperative (commands), and exclamatory (exclamations).

SUPPOSE you are standing at a curbside, watching a parade. Suddenly, a huge balloon shaped like Slimer of Ghostbusters fame breaks loose from its tether and starts flapping wildly in the wind.

LISTEN to what the bystanders say, and copy down (1) one declarative comment, (2) one interrogative comment, (3) one imperative comment, and (4) one exclamatory comment.

B   *Check out those nouns.* .... **Nouns: Number and Gender**

■ After you look over sections **725-728**, decide the number and gender of the following nouns. (Be careful! Some could be more than one number or gender.)

ewe	ship	cousins	stallion
aunt	cacti	hen	skirt
skateboard	gentlemen	trout	children
senator	oxen	pastries	mice

TRY to INVENT a couple of tests that will help you prove the gender and number of a noun.

C   *Nice Doggy* .... **Person of a Pronoun**

■ Suppose a pizza-delivery person decides to take a shortcut through a dark alley. He (or she) gets halfway over a wooden fence, one foot over with a pizza box held high in one hand, when a low, very fierce-sounding growl is heard close at hand (or should we say close at foot)! What happens next?

TELL what happens next, but do it in two different ways. First, USE first-person pronouns. Second, TELL it again, using third-person pronouns.

For help using pronouns, CONSULT sections **737-739**.

D   *Then don't shut your eyes.* .... **Number of Verbs**

■ CHANGE the verb in the following sentence to a plural verb, and
MAKE any other changes required by the change in verb:

        A ghostly shape appears every time I shut my eyes.

SEE sections **750** and **751** for definitions of singular and plural verbs.

A   I get a kick out of this. .... Active and Passive Verbs

■ Review the definitions of active and passive voice in verbs (**753-754**).
CHOOSE a sport that involves hitting or kicking a ball.
WRITE a paragraph describing a moment of intense action in that sport from the point
  of view of one of the players; USE active verbs.
REWRITE the paragraph, describing the same action from the point of view of the ball;
  USE passive verbs.

B   Food from the Table .... Using Tables

■ Study the pages titled "Planet Profusion" in the Student Almanac (**809**). Pay special
attention to the table of facts about the planets.

PICK OUT three quite different planets from the table.
STUDY the facts about each one—gravity, length of year, temperature, etc.
PRETEND you are on the planets, equipped for survival.
WRITE an imaginative observation report telling what your experience is like on each of the
  three different planets.

C   Have I got problems. .... Word Problems

■ Study the "Guidelines for Solving Word Problems" in the Student Almanac (**849-855**).
THINK of a situation in your own life that involves measures, distances, times, costs,
  weights, rates, or fractions.
WRITE up your situation in the form of a word problem (also known as a story problem). USE
  the tables in **803-808** and **843-848** if they will help.
GIVE your word problem to a neighbor in class to solve.

D   Travel Log .... Journal Writing

■ Let your imagination turn part of your ordinary day into the travel adventure of a
lifetime. You could, for example, pretend that, while passing between classes, you
suddenly found yourself on a dangerous journey in an alien world.
WRITE a journal entry, expanding on your travel adventure. (See **130-132** if you need help
  with journal writing.)
SHARE your writing with one of your classmates. (Continue writing about this adventure
  in future journal entries.)

| **A** | *It's a monkey world.* .... | **Using Metaphors** |

■ You don't often hear people practicing their metaphors like they practice free throws or slap shots. Yet, the ability to see, understand, and create metaphors is one of the most important thinking and writing skills you can master.
READ about "metaphor" in the list of "Writing Techniques" (**124**).
WRITE two effective metaphors of your own using the handbook example as your guide.
Note: An effective metaphor speaks truthfully, accurately, and creatively about its subject.

Special Challenge: Use one of your metaphors as the starting point for a story. For example: "My room is a compost heap" might prove fertile ground for story writing.

| **B** | *Get your ducks in a row.* .... | **Parallelism** |

■ Usually you are encouraged not to repeat yourself in writing. However, repetition can lead to very powerful writing—if it is used in a special way.
READ about "parallelism" in your handbook (**125**) to learn about the effective use of repetition.
Then WRITE two interesting sentences, each one containing at least three parallel ideas.
SHARE your work with your classmates.

| **C** | *Before I say another word . . .* | **Understanding Vocabulary** |

■ DEFINE the term "prefix" using the information on prefixes, suffixes, and roots in your handbook as your guide (**374-384**).
Then CLOSE your handbook and UNDERLINE the prefixes in the following words:

Prefix Definition

<u>co</u>pilot	*with, together*
<u>mal</u>practice	*bad*
<u>pen</u>tagon	*five*
<u>pseud</u>onym	*false, assumed*
<u>ultra</u>modern	*very, extremely*

WRITE a definition for each prefix based on your understanding of each example word. (Your handbook should still be closed.)
DISCUSS your responses with a classmate.
CHECK your work together, using the list of prefixes in the handbook as your guide.

A Job Buster .... Managing Your Time

■ Think of an extended school-related project that you would like to organize—a play in your language-arts class, an awards banquet, a field trip, a going-away party, etc. Then READ "Turn big jobs into smaller jobs" in your handbook (**452**).
WRITE a paragraph explaining how you could turn your extended project into several small jobs so that it would be more manageable.

Special Challenge: Apply the "job buster" idea to a project you are currently working on or will soon begin.

B Table-able .... Reading Tables

■ Read about tables in your handbook (**818-822**).
Then LIST the title and location of four tables in other chapters in the handbook.
SELECT one of these tables to study carefully and thoroughly.
SHARE your knowledge with a classmate. (Discuss the subject of this table, the way it works, the times it would be most helpful, and so on.)

Special Challenge: Design your own custom-made table.

C Lewis and Clark Rap .... Using Time Lines

■ Survey the "Historical Time Line" (**889-898**).
CHOOSE events that occurred during a 10-year period to write about in an imaginary conversation.
CREATE this conversation between two friends who are discussing one or two of these events, as if they had just occurred.
SHARE your work.

D Dig into History .... Using Time Lines

■ Survey the "Historical Time Line" (**889-898**).
CHOOSE one important person listed in the time line.
FIND information from an encyclopedia or from another reference book about your subject.
WRITE five questions and answers about this person.
Then SEE how much a classmate knows about your subject in a question-and-answer discussion.

STUDENT SOURCEBOOK 6000 INDEX